Praise f(
A BEAUTIFUL DEATH

"A truly beautiful account of a truly beautiful death."

—KEN WILBER, author,
Grace and Grit

"In this skillfully crafted first-person account of her profound healing journey, Cheryl Eckl provides wise guidance to help each of us face life's inevitable losses with creative compassion and messy, elegant grace."

—MARK BRADY, PH.D., author,
The Wisdom of Listening and *Right Listening*

"A gem of inspiration and wisdom. Whether you are a family member, friend, or caregiver of a loved one who is passing on, these real-life lessons can help you love, heal, and experience each other more deeply. As much about how to live fully as how to let go gracefully, *A Beautiful Death* is a precious and indispensable guide to making our final journey through life a fulfilling voyage of resolution, discovery, and promise."

—PATRICIA SPADARO, author,
Honor Yourself: The Inner Art of Giving and Receiving

"Cheryl Eckl writes beautifully about the transformative power of her husband's final journey—of experiencing life's deepest joys while facing life's deepest sorrows. She shares a profound and universal message of hope while chronicling her intensely personal story."

—BEV SLOAN, President and CEO,
The Denver Hospice

"Cheryl Eckl is doing the work of a Warrior in the World. *A Beautiful Death* does far more than simply honor those of our beloveds who have passed; it is a sacred vessel that provides healing, equanimity, acceptance, and rest for all of those who have lost or are losing another. In fact, after exploring Cheryl's profound work, we find that we have not lost anything at all."

—BRANDON P. THOMPSON, Global Faculty,
Institute of Transpersonal Psychology

"For those with cancer and those who love and care about people with cancer, this book is an invaluable resource to help people face the hard realities, cope with the physical, emotional, and spiritual pain, and move toward a more positive and constructive outlook."

—JOHN J. HORAN, Chairman of the Board,
The Denver Hospice

A Beautiful

DEATH

A Beautiful DEATH

facing the future with PEACE

Cheryl Eckl

FLYING CRANE PRESS

For information address:
Flying Crane Press
P. O. Box 355
Littleton, CO 80160-0355
E-mail: info@flyingcranepress.com

For foreign and translation rights, contact Nigel J. Yorwerth.
E-mail: nigel@publishingcoaches.com

Library of Congress Control Number: 2010931352

ISBN: 978-0-9828107-0-5

Cover design: Nita Ybarra
Interior design: Alan Barnett

Distributed by SCB Distributors

For Stephen

CONTENTS

*All spiritual seeking is aimed at awakening us
in order to know one thing and only one thing:
birth and death can never touch us
in any way whatsoever.*

—Thich Nhat Hanh

A NOTE TO THE READER:
YOU CAN DO THIS

There is a Power whose care
Teaches thy way along the pathless coast,
The desert and illimitable air,
Lone wandering, but not lost.

—William Cullen Bryant

SOMEONE IS DYING. And for all concerned, life will never be the same.

You cannot comprehend the impact death will have on your life until you meet it face to face. Until you sit with it a while. Until you watch it hovering for years—or perhaps for just an instant. Until you feel the nothingness it leaves behind as it steals away with your beloved. Even then, you may not really know death— but I believe you need to try. I also believe you have the inner resources to face it, even if you don't know that you do. I learned that from my mother when my father passed away, and she had learned it years earlier from her friends in the Arizona retirement community where they lived.

"How could you be so calm and in control?" she had asked a courageous woman who had recently lost her husband. "I'm afraid I would just fall apart."

"You won't," her friend had answered without hesitation. "The strength will be there when you need it. I don't know exactly how it happens, but you will be sustained."

And it was true. When my father died after a long illness, my mother was calm, poised, organized, and capable. Her collectedness was truly inspiring, and she gave me a powerful role model to follow when my husband, Stephen, passed away.

When we faced his imminent death from colon cancer, we were often surprised by the strength we felt from our own inner reserves as well as from the prayers of family and friends. We were also amazed to encounter less fear for ourselves than for each other. I was afraid Stephen would suffer, and he was afraid I would be lost without him. What we did not fear was death itself. He had faith in a loving afterlife, and I believed I could help him get there.

Facing death—either your own or that of someone you love—can be the worst thing that ever happens to you. It can also be your most important life experience because of what it teaches you about love and compassion, about serving another person in the hour of greatest need, about the resilience of the human heart, and about the unimaginable blessings that can flow to you and through you if you accept death as a natural part of life.

Ever since I was a child, I had looked at my existence as a continuum that moves from this life on to what philosopher William James called "something more." If it was Stephen's destiny to die young, as I tend to believe it was, he could not have picked a better partner than me because I was more inclined to the ethereal than the physical, and much preferred the realm of imagination, where my mind could soar, to the material where, as I was a sickly child, my body often failed me.

My family did not shrink from the idea of death, so I always accepted it as part of life. It was an indisputable fact that people we knew and loved got old or sick and died. My father's elder brother was a mortician. Everyone we knew owned burial plots. We regularly visited the graves of loved ones. And I attended my grandfather's funeral when I was seven years old. I remember people crying, but more vivid is my memory of how serene he looked in his coffin.

We believed in an afterlife, but I thought my parents were profoundly un-curious about what actually happened "over there." I, however, found it fascinating to imagine a world beyond the physical where people went when they died and where one day I might go too. I was especially intrigued by my Grandma Cody's near-death experience that had left her somewhat clairvoyant and with a gift we called her "hotline to God." While lying gravely ill with childbed fever after the birth of her fourth child, she heard what she described as angels singing outside her window and she felt a divine presence that remained throughout her life.

One summer, when I was about nine years old, we were at Cody's house for lunch and she was saying grace in her quaint little way: "Now, Jesus, you take care of these dear children." (She always talked as if he were her best friend.) With my head bowed and my eyes closed, I suddenly felt the room fill up with a radiant energy. Peeking around, I couldn't see anything, but I could feel it. And I silently announced to myself, *I want what Grandma Cody has.* She clearly had friends in heaven and I wanted them too.

Later that summer, I got my first real glimpse of the Other Side. I was lazing on my swing set in our backyard, enjoying a balmy breeze, thinking about the book on ancient Greece I had been reading. I was imagining the hot Aegean sun beating on my face, making diamonds of light on the azure-blue sea, with iridescent marble columns a short distance behind me. It was a scene so vivid I could almost remember being there—but not quite.

As I sat motionless on the swing trying to will myself back to antiquity, I was transported. In my mind's eye I no longer saw the brilliant white of Greek temples, but rather a tunnel of light—and I had the clear idea that this was where both Jesus and Buddha came from. Even though I had been raised with traditionally Christian beliefs, this concept did not seem strange, because I had become familiar with the Buddha in my world history books and my beliefs about Jesus were already expanding beyond Sunday-school stories. Neither of them actually appeared in the tunnel I saw; but I instantly knew the light was where they came from and where they lived. And I felt myself being comforted with a promise that, if I would follow that radiance, one day I would remember ancient Greece—and much, much more.

As I grew up, I didn't see any more tunnels of light, but I decided I was a mystic—a person who desires union with the Divine, however they define it. In my late teens and early twenties, I had many experiences of synchronicity—unexplainable coincidences or serendipitous events that I ascribed to being in tune with angels or other spiritual beings. I did my best to follow the light I had seen in the tunnel, but for many years, my path consisted mainly of singing in church choirs; reading books on Edgar Cayce, Tibetan Buddhism, and ancient civilizations; and pursuing a career in musical theater. For me, being creative was uniquely holy. Yet all the while, I felt a persistent inner hunger—an intense longing for the spiritual connectedness that I had trouble maintaining but that seemed so natural to my grandmother.

In 1998 I caught sight of that connection at the passing of my elderly father. I was not afraid to sit with him in his final hours because a couple of years earlier a friend had told me, "If you ever have the opportunity to be with a loved one when they are making the transition, do not hesitate. You'll be glad you were there to share such a remarkable moment." Indeed, I am grateful I was.

While in a coma, my father appeared to be carrying on an animated conversation with people he was very happy to see, because he smiled and gestured as if greeting old friends. His breathing was labored for the next several hours; but when he died early the next morning, a gentle, sweet smile came over his face, giving him a serenely childlike expression. For years I carried this beautiful image in my heart, but I did not dig deeper into the mystery of life and death until I was forced to.

Ironically, it was not until the horrible gift of my husband's illness and eventual passing that I really began to understand what it means to live each day to the fullest. Stephen may well have laid down his life for me to learn that when we conquer our fear of the Great Unknown, life becomes unspeakably sweet. In fact, my journey through his illness and death convinced me that we are both able to and *meant* to fully engage the intensity of life's deepest sorrows because, through that process, we may actually experience some of life's highest joys.

During this heartbreaking process of losing Stephen, learning to be alone, and finding my way into a new life I had to learn to want, I have come to believe that making the transition from this world to the next is as natural as a sigh. That, while rarely easy, the experience can be beautiful. And that, in the end, those whom we have lost are not so far away as we might think.

I promised Stephen I would walk up to the door of death with him, and our experiences in his final hours convince me that I did. In sharing our touch of heaven, my hope is that, whatever your beliefs, you may begin to see death of the physical body as but the doorway we must each pass through on our way to the exquisite joy that awaits us.

Of course, getting through that door is the hard part. Facing death is a soul-wrenching experience. But Stephen and I discovered a way through its hardships that lifted us up rather than grinding us to pieces—which is the process I encourage you to embrace. Being with my husband as he lived and died transformed me, even as he was being translated to the Other Side. When something that extraordinary happens to us, I believe we have an obligation to share it, in hope that our experience may light the path for others we chance to meet along the way.

Part One

A
BEAUTIFUL LIFE

My true love hath my heart, and I have his,
By just exchange, one for another given,
I hold his dear, and mine he cannot miss,
There never was a better bargain driven.

—Sir Philip Sidney

One

THE HEART MUST BREAK

And tho' the hope be gone, love,
That long sparkled o'er our way,
Oh! We shall journey on, love.

—Thomas Moore

It was late spring of 2008—one of those warm, crispy-clear May mornings in Colorado—a great time to be driving south along Interstate 25, as I had done so many times before. Today I was going to Pueblo to present a couple of workshops at the local community college, but I was actually happier for the solitude than for the work.

I put on a bluegrass CD, my favorite kind of traveling music, enjoying the banjo's bright rhythm and the singers' high-lonesome harmonies, when I suddenly started to cry—the deep, soul-wrenching sobs that erupt, uncontrollably, from a broken heart.

My husband, Stephen, was dying of cancer. And, despite over four years of chemotherapy, radiation, and some alternative therapies, there was nothing we could do about it. Stephen was still working, but the weight loss and jaundice that are symptoms of end-stage cancer in the liver were starting to appear. He was getting very weak and needed more care, and I had started cutting back on my business travel so I could be home with him more. We didn't focus on the changes, but we both knew that life was about to get much harder.

It was a relief for me to cry alone there in the car, without burdening Stephen. He already felt that he was ruining my life by dying, so I tried not to make him feel worse by getting weepy. We were doing our best to be brave and positive, and we had come to terms (more or less) with the fact that we were facing the end of our nearly eighteen years together. But sometimes, you just need to let the tears come. "Un-cried tears are toxic," my mother had warned. "Just let them flow when they start." Right now, letting them flow was not a problem.

I was just north of Colorado Springs, with April snows still glistening on Pike's Peak up ahead, when my mind suddenly flashed back to my freshman year at Colorado College, to a time, over forty years earlier, when the rising sun created a kaleidoscopically fresh view of that peak every morning as I walked to class. My whole life lay before me, and like other eighteen-year-olds, I was full of anticipation and yearning—for true love, a meaningful career, and a spiritual path that would unlock the mysteries of life I often found confusing.

Earlier that year—1967—I had stood in my bedroom at home and declared to the heavens, "Please, God, please—don't let me be normal!" This was a line from the popular musical *The Fantasticks!* It was also my life's rallying cry. My parents were opposed to my dream of singing and dancing my way into the hearts of millions as a professional entertainer; but I wanted to create a life of interest, maybe even adventure, and surely one that was different from the middle-class conventions that seemed destined to trap me forever.

Nevertheless, being an obedient child, I wanted to please the authority figures in my life, so I went off to become a French and history major—a pretty disastrous choice, as it turned out. In less than a year, academia and I parted ways and I transferred to a theater arts program in Texas, beginning in earnest a lifetime's search for meaning and my true place in the universe.

After receiving a Bachelor of Arts degree, I followed the career path of countless music and theater gypsies before me—taking performing gigs when I could get them and waiting tables when I couldn't. I honestly had no idea how the world worked. All I knew for certain was that if I listened to the inner voice that had spoken to me since childhood, I would eventually know what to do. Unfortunately, that inner "knowing" took its own sweet time, while I made a few wrong turns, including a brief, unhappy marriage. Finally, in 1978, I landed safely in a spiritual community where I would spend most of the next twenty years.

When asked how one with so much potential (as the adults in my life persistently reminded me) could run off and join what my parents considered a religious cult, I reply that my soul seemed to have its own agenda. In many ways, I just went along for the ride.

After divorcing my first husband in 1975, I joined a musical-theater troupe that performed in San Francisco and then got the wild idea to do a nightclub revue in Omaha, Nebraska. That show closed before it made any money, leaving me too broke to return to California, where I had an apartment and a boyfriend. So I stayed with a friend in Denver and worked for several weeks at my old waitress job until I earned enough cash to get home. I was about to load up my black-and-yellow Porsche 914 (a divorce present to myself) for the drive back to California when I had a premonition that I was going to die in a car accident out in the middle of Nevada.

I took this warning very seriously because, through the years, I had learned to trust the inner voice, which often spoke to me—not just through intuition, but in powerfully commanding tones—in matters of great importance, such as: "Don't get involved with him" regarding my first husband (which, regretfully, I had ignored) and "Get out now, he's killing your soul" (which I had readily obeyed). Also, separate car accidents had recently killed two cousins who were my same age. So I was genuinely afraid to set out on that highway; I didn't want to become casualty number three.

While delaying my trip, I felt prompted to go see some friends perform at a local dinner theater. I knew they were involved with a spiritual community in California, so after the show I mentioned my trepidation to them. They, in turn, spent the next several hours telling me about the teachings they followed, which included protection afforded through prayers and mantras to Archangel Michael and other spiritual beings.

The teachings they explained during that all-night discussion thrilled my soul. This was the path I had been looking for. These were the mystical ideas that spoke to my childhood vision of the tunnel of light—truths that aligned with my own beliefs about guardian angels, reincarnation, karma, and an ongoing life in the spirit for which physical death is but the doorway.

The next morning, my friends armed me with books and prayers, and I was on my way. I packed up my car and set off for California. I faithfully recited the mantras to Archangel Michael, visualizing him protecting me, and I made it safely back to San Francisco. However, there was a point, out in the barren wastelands of Nevada, when I looked in the rear view mirror and had the very strong impression that I had just passed the spot where the accident I had seen in my premonition would have taken place, had I not listened to the prompting to go see my friends.

A few months after I got back to San Francisco, these same friends invited me to join their summer melodrama and musical revue in Vail, Colorado. I jumped at the chance to return to the mountains of my home, to do music and theater again, and to spend time with people who were actively pursuing the path I wanted to know so much more about.

In September, after the melodrama closed for the season, another college friend joined us to form an acoustic band that performed folk music, bluegrass, jug band, and original songs, plus comedy skits. We all were theater majors with a penchant for improvisation, so our musical sets often contained more skits than songs. Audiences had never seen anything quite like us, and we were a hit.

For the next eighteen months, we had a blast touring the Holiday Inn circuit in our Ford van along the old Oregon Trail. This was the late 1970s, and we were free spirits of our generation—growing alfalfa sprouts in Mason jars, studying spiritual teachings during the day, and singing at night—absolutely *the* most fun I have ever had in any job at any time in my life.

Our goal was to save enough money to attend a conference at the California headquarters of the organization that published the teachings we were studying. In December of 1978 we arrived in the Malibu Mountains for the New Year's event. I remember driving through the community's gates and feeling that I had been there many times before. It was not a new experience, it was a homecoming. And the conference was electric. I instantly recognized the leader as my spiritual teacher, and my soul rejoiced. This was where I belonged.

After the conference, we returned to Colorado to discover that all of the jobs we had been counting on for the next few months had fallen through. By this time, the frictions that plague most bands were beginning to surface, so we took the abrupt loss of work as a sign to move on. We sold our sound system and dissolved our musical partnership. It was time for dramatic change.

The California community had a teaching center in a beautiful old Colorado Springs mansion where members of all ages and backgrounds could live, help conduct services throughout the week, and pursue more rigorous spiritual discipline. I applied to join the staff there, but was told in a letter from my teacher that I must first attend a 12-week session of her "spiritual university." Since the next quarter was starting in less than a month (and, as usual, I was low on funds), I cashed in a life-insurance policy, vacated my apartment, sold or gave away my theatrical wardrobe, and moved in with a friend until it was time to leave for California.

The spiritual university was sublime. I loved these teachings, depicting Earth as a schoolroom where we are assisted by beings of light that help us meet the challenges of the spiritual path. Our teacher believed that the great wisdom traditions of both East and West had been born of the same essential concept: Love. She spoke eloquently of the unconditional love of a Father/Mother God and the opportunity for individual souls to return to the Creator in what she called the ritual of the ascension.

Most instruction was held in the lovely Gothic-style chapel building erected by the previous owners, Catholic Claretian Fathers who had operated the Malibu property as a retreat site. I remember listening to a taped lecture in a classroom that spring (it was 1979), watching new leaves burst forth on elm trees just outside the window. Whenever the hot sun caused a bud to release its baby leaf, a tiny spray of moisture would shoot out at the same time.

That's the way my soul felt—just popping with new life and gratitude that I had actually found a place where I could pursue this unique lifestyle with hundreds of like-minded people. Our mission was to build a self-sufficient spiritual community in which we could live apart from the world, yet close enough to minister to people who were likewise searching for perennial truths in an age of social and religious upheaval. Many of us were refugees from the hippie era. All of us were enthusiastic, courageous, and dedicated to our teacher's version of the path to self-mastery.

The three months of spiritual instruction flew by. As soon as they were over, I knew what I was meant to do: I joined the headquarters staff in Malibu and prepared to stay for the rest of my life. It was here that I gained most of my professional skills and experience. And it was in this community, nearly a decade after I leapt into what I absolutely believed to be my destiny, that I met and married Stephen—the man of my dreams—the one who was now about to leave me.

Oh, yes, I remembered—as the traffic on the highway brought me back to the present—Stephen is dying. It's amazing how so many vivid recollections can flash before the mind's eye in an instant. And it was even more astounding, I thought, that in the forty-odd years since high school, I had attained all three of my life's great desires: for meaningful work, true love, and a spiritual path. Any one of them would be sufficient for a lifetime. Yet here I was—not even old by current standards—having seen all these dreams come true!

In the thundering realization of what I had truly been given in this life, I felt a huge crack open in my heart. For weeks, as we tried to hold back the crushing weight of an end we could not prevent, it had been breaking a little more each day. In this moment of insight, it broke wide open and the tears flooded through. But then it came to me that my heart *must* break. In fact, I realized, it is actually my *right* and an essential part of my spiritual path to feel this deeply—both the exquisite joy of true love and the unspeakable sorrow of loss.

Living with a heart that could break made me more than merely human. The ability to grieve was grace for transformation. I saw how walking through this pain with Stephen was the way I would build the "soul stuff" of courage and character that I would need for whatever my life without him might hold.

SEARCHING FOR MY ANAM ĊARA

My bounty is as boundless as the sea,
My love as deep: the more I give to thee,
The more I have, for both are infinite.

—William Shakespeare

I HAD LOOKED FOR STEPHEN my entire life. Even as a little girl, I was always searching faces for the eyes that would say, "I'm the one." There seemed to be somebody missing from my life—and not just the romantic soul mate that many people yearn for. What I was seeking was my *anam ċara*, Gaelic for "soul friend." To me, my *anam ċara* would be the one with whom I would feel no separation, the one with whom I could share a soul unity that would keep us attuned to one another across the limits of time and space.

I knew he was out there; I just couldn't find him. But that didn't stop me from looking. My college roommate still remembers, "You always needed a boyfriend"—which was true. My best friends were female, but I really preferred the company of men to that of women. One night, I dug deep into my soul's longing and wrote the following poem.

Penance

And I who once in loving sought God only,
Yet found you standing tender at my door,
Now for the sin of loving you too dearly
Must now seek God, my soul yet to restore.

For loving wakened mem'ries of our partings—
Of sorrows, specters of our trials and hates
That, though you rained sweet comfort's joy upon me,
My melancholy fear would not abate.

Oh, can such rapture truly be deservéd
Or should my heart, desiring you, e'en break
And deign the gods their leave to take you from me—
Their schemes of vengeance on God's own create.

Thus love of love affixed in my remembrance
Rejection's fear yet threat'ning out of sight,
I foundered on the rock of indecision
And slipped away from you into death's night.

If love of Truth be not my higher master
And fire of Justice not my daily fare,
The love I bore you once shall have been wasted—
Devotion withered on the vine of care.

Ah, love, I long so often now to touch you,
To feel the warmth of your remembered breath.
Yet I know angels stand firm guard between us.
In God's time only may our dreams cheat death.

This poem was not just expressing a natural desire for companionship or romantic love—or even for a husband to have a family with. I was an independent career girl who never wanted children. In fact, the only time I ever wanted a baby was some months after Stephen and I got married, and by then the sands in my biological hourglass had run out.

No, "Penance" was a deep memory of twin souls struggling to reconcile their love for each other with their love for God. I wasn't just writing a poem, I was living a memory. I was *in* the scenes I was imagining. It was a painful recollection that shocked me as soon as I wrote it, but then rang true with an overwhelming sense that finding my *anam ċara* really was, for me, a matter of life and death.

Naturally, this deep longing was more than a little inconvenient in a community made up mainly of people who were celibate. Like the historical Essenes who authored the Dead Sea Scrolls, the Catholic Church in fifth- and sixth-century Ireland, and even the earliest followers of Jesus, we were a "dual monastery" where both genders served equally. Women enjoyed equal standing with men, including similar access to spiritual teachings, participation in rituals and sacraments, and even ordination. There was, however, purposeful separation of the sexes. Men and women might work side by side, but when they attended certain prayer services, they sat on opposite sides of the chapel. Casual dating was not allowed. Anyone interested in pursuing a romantic relationship with another staff member had to write to our teacher for her approval.

This code of conduct seemed onerous, even absurd, to people viewing us from the permissive perspective of modern culture; but we who lived in the community understood it as insurance against sexual advances that could easily derail one's spiritual progress. Of course, most of us young adults were still secretly looking for our soul's best friend; but we believed that dedication to spiritual discipline was the force that would eventually attract the perfect partner.

We also understood that the history of twin souls—or twin flames, as they're called in Theosophy and the Edgar Cayce readings—is often cluttered with more sorrow than sweetness. Even when the two find each other, the union can be fractious, ending in bitter division, unless they can learn to honor their special bond and work together in loving service to a cause greater than self-interest.

So I watched and waited, staying very busy with more practical pursuits. After all, I knew I was exactly where I was supposed to be.

Three

HE'S THE ONE

You have been mine before—
How long ago I may not know:
But just when at that swallow's soar
Your neck turned so,
Some veil did fall—I know it all of yore.

—Dante Gabriel Rossetti

WHEN I FINALLY MET STEPHEN, I was living in Montana on a vast property we called the Ranch, located just north of Yellowstone National Park, where my teacher had moved the entire community in 1986. We were holding our annual ten-day conference that coincided with the Fourth of July weekend, drawing thousands of people from all over the world.

This particular day was a hot and crazy-busy one, and I was distracted by all the commotion that accompanied the crowd of attendees flocking through the bookstore tent. Our teacher was a prolific author and the organization was dedicated to printing and distributing her books, so this was a very busy place.

There were no fireworks or clarion bells announcing that my thirty-nine-year search was over—just another new staff member to meet. A longtime friend introduced us. "This is Stephen Eckl," she said. "He's just come from the Chicago teaching center to work in the book sales accounting department." I was working as a traveling book-sales representative at the time, so this meant that, technically, we would be in the same department—although I was spending most of my time on the road, visiting bookstore accounts in Texas and the Southwest, which was my territory. He would be in the office.

Like anyone meeting Stephen for the first time, I was struck by his beaming smile and the fact that he was drop-dead gorgeous—the epitome of tall, dark, and handsome. I was very glad to meet him, but I did not recognize his eyes as the object of my lifelong search. Of course, he was a full head taller than I and wearing glasses, so standing on tiptoe and peering into his face to actually get a good look at those deep-set, sea-green eyes would have been a bit awkward.

At the time I thought he was rather quiet, and soft men did not appeal to me. In fact, the next time I took particular notice of Stephen was nearly eighteen months later in the spring of 1990 during a large construction project the community was undertaking. I was now working in the audio-video department and he was driving heavy equipment on what was affectionately known as the "dirt dog" crew.

I happened to be sitting behind him in a prayer service and was struck by how virile he had become since changing departments. No sooner had this thought wandered through my mind than I heard that famous inner voice declare: *He's the one.* I was stunned and didn't know what to do—except figure out how to get better acquainted with Stephen Eckl.

I got my chance a couple of months later when he and I were both working at the construction site. Of course, I immediately made a goon of myself, practically choking with embarrassment when I had to ask him a simple question. As the days went by and I had occasion to engage him in casual conversation, I realized I was totally falling for this guy who didn't say much in a crowd but who was downright talkative one-on-one—and he seemed to be interested in me.

At lunch one day I was sitting across a table from him while he talked to a buddy about growing up in Rochester, New York, and visiting his parents, who now lived in Colorado—or something like that. I wasn't paying much attention because I was looking at his ear (did I mention he was gorgeous?), deciding it was the loveliest ear I had ever seen. (Oh, my!)

But I was in a quandary. Inner voice or not, I had been very wrong about men before; and, as I well knew, in our community you didn't just ask somebody out on a date. For several days I deliberated. I was seriously considering asking our teacher for permission to pursue a relationship with Stephen when he abruptly stopped talking to me, obviously going out of his way to avoid crossing paths if he saw me walking in his direction. Clearly, his mind had changed from the warm signals he had been sending only days earlier.

Well! So much for divine inspiration, I thought. *Thank goodness I didn't embarrass myself by writing to our teacher about him. Maybe I'm just not supposed to be married again. Whoever my twin flame may be, he's not here. He may live in Outer Mongolia or he may be five years old, but I'm not going to find him here.*

And with that thought, I decided to give up looking for a husband and focus my attention on creating a stronger bond with the Divine Presence in my own heart. "I'm claiming God as my spouse," I declared aloud in my room one evening before bedtime prayers, and then I started visualizing a symbolic wedding band on my left hand—a lovely gold ring with a brilliant blue stone.

Nevertheless, there was weird magic afoot. I tried putting Stephen out of my mind, but whenever I did think about him, my heart and stomach did a breathtaking flip-flop—which I suppose was not all that strange. What was strange, however, was that one day, in my mind's eye, I saw Stephen's intense, blue-green eyes staring right into my face, and I felt the brown plaid work jacket that he always wore somehow present in my aura—as if I were wearing the jacket myself. *That* was truly disturbing.

A couple of weeks later, my division of the A/V department finished its work at the conference site and we returned to our normal offices at headquarters. While I occasionally noticed Stephen at prayer services, he was still keeping his distance, and our paths did not cross for several months.

Soon it was July conference time again and the entire community was in a flurry. During the massive preparations, I had an opportunity to speak to our teacher, not saying anything about Stephen, but mentioning to her that I had never been able to completely forsake the idea of being married.

"It's not something you necessarily have to deny," she explained. "But if it's not happening, you should work to raise up the light in your consciousness. If the person isn't here, he can't get here if you don't resolve your psychology."

It was painful to admit that I would probably never find my true love, but I was very busy with my duties in the A/V department as well as practicing for the musical revue that I and several other former professional musicians were preparing for conference entertainment. So I hardly noticed when Stephen Eckl began eating his lunch in the big tent where we were rehearsing.

"What is he looking at?" I wondered aloud one day—and then went back to practice. On Sunday night, following the final conference event, I found out. I was standing outside of the main chapel building when up walked Stephen Eckl.

"Can I talk to you?" he asked. I froze. Stephen had not spoken to me in months. The idea shot through my mind that I was really in trouble for still fantasizing about him. *He's going to reprimand me for having my energy all over him,* I thought, remembering how often I had actually dreamed about him during the past few months.

Instead, he told me that in April he had written to our teacher about dating me. Rather than giving her approval, she had told him that it was not meant to be and that he should concentrate on overcoming certain negative aspects of his human consciousness.

"It was really difficult," he said, "but I did it. It was important for me to follow her guidance because I knew it would be the decision of a lifetime. Then, just before the conference, I got word from her—totally out of the blue—telling me that I was now free to contact you to determine if there was any basis for a relationship."

For the first time in my life, I was utterly speechless. All I could get out was, "Really?" And then, "Is that why you've been watching our rehearsals in the tent?" Odd things were beginning to make sense.

"Yes," he went on. "Frankly, I had so completely surrendered the idea that I didn't know if I was still interested or not. In fact, I really wasn't sure until today. I was concerned that your being a performer might be a detriment to our relationship. But after this evening's worship service, I knew that I really did want us to be together."

"What do we do now?" I gulped. I felt as if I had been struck by lightning. For so long I had wanted to be in a relationship; but now that I was suddenly faced with it, I was terrified. I could hardly form a complete sentence, and I was very uncomfortable. I wasn't even sure I loved Stephen. It all seemed so clinical.

"You look frightened," said Stephen.

"I am," I admitted. "This is all pretty amazing." I knew that God would not do this to me if it were not real. But it didn't feel real. I kept thinking, *Where is the romance?* This wasn't how I imagined it would be.

That was Sunday night. All day Monday I was in turmoil. But on Tuesday morning I awoke in what can only be described as a pink bubble of love and light—a bit like the one that surrounds Glinda the Good Witch in *The Wizard of Oz*—except this wasn't a fairy tale. I was quite literally enfolded in love!

"I'm not afraid anymore," I told Stephen as soon as I could reach him by phone.

"I'm so glad," he said. "You had me worried."

"I'd love to see you tonight," I explained, "but we're opening our own dinner theater next weekend, so for the next two nights I'm busy rehearsing the new show. Why don't you come to dress rehearsal on Thursday evening? You'll be part of an invited audience and we can talk afterwards."

"That sounds great," he agreed immediately.

"The conference show was just a warm-up," I warned him with a laugh. "You'd better see what it is that I really do so you know what you're getting into."

On Thursday night Stephen sat in the back row of the theater, observing. Whenever I caught a glimpse of him, he was smiling, apparently not changing his mind. At least he stayed for the entire show and talked enthusiastically about our being together as he walked me home that night under a starlit Montana sky.

A few days later, on a picnic beside the Yellowstone River, he proposed. I accepted "with all my heart" and we got married three weeks later. When you know, you know.

At the picnic I gave him a copy of the "Penance" poem and we discussed its powerful description of reincarnation—a belief we held in common with many cultures, both ancient and modern. I definitely felt that we had been together in past lives and Stephen seemed to agree.

That came home to me in one dramatic moment on the day we spent shopping for wedding paraphernalia. Stephen was trying on tuxedos. He would eventually settle on a white one, which best matched my wedding gown. But when he emerged from the dressing room in a gray morning coat with tails, the room went all fuzzy-light before my eyes and I felt as if I were looking at him through a window into another time when he wore this formal attire every day. The sensation lasted only an instant, but I knew I had witnessed this scene before.

Between the proposal and the wedding there was one more event that confirmed forever my belief that this was a match if not made in heaven, then certainly ordained by it. About a week after we set the date for our wedding, Stephen met me for lunch in the cafeteria and said with a twinkle in his eye, "I have something for you."

"What is it?" I asked excitedly.

"Just a minute, it has a story." He smiled. "I've never worn this," he explained. "I bought it from a friend in Chicago when he needed some money, but it never appealed to me to wear it. I guess it was always for you."

Given the fact that we were both working for a very small monthly stipend, it had never occurred to me to expect an engagement ring; but that's what he pulled out of his pocket. He opened his hand and there was a lovely gold ring with a blue topaz stone at its center: the *exact* same ring that, months earlier, I had been visualizing on my left hand as my wedding ring from God. I was, once again, speechless.

Four

TWO HEARTS MAKE A WHOLE

I love thee to the depth and breadth and height
My soul can reach.

—Elizabeth Barrett Browning

FRIDAY EVENING, AUGUST 10, 1990, was opening night of a new Broadway revue. I was singing and dancing with the troupe at the dinner theater we had created in the huge back room of the Ranch's commercial restaurant. It was located on the highway that ran north from Yellowstone National Park, so we were getting a lot of local tourist traffic and our shows were regularly sold out. To keep people coming back, we opened a new show every month.

This Friday night was also the rehearsal dinner for my wedding to Stephen. Our families had met the day before and were seated right up front, where they could catch all the action and where I could see their every response. I was taking a huge risk by inviting them to the show, but with a Sunday wedding, there was no other way to arrange the weekend's events.

What a way to get to know your future in-laws, I thought as my big comedic solo began. This was truly appalling. Here I was, sitting on a stool in the spotlight, my hair tied up in a scarf like *I Love Lucy,* singing "Adelaide's Lament" from the musical *Guys and Dolls* in a fake Brooklyn accent (to people from New York, for heaven's sake!) about a not-so-young woman who's afraid she'll never get married. This was certainly art reflecting life.

What must Stephen's family be thinking? I worried. I could only imagine their response to the final lyric: "From a lack of community property and a feeling she's getting too old, a person can develop a bad, bad cold."

At least they're clapping, I thought as I took a bow and scurried backstage for a quick costume change. *Maybe they don't think I'm too weird.* At that point, there was no telling for sure.

Less than a month earlier, when Stephen had called his parents to announce our engagement, they were in New York for his grandfather's funeral. "This is the best news you could possibly have given us," his mom had told him. I think they had given up on the idea that he would ever marry. He was thirty-seven years old and had never had a serious, long-term relationship.

His mom and brothers (John, seventeen months older; Rick, eight years younger) were thrilled with the match, but his dad had clearly been disappointed at our first meeting when he quizzed me about what sports I pursued. All the Eckls were skilled athletes, so it was assumed that Stephen would marry someone similarly inclined.

"Do you ski?"

"No."

"Play golf?"

"No."

"Tennis?"

"No."

"Well, what do you do?" Papa John Eckl had a way of stating the awkwardly obvious.

"I sing and dance," I had offered with a weak smile, trying to sound confident and worthy of marrying his much-beloved son. He did not appear convinced.

My own parents were accustomed to my crazy antics on stage, so I wasn't worried about their response to the show. Their main concern was the fact that, until three weeks ago, they had not heard a single word about this guy I was going to marry in two days.

"Hi, would you like to come to a wedding in Montana?" I had chirped when they both picked up the phone, hearing only stunned silence on the other end of the line.

"I guess so, if it's yours," my father had finally managed. But they were understandably apprehensive. So far, they thought Stephen was cute and they liked his family very much, but this was all quite sudden.

Fortunately, music and comedy worked their magic, and by the end of the evening, both families seemed very much at ease, laughing and talking—even slapping Stephen on the back in congratulations. It was all smiles and hugs after the show and I could tell that Stephen was relieved. Me too.

Our wedding day—Sunday, August 12, 1990—dawned gloriously full of sunshine and promise. In three short weeks, all the preparations had come together in miraculous fashion. The whole event seemed touched by angels. Our community owned a stock of designer wedding dresses that had been donated by an exclusive bridal shop on Rodeo Drive in Beverly Hills. The one I chose, an exquisite gown that glistened like spun ice, fit perfectly because it had recently been altered by another bride who was just my size. And the two pink bridesmaids' dresses that were part of the same collection fit my attendants perfectly.

Despite the short notice, both sets of parents and Stephen's two brothers and their families had flown in, and his grandmother, now a widow, had made the trip from New York. Without knowing it, we had decided to get married on the senior Eckls' fortieth wedding anniversary. It was also two weeks before my parents' fiftieth, so at our reception we surprised both couples with their own little heart-shaped anniversary cakes to cut and feed to each other. My musician friends sang "Because," which had been sung at my parents' wedding. Truly, there was not a dry eye in the house.

And Stephen and I were ecstatically happy. For months after our wedding, we would sometimes weep from the sheer joy of finally being together. When we moved into our tiny studio apartment on the Ranch property, it was as if two pieces of the same puzzle had finally locked into place. It felt like we were just picking up where we had left off in a previous lifetime, rather than being two people who hardly knew each other.

The walls separating our apartment from the one adjoining proved to be embarrassingly thin. One day I overheard our neighbor joking with her friend, making smoochy noises, and laughing at the way we whispered and giggled at all hours of the day and night, calling each other silly names. We had started out saying "Honey," but that had quickly expanded to Honey Bunny, eventually morphing into Bunny or Bun—which remained our pet name for each other throughout our marriage. We might have appeared ridiculous to others, but we were perfect in one another's eyes.

One week after our wedding, Stephen wrote me this card:

To my dear wife whom I adore with all my heart,

As I contemplate the last seven days—the first seven of our marriage—I am, of course, reminded of the intense joy you have given to me. As we start our journey together in this life, I send you my deepest gratitude, not only for your care of me and all the expressions of life and love you do so well, but for your presence within me that I feel even when you are not physically near me. I am made whole!

The most precious gift of our union, however, has been the standard of "Being" that we have established. The level of our Love is so dear to me that I strive daily to let nothing trespass that ring of fire. I look forward to this so very sacred adventure of proving what two souls united in Love can do for God.

I am yours, serving the flame in your heart which is within mine.
All my love,
Stephen

Several weeks later, I was talking with an acquaintance who had also been recently married. She was complaining about how difficult it was for her and her new husband to live together. They were in their early forties, about the same age as Stephen and I, but so set in their own quirky ways that they disagreed on practically everything having to do with daily routines.

I was amazed; Stephen and I just fit. It had never occurred to us that the sudden adjustment of living together could be hard.

I have heard philosophers describe the soul as shy—not wanting to be entirely known. Stephen was like that—in many ways, more of an observer than a participant. An introvert born into a family of extroverts, he had long ago learned to keep his own counsel. He was highly vocal and competitive when engaged in sports (especially with his brothers), but except for the occasional card or love note hidden where I would find it by accident, he kept his deepest feelings to himself.

So I learned about Stephen by experiencing him, not so much by what he told me. We anchored each other. I felt safe and grounded with him. He was so steady and reliable, and he absolutely adored me, as I did him. However, adoration did not mean indulging my attempts to manipulate him; in the face of even mild emotional outbursts, Stephen would become an immovable rock. But he looked out for me and began teaching me by example that maintaining a harmonious attitude can smooth out a lot of bumps along life's highway.

At the time we were married, Stephen was still working on the heavy-equipment crew. He was feeling the need for a change, and we both worried about his continued safety—especially when the supports on a water tank he had been working on collapsed just a few minutes after he had crawled out from under it. We prayed for a solution and one came within a few days—as the "coincidence" of divine intervention often does—in a most unanticipated way.

Ever the intrepid "dirt dog," Stephen was helping a backfill crew, using his left leg on the shovel. I still don't know why he was using that leg, because his left knee was a mess. He had torn his anterior cruciate ligament in high-school wrestling, and it had been only partially repaired by surgery when he was in college. So while he was shoveling, a piece of cartilage broke loose and lodged itself in his kneecap. He didn't notice it until he got up from dinner later that evening and nearly crashed to the floor in pain. An orthopedic surgeon confirmed that he needed a complete ACL replacement, which took place within a couple of weeks.

The surgery itself was unremarkable. The doctor even let Stephen watch the procedure on a TV monitor. What *was* remarkable was my reaction when they rolled Stephen into surgery. I had nearly fainted when the nurse inserted his IV during the prep, so I was feeling a little wobbly. But when I saw Stephen being taken away, I fell apart.

It was as if I would never see him again. He wasn't just going to surgery; he was going away forever. I had never felt such utter desolation. Sobbing uncontrollably, I called his mother and then my own. I finally regained some composure and went to the hospital chapel to wait until the doctor reported that the surgery was a success. I went to Stephen's room and starting crying all over again, in joy and relief that he was not gone. My reaction was illogical, completely involuntary, and totally overwhelming.

"I'm sure it was just because you were a newlywed alone at the hospital," said Stephen's mom, recalling how distraught I had been. But it was more than that. This was the "memory of our partings" that I had written about in my poem "Penance." I was actually experiencing that devastating separation, and I was inconsolable at the thought of losing Stephen again so soon.

The knee surgery was our first real shared crisis and it only strengthened our bond. One thing I learned about Stephen from it was his astonishing stoicism when it came to bearing physical pain.

"Doesn't your knee hurt?" I asked him one day while he was still using crutches to get around. He had been transferred back to the accounting department, so he had a nice, safe desk job, but the healing seemed to be going slowly.

"Of course it does," he answered. "But there's no point complaining about it. I learned that lesson years ago from my friend Michael."

"Who was he?"

"He was the leader of a spiritual group I joined in Colorado a couple of years before I found our teachings. We studied the work and sacred dances of the Russian mystic Gurdjieff, which he had learned from Sufi masters in the East. It was quite a bit like being here at the Ranch, except on a much smaller scale. We had purchased some land in the mountains northwest of Denver and were building a meditation center there. I was working as a fireman in Fort Collins; but whenever I had time off, I would camp out in my teepee—yes, it was an authentic Native American teepee," he said, seeing my expression—"that I had pitched on the property. And I did carpentry work on the center with whoever was there at the time.

"One day we heard that Michael had suddenly collapsed at home with a peptic ulcer. As he told the story to us later, when he cried out, 'I can't bear the pain!' he heard a voice demand of him, 'Why not?' He said the force of that voice shocked him into actually embracing his agony as an opportunity for self-transformation—which was a primary focus of Gurdjieff's teachings.

"I've never wanted people to make a fuss over me if I got hurt or was ill. Michael's experience only reinforced that. I guess I'm just not a whiner."

Before I married Stephen I was concerned that I might hurt him because he seemed so mild-mannered. He certainly put that notion to rest in a hurry. Even with a bum knee, he was the strongest person I have ever met. He was a real "guy" who wore his masculinity with easy grace and enjoyed being physically strong. I was continually amazed to discover that things I couldn't budge he would just pick up and move. He was a natural athlete who could play any sport. He was rather humble about his accomplishments, but he did once confess to having been a high-school football star who covered both offense and defense—exploits that prompted one boy's parent to exclaim, "Stephen Eckl doesn't just play on the football team, he *is* the football team!"

Once his knee healed up, he was eager to get back on the bicycle he rode everywhere; and we bought me a bike so I could ride with him. Those were interesting excursions. What was a relaxing ride for Stephen was for me a total survival experience. "Don't be such a wimp!" he teased me one afternoon as I struggled through loose gravel on one of his favorite trails that went straight up a steep mountain path. "I can see I'm going to have to toughen you up because you never had any brothers. Don't worry, you'll make it."

And I did. Living with Stephen, I got stronger in every possible way. I also learned very quickly not to complain about petty human squabbles or how rotten my day had been, because discord of any kind was physically painful to him. He was a brilliant problem solver if I actually wanted his advice on how to remedy a bad situation, but whining was not something we did at our house. If I just wanted him to listen, I had to say so up front and then get on with the details. He was not very patient with long, protracted stories. "Too much drama!" he would exclaim if I started getting emotional about something. I eventually learned to think through situations more than react to them, but it took me a while.

Several years after Stephen's knee surgery, we moved to a slightly larger apartment, and his extraordinary talent for woodworking and home improvement surfaced with dramatic energy and enthusiasm. He quickly fitted our kitchenette with custom oak cabinets that he designed and built himself in the construction department's wood shop. He also extended the lawn outside our building, planting pine trees, building a rock garden—including a huge boulder that had to be brought in with the front-end loader he still enjoyed driving once in a while—and creating a beautiful walkway with scores of used bricks that we hauled in and laid by hand.

I planted flowers that flourished in the rich topsoil Stephen trucked in, and we built a storage barn (his original design, of course) to hold our extra belongings that wouldn't fit in the small but tidy space we called home. Our friend Kerry dubbed our handiwork the "Greater Yellowstone Eckl-sphere." It truly was a little paradise.

Five

PLEASE, MAKE IT OBVIOUS

God has prepared a path for everyone to follow.
You just have to read the omens that he left for you.

—Paulo Coelho

IN 1996 THINGS STARTED TO CHANGE in the community. For several years, headquarters had been under pressure from the satellite teaching centers to relinquish some control to the local groups, which would allow them to keep more of the contributions they collected from their members. This meant the need for fewer staff at the Ranch and led to a decision to reorganize and decentralize most operations.

Departments were downsized or eliminated, and staff members were given the opportunity to apply for different jobs if they wanted to change departments. People were also offered an incentive to leave the community if they or the administration felt it was time for them to move on. Sometimes this was by mutual agreement; sometimes it was not. Stephen went to work part-time in Editorial and decided to pursue degree work in philosophy through a distance-learning program.

I took a job as meetings facilitator and office manager for the professional management consultant who had been hired as president of the new organization. It was thrilling work that opened up a whole new world for me in leadership training, organizational development, and personal self-actualization—although it kept me tied up in long meetings that went late into the evening, which Stephen did not like.

I also discovered my passion for delivering workshops—almost by accident, when my boss decided not to show up for one of the many team-building sessions he was conducting for various departments that were being completely reorganized.

"Don't worry," he assured me, literally five minutes before the session was to begin. "You have all the material and you know the workshop as well as I. You can do it." Fortunately, he was right— although throwing me into the deep end to sink or swim as a trainer was a risky move on his part. But I successfully presented that workshop and many others, and every time was an exhilarating experience—even better than being on stage.

Unfortunately, the community was reeling from all the changes as people switched jobs or simply left when their positions disappeared. After completing only one semester of his philosophy course, Stephen was asked to return to full-time accounting work. I seemed to spend my life in meetings.

In June of 1997, I celebrated my eighteenth year on staff. One afternoon, as I was meditating in our apartment, I had a very strong premonition that I was going to have to pass through death, which looked like a dark tunnel. I saw that it would be a serious situation, but that I would not die—I would come out the other side of the darkness and be okay. At the time, I thought this had to do with childbirth, because we had been trying to get pregnant for several years. I immediately told God I would do it—and then promptly forgot about the whole thing.

July was a busy month and a turning point for Stephen and me. The summer conference was held in San Diego, and we both flew there to work—he as accountant and prayer-service leader and I as assistant to the president. We thoroughly enjoyed our hotel room with a view of San Diego Harbor and a friendly seagull that dropped by for snacks whenever we went out on the balcony.

But it was an intense conference. At one point, Stephen left the podium in the middle of a service because he felt his integrity was being compromised by the way the event was being handled. It is hard to convey how severe this situation had to be for him to do something like that; he was not given to fits of pique. And I found myself challenging the president to literally put his money where his mouth was—to give me the raise he had been promising for months. We were being paid actual salaries now, but my pay was still quite low.

After the conference, we extended our stay in San Diego for a few days' vacation with my parents, who had driven over from Phoenix to join us; then we flew to Denver for a visit with the Eckls. When we returned to Montana, Stephen was ready to leave the community, but I was torn. I had promised the president I would work for him for two years and it had been less than one. I found myself in an uncomfortable situation, actually running out of work to do because, due to an odd legal circumstance, he was not coming to his office for days at a time. In fact, one afternoon I realized that I had completed every single pending project; I had nothing else to do. So, standing in the middle of my now completely organized office, I declared aloud to the heavens: "You've got to show me what to do and, please, make it really obvious!"

Oh, do be careful what you pray for!

Not more than two weeks later, Stephen was flying back to Montana on a Saturday evening from a finance conference he had attended in Washington, D.C. I was supposed to pick him up around 8:00 p.m. at the airport about ninety miles away. My plan had been to make the drive after dinner because it was August and it would still be light then. But around 4:30, I was cleaning our apartment when I suddenly exclaimed, "I have to leave right now!" I had learned to pay attention to these abrupt promptings, so I hurriedly packed up the car and took off. I remember stopping at the convenience store for a cup of coffee, but the rest is a blank—a bit like a black tunnel, in fact. To this day, I do not remember the car accident—except that I came out the other side of the darkness, and I did not die.

What seems to have happened is this: A few miles north of our property on the two-lane rural highway that was both a main trucking route and a wildlife migration corridor, I looked down to change a cassette tape and veered off the road toward a mile marker. I must have looked up, swerved to miss the post, and lost control of my car. I over-corrected and ended up driving along the drainage ditch on the right side of the highway.

In that part of the country, driveways are built up across these ditches to allow access to the properties beyond. While still going fast, I hit one broadside and it acted like a ramp, launching my car into the air. I soared over sixty feet, finally landing "ker-splat" in a field—amazingly right side up, but with a serious concussion and a compression fracture in my lower back.

I am convinced that my guardian angel was working overtime that day—and that somehow my being obedient to the prompting to "leave right now" saved my life. Incredibly, I did not run into either oncoming traffic or any of the deer, elk, or curly-horned Rocky Mountain sheep that lived in the area. Apparently, I got out of my car and flagged down a passerby, who called an ambulance that took me to the hospital about fifty miles away. Somebody got word to friends, who dispatched people to the hospital to sit with me and to the airport to pick up Stephen. He was as upset as I had ever seen him when he appeared at my bedside.

It was all pretty amazing—especially considering the car accident premonition I had had eighteen years earlier. Perhaps this actual car accident I had just survived was the same one but further mitigated by my years of prayer and service in a spiritual community. If you believe in the law of karma—what goes around comes around—you might suspect there was an ancient obligation that still had to be fulfilled by my having a serious accident. Fortunately, my passing out of embodiment was no longer a requirement.

These are things we will never know until we get to the Other Side. By then, of course, it won't matter a bit. What did matter in 1997 was that our car was totaled. My head and back were a mess. I couldn't focus my eyes, let alone work. Stephen was ready to leave the community, and it was now *quite* clear to me that it was time for us to go. So we did.

Six

THE BEST YEARS OF OUR LIVES

*The life of the human soul is not
a "being" but a "becoming."*

—Alfred Adler

"Oh, it's a reward for all your years of service!" exclaimed Stephen's grandmother as she walked into our new home.

I loved Nana. Although she was a devout Catholic, at our wedding she had immediately accepted the correlation between her saints and those from the spiritual traditions of both East and West that we included in our rather complex belief system. (The chapel where we were married included life-size statues of the Virgin Mary and the Chinese figure of Kuan Yin, known as the goddess of mercy.) And here was dear Nana again, expressing exactly what we felt about the darling townhome we had just bought.

Truly, Stephen was born to be a householder. Almost as soon as we moved in, he started plotting what and how he would remodel. I would catch him just staring at the ceiling, walls, or floors, visualizing the best way to transform this ordinary dwelling into a work of art. He was like a painter with a huge new canvas who can hardly wait to start creating his magnum opus.

He managed to contain himself until after our first Christmas in the house because my mother was coming from Arizona to spend the holidays with us, alone; my father had died the previous January. But the day after she left for home, Stephen started ripping up carpet and tile, knocking out a half-wall between the living room and dining area, and tearing out ugly baseboards—proving Pablo Picasso's assertion that "creativity is first of all an act of destruction."

If Stephen had a celebrity hero, it was Norm, the master woodworker from *This Old House* and *The New Yankee Workshop* television programs on PBS. Like Norm, Stephen was meticulous in his old-school approach to building, and he aspired, also like Norm, to own the perfect tool for every project.

It was never hard to buy for Stephen on Christmas or birthdays, because he almost always wanted some kind of power tool that he used to fashion gorgeous tile work and furniture-grade cherry cabinets for the living and dining rooms. He also installed hardwood floors, cut new windows in a big, blank living room wall, created decorative beams and wood ceilings on the first floor, and designed the kitchen remodel, though we had it professionally done to save time. He was good, but he wasn't fast.

Stephen was the master builder, but I was a very competent assistant who did the interior painting. I even gained enough confidence to try my hand at some decorative faux. The dining room was my one success; the other walls appeared to have the measles and had to be repainted a solid color.

Remodeling is not without its bumps. In fact, I've heard that do-it-yourself projects and major remodels (especially kitchens) are responsible for nearly as many divorces as rank infidelity. We were never quite that bad, but in the early days I had trouble visualizing the dramatic changes that were so clear in Stephen's mind. "Why can't you just trust me?" he complained more than once—until I finally learned that anything he created was going to be beautiful.

∞

Stephen and I may have been twin souls at a spiritual level, but we were not identical people. By the time we left the Ranch in late 1997, we had been married for over seven years and the differences were showing up more acutely.

Probably the biggest distinction between us—aside from my having the more extroverted personality—was that when we left the community, Stephen's inner world was intact. His intention was to find a job that did not interfere with either his spiritual practice or his leisure time. He was a great friend to his own imagination and found enormous pleasure in leaving it free to explore the almost limitless possibilities he felt within his being.

When he was in his early twenties, he had had a spiritual breakthrough while hiking in the Maroon Bells wilderness area near Aspen, Colorado. He had gone there with some friends who were experimenting with a mild hallucinogen. In characteristic fashion, while his buddies were hooting with laughter, he went off by himself to be quiet.

At this point in his life, Stephen was not the disciplined mystic I married years later. After dropping out of graduate school, he had worked at various unsatisfying jobs. He didn't know what he wanted to do with his life and was probably in a certain amount of psychological turmoil because—like most of us seekers in the '70s— he didn't really fit anywhere. He had no definite spiritual direction and was just beginning his practice of daily meditation. He was searching for answers but had no clear way of finding them.

Years before, as a boy of 12, he had heard a voice speak to him one Sunday morning in church, saying, *Be a priest.* He thought, *I can't; my family wouldn't approve.* Perhaps it was a coincidence, but soon afterward he started getting migraine headaches, which continued throughout high school.

He probably wasn't thinking about that day as he sat by the still waters of Maroon Lake, gazing at the reflection of the majestic mountains that rose thousands of feet above it. But as he meditated on the quandary of his life, he felt a warm spinning sensation in the center of his chest and heard a voice say, *Build my community.*

Stephen was so startled that he blurted aloud, "All by myself?" The voice did not reply, and the spinning in his heart stopped; but the feeling of a powerful presence stayed with him. The seed was planted. He was changed, and he began in earnest his search for a spiritual path that eventually led him to our teacher's community.

So Stephen was now comfortable in our home with his daily meditations and the routine of his life—but I floundered. When my car went flying off that country road in Montana, I had lost the support structure that I had relied on for nearly twenty years. Leaving the comfy nest of Ranch life was very hard for me. I missed my friends and the certainty of my part in the mission of building our community.

It had been only a few months since the car accident and I was still recovering from a concussion and fractured back. I was in the throes of full-on menopause, complete with migraine headaches of my own. I did not especially like the secretarial position I had taken to tide us over until Stephen found a good job with benefits. And then on January 6, 1998, the day he found that perfect job, my father died.

Any one of these factors would have put me in the top ten categories for stressed-out people. I was absolutely in the soup of emotion. I felt lost and cranky, and I'm sure I made Stephen's life pretty uncomfortable because I was so ungrounded.

He was willingly and consciously tearing up old physical patterns in our house, creating an entirely new look and feel about the place. At the same time, I was unwillingly and unconsciously being pushed to tear up old psychological patterns of thinking and feeling, creating new ways of being in my own life. Both types of deconstruction are messy and can raise a lot of dust before the new form emerges.

It is testimony to how dearly Stephen loved me that for the most part he didn't react to my ups and downs, but just kept going along in his sure, steady way, always reinforcing his approach to the tough times in life: face your situation one day at a time, find a way to enjoy the process of carving out a solution, and use Spirit as the foundation and inspiration for whatever you do.

Okay, there was that one big blow-up we had over money when the professional-development training business I launched on

Tuesday, September 11, 2001 didn't make any money. Stephen wanted me to go back to regular employment with a dependable income and benefits. This suggestion triggered all my old fears of getting stuck in a "normal" (read "boring") job, and I rebelled.

"We've had our junket in this life," he explained firmly. "In the community we were not saving any money and we were not contributing to Social Security. We have a limited number of years to create a nest egg for our retirement. I don't feel like you consider this very important or that you're holding up your end of our partnership."

"I'm not dead yet," I countered, shouting. "Some people don't even make it to retirement! I have no intention of wasting away in an airless office, working for some creep who doesn't care a whit about my creativity or my soul."

It wasn't pretty. However, when I calmed down, I realized that Stephen was probably right. (He usually *was* right—which it irked me to admit—because he thought things through so carefully.) So I called a friend in the temporary-employment industry and asked her to find me a job where I wouldn't suffocate. Thankfully, she did. And the temporary situation she found for me in human resources at the state community college system headquarters turned into a permanent job that offered me unforeseen opportunities to write and hone my skills as a facilitator and trainer.

Despite our differences and this brief period of disagreement, Stephen and I were becoming more devoted to each other all the time. We were complete within ourselves, so happy together that sometimes Stephen would spontaneously exclaim: "Bunny, these are the best years of our lives!"

A lovely consequence of my returning to an office job was that we were able to drive to and from work together. For a full year, my office was right across the street from his. Even after my company moved across town, we were still able to share the morning commute.

Rather than chit-chat about work or complain about crazy drivers on the road, we listened to inspirational music and audio books of classical literature, Romantic poetry, and spiritual teachings. These precious hours in the car did more to deepen our love and mutual understanding than almost anything we did—other than our weekly Sunday readings, which had already become the mainstay of our spiritual development.

Our ritual was to set aside at least an hour first thing on Sunday morning to reconnect with our deepest sense of the Divine. Often still in our pajamas, we would take turns reading aloud from whatever spiritual materials we were studying together at the time. When Stephen and I left the Ranch, we decided to take a break from our teacher's particular approach to the path of self-realization. We highly valued our experience with her, but it was time for a change—so we created our own curriculum that included the poetry of William Wordsworth, Ken Wilber's integral philosophy, *A Course in Miracles,* and Stephen's personal favorite: *The Urantia Book.*

Stephen was a kind and happy husband during these years. I think at least part of this tenderness derived from his belief in a romantic universe. More than once he said to me, "Life is a love story—a tale of yearning from both sides of life, of God reaching down to man and man reaching up to God." And to Stephen, our love was a sacred adventure in which we were betrothed to one another, but—first of all—to the Divine.

Part Two

ROUGH
WATER

"Courage!" he said, and pointed toward the land,
"This mounting wave will roll us shoreward soon."

—Alfred Lord Tennyson

Seven

SHOCKS

Pearls lie not on the seashore,
If you desire one, you must dive for it.

—Oriental Proverb

WHAT A HAPPY BEGINNING to the new year of 2004! Stephen was so proud of the progress I was making professionally. "Do you see now that life doesn't have to be an either/or proposition between earning a living and being creative?" he teased me one day. "It looks to me as if you're doing both."

He was right. As a result of a successful leadership academy that I had designed and led at work, I was now doing custom workshops for the various colleges that the state community college system comprised. In addition, I had passed the first level of interviews to begin contract work with a prestigious training company on the East Coast, and I was working very hard on a book about business excellence that I hoped to complete and publish by the end of the year.

After more than thirteen years of marriage, Stephen and I were doing great. Our Sunday readings and early-morning discussions on the way to work were deepening our relationship and clarifying my spiritual path. In many ways, I felt that I was coming out of a dark shell of fear and self-limitation that had plagued me since childhood.

Since 1998, I had been keeping an infrequent journal as a way to help me figure out my marriage and my place in the world. Journaling had become a much more important process for me in the new year as I found my writer's voice and discovered new ways of giving shape to the thoughts and feelings that arose with greater intensity as my creativity and career began to unfold more rapidly.

January 15, 2004

These days I feel such clarity of purpose for our relationship—and for how Stephen adds value to my life, particularly when I get anxious about the opportunities that are beginning to emerge. I am beginning to more fully appreciate how he acts as my teacher of philosophy, spiritual freedom, personal mastery, and self-care.

We talk about truth and beauty—about how much we relax when seeing the beauty in life, how we are uplifted in beautiful surroundings, how much inner peace we gain from sharing these thoughts. Stephen values his peace above all else. He is careful of himself and his path. One day recently he said, "If I did not have the opportunity to share with you what I have learned in my study, my life would be meaningless."

In me, Stephen had a partner who appreciated and encouraged his uniqueness. "You let me be myself," he said more than once. Actually, I never considered that a choice. He was always completely himself—comfortable in his own skin, with a quiet way of taking care of his own needs. If a social obligation became too intrusive, he slipped away. If he found a situation toxic, he removed himself—and people ultimately respected him for it, even if they did not fully understand his actions at the time. I think this was a survival technique he developed early in life to protect the sensitivity of his heart.

"I didn't know if he was being a Buddha or a prick," our mutual friend Kathleen told me once. She had been at the Chicago teaching center when Stephen lived there. "For several months, he was the only guy in a household of nine women. He was very patient with us, always cheerful and willing to do the heavy lifting around the house. But if we got too demanding or shrill, he would disappear into his room in the attic and not come out until he was ready."

Not much had changed since he married me.

January 29, 2004

Today I'm on my way back home from Reston, Virginia, where I did my audition workshop for the training company to determine if they will consider hiring me as one of their instructors. I think I made a good impression. The managers who attended my demo seemed to like my perspective of teaching people how to identify and appreciate their own uniqueness and that of others.

I had focused the workshop on the need to hire and retain great people in jobs that fit their innate talents—not just their skills, knowledge, and competency. The day before, at breakfast in the Denver airport, I had met a woman who was doing this very thing. She had started a mentoring program for structural engineers who had suddenly become managers, finding themselves completely out of their comfort zone. Instead of building bridges or highways, now they were pushing paper for human resources and dealing with people problems that just "blew their mental circuits."

So I was excited about doing similar work as an instructor. I would have students from all over the country, perhaps even the world, and I would be mentored by highly skilled professionals who knew how to achieve excellence in the classroom. This was truly a turning point in my life and in my career.

A Course in Miracles, which Stephen and I were reading about this time, says that each of us has students in this life, and they must find us. I felt it was time for me to break out of my shell and put myself out there where my students and I could find each other. There seemed to be so little time. Connecting with our students is one thing, but how do we really move forward in our goal of union with Spirit? One day in February, Stephen explained that process to me.

"Gurdjieff taught that sometimes the universe will precipitate a shock to jolt us out of one level of consciousness to the next," he said. "The process is often painful because it requires breaking through the artificial limitations we have created from erroneous interpretations of life experiences—or from outright lies we have been taught by even well-meaning authority figures. We move into the next level with a certain quotient of awareness—the combination of experience, insight, and desire we have accumulated so far. But we can be entirely wrong in our perception of the event's purpose. Because, to the Divine, all that matters is the soul's evolution."

March 1, 2004

I am back in Reston, Virginia. I have been tentatively accepted as an instructor for the big training company, so now I'm attending their train-the-trainer course as the next step.

As is becoming my custom on the plane, this morning I was writing in my journal—today commenting on how judgmental I was toward other people in the airport. There was a lot of anxiety—with people jostling for a place in the security line or to board the plane—and I was disappointed to discover how easily I got caught up in the emotional turmoil.

Suddenly, the familiar inner voice took over my journal entry, which has happened several times of late. But today it took a different, more authoritative tone. I honestly don't know what that means, but this is what it said:

Can you love these people rather than judging them? You are being sent out to love, not judge. You cannot fulfill your mission if you are consistently unloving toward others. You must be a servant twenty-four hours a day. The same goes with Stephen. You must take care of him. He is fragile and the world could damage him. He needs to meditate and think and pray. That is his service. You must meet your own needs and not blame him for not acting like one of your girlfriends.

Some people have an obligation for stillness. They get out of sorts if they don't have it. It is good when they marry someone who can share the burden of life in time and space and not blame them for supposed lack of ambition. Stephen is appropriately ambitious for the things that are his to do. So find your own way. Nurture yourself. Love Stephen deeply and care for him. Have faith that what you are pursuing is also pursuing you.

The training course was rigorous but very practical, and I returned home full of enthusiasm for what felt more and more like my true work. I was finally finding my purpose in life. I felt like a burden of limitation had been lifted from my psyche. I determined to leave behind many old insecurities of the past, to claim my identity as a creative person. And to realize how fully I was loved and supported by my husband and the universe.

That was in March. April was an exceptionally busy month, with lots of workshops at the community colleges and ongoing preparation for the next step in my "trainer training": a co-teaching event that would take place in June at the training company's New York education center. I would teach the full course, but with another instructor in the room as backup and mentor.

In my spare time, I worked on my business book and designed a website to advertise the professional-development workshops I continued to offer through my freelance coaching and consulting business. While the community college leadership academy was winding down for the school year, I was intently focused on the next phase of my career, which was taking off like gangbusters.

About this time, I also started feeling strangely disconnected from Stephen. I was working only part-time for the community colleges now, so we no longer drove to work together each morning. It seemed that the more involved I became in the business world, the more difficult it was for me be still and enter into the spiritual world that Stephen inhabited so naturally.

He seemed to be retreating into himself and I couldn't reach him. He was settling into a steady routine of work, watching sports on television, doing his solo hobbies, and meditating—none of which included me. The more agitated I became, the more distant he was—except on Sundays, thank goodness. But even then we were not always in sync, because I really wanted to talk about business and Stephen seemed more concerned that I keep my eye on spiritual goals. I felt that he was nagging me and that he didn't realize what a big deal this new career opportunity was for me.

I finally went to a psychiatrist, who labeled Stephen as having an antisocial personality disorder. That really put me off and I never went back. I could complain about my husband's introversion, but nobody else got to do that. I still had a blue topaz ring on my finger as proof of why we were together.

"I think I'll get a flexible-sigmoidoscopy like you did last spring," Stephen said casually one day in early June. I was consumed with preparations for my upcoming first teaching event, so I didn't pay much attention.

"That's probably a good idea," I said somewhat distractedly, "and the test really isn't too bad. Mine was a piece of cake." We were both in our fifties—the age when some kind of colon exam is recommended. I had opted for the minimally invasive flex-sig procedure, which checks the large intestine. Like many people, I thought the idea of getting a full colonoscopy sounded icky and painful.

In mid-June I was off to New York to teach my first public management course—and coming up against my old sense of limitation and inexperience. The raw material was there but it needed forming. After the first day of the three-day course, my mentor insisted that we spend hours going over every single slide in detail until we were both exhausted.

I was terrified that I was about to fail. I felt like I was simultaneously up against a wall and falling into an abyss—only the floor refused to swallow me up, so I had to push through my fear and go back to class the next day. Somehow I got through the experience and, miraculously, ended up with glowing student evaluations. My mentor was ecstatic, and some of the training-company administrators even sent me congratulatory e-mails.

"Good job, Bun!" Stephen exclaimed when I got home on Saturday. "I knew you could do it." And he gave me a big hug—something he didn't always do, even when I had been traveling.

"I went to the gastroenterologist for the flex-sig exam while you were gone," he said. "I didn't want to tell you before you left, but the reason I decided to go was that I had begun to notice some pink mucus in my stool." *Was that why Stephen seemed so preoccupied of late?* I wondered.

He went on. "The doctor didn't like what he saw on the screen during the test and decided to do a complete colonoscopy right there."

"Without anesthesia?" I asked. "I didn't think they would do that. Wasn't it painful?"

"No, it wasn't too bad," Stephen answered in his classic stoic style. "Anyway, the full scope revealed only a single polyp, which didn't look particularly suspicious, but the doctor did a biopsy and sent it to the lab just to make sure. He said he would have the results next week. I don't think it's anything to worry about. The rest of the colon was clean."

"I hope you're right," I said, trying not to sound apprehensive—and we said no more about the situation for the rest of the weekend.

On Monday, Stephen came home from work with an odd look on his face. "I heard from the doctor today," he said more quietly than usual. "He said the polyp they found is cancerous. They want me to have surgery as soon as possible."

Sometimes we have to look back to pinpoint the exact moment when our lives change forever. The day I drove my car off the road in Montana, it was quite obvious that life was going to be different. But today, I didn't even notice that my entire world had shifted. We were standing in our breakfast room where we ate every morning. The room looked the same, so I did not feel the touch of death's dark wing as it brushed past and took up a seat in the corner, waiting.

In fact, I wasn't really surprised that the doctor had said, "Cancer." It was almost as if I had been expecting it—although I certainly had never consciously entertained the idea. Stephen was trying not to be alarmed by this turn of events, and I followed his lead. Besides, his situation wasn't really cancer; it was just a polyp that needed to be removed.

At the moment, I was actually wondering how Stephen's surgery was going to fit in with my teaching schedule. I had already arranged to conduct a two-day communications workshop for the training company's operations staff at their headquarters in mid-July, and other teaching events were coming up soon. In truth, I was more concerned about teaching than I was about Stephen. It wasn't that I was blasé about his having surgery. It just never occurred to me that the operation would be anything other than a minor inconvenience in our lives.

The next two weeks were a flurry of consultations with the surgeon and preoperative tests. With each appointment, the potential gravity of Stephen's situation became more alarming. Increasingly worried about what really lay ahead of us, I conducted the workshop in Virginia and then flew straight home for Stephen's surgery on July 19, 2004.

And just like that—quietly, stealthily—life dealt us the first of many shocks, just as Stephen had so clearly described only a few months earlier. A chasm was opening and we were about to start a long, slow-motion tumble into a darkness neither of us could imagine.

Eight

PLAYING THE ODDS

If you are not strong,
ask for troubles to make you so.

—Leo Tolstoy

July 23, 2004

The start of a new journal. The beginning of a new phase in our lives—the one where Stephen has cancer.

Life has been imaginary until now—lived mostly in my head and emotions. Events have come and gone like so many lovers. I got my heart broken a time or two. There were victories and disappointments. But nobody died, or threatened to—until now.

Surgery was Monday. On Tuesday the pain was so bad that Stephen could cope only with drugs and music—something to distract him until Wednesday. Thursday was better. Now it's Friday, and he's home to heal. I breathed a sigh of relief to finally have him in my care, where now it's my job to feed him and make him comfortable. And he's able to be sweet again.

For three days I was a lost soul with no concept of time, unable to sleep, and of absolutely no use to Stephen. He's never had much patience with agitated people, and my persistent, bouncy need to connect sometimes jangles him, even on good days. So he actually couldn't tolerate my visiting for long in the hospital.

Just as well. I went home, watched a lot of movies, ate popcorn, tried to knock myself out with gin-and-tonics. And I floundered. Stephen is my rock who keeps me anchored. Without him I am lost. But I cannot expect him to hold me together. He must fight for his life. He must gather his strength and push back against the energy of death that has been gathering around him for some time. I cannot do that for him, but I can push back against death in my own world.

I knew we were in for a change, but I had no idea it would be so dramatic. Now all the years of seeking and learning must coalesce into a true path to life, to a destiny greater than one body or one lifetime. This is where Stephen and I marshal our forces and conquer death in all its subtle traps.

This is not *the* end, but it may be *an* end. We may not come through this physically intact. But we will come through spiritually, and that is what the whole journey is about. I heard the inner voice:

Will you love life more than death? Will you understand what is important? Will you strive with the Divine for truth? That's the deal.

I can hardly bear to write the awful report from the operating room: The single tumor was four centimeters, or about two inches. It had perforated the colon wall and was very low in the rectum. Stephen was fortunate not to need a colostomy. On a scale of 1 to 4, it was a 2; only moderately differentiated. But worst of all, two of eleven lymph nodes were cancerous and had to be removed.

This means chemotherapy and radiation. Hideous words. How to kill the cells that are now hostile invaders, traitors to the body's integrity. Parasites that kill their host. Now it's for real. Death lurks, and no longer in the imaginary shadows.

We are determined to fight on our own terms, not death's. We are not people who die; we live. And we still have so much to live for—especially for each other. Would it help to cry? Perhaps. I'm sure I will. Yet life is more powerful, and people do survive for years. And still—the premonitions of my being alone were so strong—I wonder.

Stephen recovered well from surgery and regained his strength. I couldn't help but imagine him as a calf being fattened up for the slaughter. His newly constructed rectum had to heal up before it could be attacked with radiation. If we had known how painful the radiation would be, I'm not sure we would have accepted this treatment. But medical doctors are focused on solving a problem, so they don't always tell you enough about the pain you will experience. Or perhaps, even when they tell you, there is no way to comprehend the severity until you actually go through it.

August 6, 2004

Today we saw the radiation oncologist. This is going to be worse than we thought, but adding radiation to the chemo increases Stephen's survival chances from 50 percent to 75 percent. We're playing the odds here. It's a crapshoot, regardless. They don't know if there is more cancer in his system or not.

He will have six weeks of weekly chemotherapy, then six weeks of weekly chemo plus daily radiation, then six more weeks of just chemo. There will be breaks between each six-week regime so the body can recover (sort of). The whole process will last until next February, at which time the doctors hope to see no cancer in Stephen's system. Actually, they don't see any cancer now; all of this is just a precaution. Poor Stephen. I just hate this for him.

"Maybe we could go away for our anniversary," I suggested.

"I'm sorry, Bunny, I just really don't feel like it," he apologized. "Maybe you could do something with your girlfriends."

Stephen realizes that I need some kind of escape—but it's not much fun to do anything without him. The thought makes me feel like a widow. I need to spend as much time as possible with him, not away from him.

August 14, 2004

I don't want to go to support groups. I can't bear other people's grief. And I don't want to be with those who have made cancer their cause célèbre, literally a religion. An entire culture has sprung up around cancer: cancer research, cancer prevention, walks for a cancer cure, big events for cancer research. It's like a cancer community. I know the support is tremendously important to many people, but I feel that the cancer culture focuses on killing the disease, not on enhancing the life force of the person who is dealing with it. This may not be a fair assessment, but it's how I feel right now.

I feel as if I am confronting the consciousness of death everywhere—as if it were a specter trying to suck the life force out of me as well as Stephen. I remember our teacher's sermon on choosing life, not death. She said there were so many aspects of our culture that try to lull us to sleep, pretending to be the truth; telling us we are unworthy, unimportant, dull; eating away at our happiness, our inspiration, and our drive.

"I am awake!" she quoted the Buddha as saying—meaning that he had awakened to the reality of his own divine nature. That is the focus I want, the perspective I must maintain, lest either Stephen or I should "slip away into death's night." Another line from my poem "Penance." Another reminder from the past. We were not always victorious. But today I will not speak of death, only life.

One night Stephen and I were talking about the fact that we were not angry—which is supposed to be one of the emotions you feel when facing a potentially fatal disease. Posing philosophical questions was one of his favorite forms of dialogue, so he asked me, "Why do we choose to get angry?"

"I think I get angry as the result of situations I have set in motion by bad decisions," I said. "Or from simple lack of awareness about a situation. I get upset at injustice, dishonesty, misuse of power, and at things that scare me. But I'm not sure why."

"I think we allow conflicts with our worldview to upset us," Stephen offered. "We get angry when we can't control people and make them behave the way we think they ought to. The anger is a habit, a threat, a control mechanism."

We both believed that much of this anger was really anger at God. People ask, "How could a loving Father allow such evil to persist? How could he allow such suffering?" Stephen and I just didn't agree that it was God's fault. Bad things may happen due to our own shortcomings. We may simply find ourselves in the way of other people's error. And sometimes, things just happen. We often don't know the cause, but we do know the remedy: to respond in peace, not anger.

"So why do we choose anger over peace?" Stephen continued. "Does the cost of peace seem too high?"

"It does to the ego," I suggested. "Because to have peace, we must resist the ego's telling us that anger is justified and that we have a right to be upset. It is human and natural to be upset over situations we don't like. But what do we gain from anger? Separation, pain, depression. How could that possibly be preferable to peace, unless we believe we are not worthy of peace?"

Stephen agreed. So the way out of anger in life is to rout out the negative wherever we find it—thoughts, words, deeds. Focus on the positive. Build a force field of life energy around the self. Clean out the basement of consciousness; get rid of the junk. These are blocks to the flow of life energy, and all of us need as much life energy as we can get. If we are in a positive frame of mind, we are less susceptible to being upset. We champion life, not death. Allowing the self to become upset also means accepting existence in a hell of our own creation.

August 16, 2004

Last night I had a dream: I am on top of a very tall ladder leaning against a building. I have to jump across what looks like a huge space to land on the roof of the next building, where I'm supposed to be. I'm terrified of the height and the gap, and I wake up before I get across. Tonight a poem came to me that rather shockingly explained the dream.

The Net

Were the consequences so dire
Of one false crossing
On board a ship
Across black water
Cold and dark—
So frightfully alone, that now you falter?

Freedom lies across the gap—
A mediocre safety on this side.
Will you dare to jump
And risk the drop?

The prize you seek awaits
But you can never walk around.
The only way is there—
Across the gap.

What if it's nothing—
A mirage, an illusion?
An abyss made of dreams and rumors—
Another lie to be dispelled?

Let go the edges.
Have faith, for once.
You've never seen the net
That's been there all along.

You are the net yourself.
Step out.

Nine

CANCER IS NOT US

*When you catch yourself grasping at
beliefs or thoughts, just see what is.*

—Pema Chödrön

August 19, 2004

I wonder how long I can deny cancer any power. It is not real, and I don't want it to become real. A situation can be a fact without our allowing it to determine how we feel about our lives. Taking Stephen's long view of his situation, death may kill the body but the spirit lives on.

So why allow cancer any authority over the path the soul has chosen? Cancer may cause chaos for a while, but it is nothing compared to the eternal power of Spirit. Yet it *is* evil and slippery and sly. Like what? An intruder. A burglar. A rapist—violating our sanctity and our home. Forcing us into a battle we thought only "other people" had to face.

Of course we couldn't deny that Stephen *had* cancer. We talked frankly about our situation. I did hours of research and quickly learned much more about the disease and its treatment than I had ever wanted to know. We felt it was essential that we be informed and actively engaged in treatment decisions. We did not hide from the challenges, which gave us permission and energy to confront them head on.

I will continue to deny it as long as possible. Perhaps until Stephen really starts to suffer, which he will, poor man. I am not denying that we must both engage all our forces; I am denying that cancer has any power to change who we are or who we will become. Cancer is not us! People do survive colorectal cancer. They fight, they endure, and they live. So will we.

The sneaky thing about rectal cancer is that it can pop up again anywhere. It seems to get into the bloodstream and travel. We have to die somehow—but, please, God: not so young and not Stephen. Chemo starts tomorrow. We're like soldiers on the eve of battle— dreading the melee but eager to get on with it. You might say the anticipation is the worst part, but I doubt it.

August 20, 2004

And so it begins. Stephen received his first infusion today after we watched a bizarrely cheery video and heard more rehearsal of the side effects. The whole thing is so gruesome. I felt ill and faint the whole time—partially from the subject and partially because we were crammed into a jumbled, stuffy room with desperately sick people.

I wanted to scream STOP! when they hooked him up to the IV and the drip began to flow into his veins—poisoning this hand- some, sweet man. Now he's being sucked into the chemo juggernaut, because this is what you do when you have cancer. Fortunately, the oncology staff is really nice, except the pharmacist who did his best to scare me about Stephen's drugs. I'm already scared—don't make matters worse.

Somehow I had to come to terms with this "kill the cancer" approach, even though accepting it went so totally against my negative feelings about Western medicine—submitting to a poisonous treatment that seemed to be little more than rolling the dice. The doctors didn't actually know if Stephen needed chemo, and I just couldn't believe that he did.

I would have liked Stephen to embrace more alternative treatments, but I didn't know what I would encourage him to do even if he were willing. There are so many "cures" out there, and it was so hard to know what would work on his type of cancer. Does anybody really know how to reset the body's chemistry once it decides to let cancer grow? I knew there were success stories attributed to changes in diet, massive doses of dried aloe vera extract, coffee enemas, foul-tasting herbal concoctions. But what actually worked?

In the absence of any other clear direction, Stephen chose chemo and radiation. *It's his body and his life,* I told myself, *and I have to respect his wishes.* He did not make rash decisions; I knew he had thought deeply about what to do.

I was so angry today. Angry at not really knowing what to do to combat this cancer. Angry at Stephen for getting sick, for dragging us through this nightmare, for not going to the doctor earlier, for not saying anything to me about the pink mucus he noticed in the spring. Was it to protect my new career opportunities? Was he too apprehensive to learn it might be cancer? Or was he just being a guy, not stopping to ask for directions?

Of course, this isn't fair. Stephen never blamed me for nearly getting myself killed when I wrecked our car in Montana. But today I don't care; I just don't want this horror to sink into my life. I am determined that cancer will not define us; it's just that this whole experience is getting really bad really fast.

Ten

SURFING THE WAVES

The soul is its own witness and its own refuge.

—Robert Southey

August 21, 2004

The day after the first chemo treatment. The nausea was bad, but manageable, and Stephen is eating pretty well. I don't want to go anywhere; I just want to be with him and do what I can for him. He is receiving my ministrations with such kindness and love.

I know this openness will be difficult for us to maintain—just as I have always had trouble staying in the contemplative "zone" that we create in our Sunday morning readings. I am so easily distracted by the necessities of running the household. It's the challenge of the Bethany sisters, Mary and Martha. Jesus said that Mary took the better part because she sat at the Master's feet, growing in understanding, while Martha was concerned with more worldly matters. But somebody has to wash the dishes, don't they?

Despite my inconstancy, Stephen and I are going very deep into each other and that is healing in itself. We need to stay locked into each other at the highest possible level. I am determined to create a cocoon of healing for him here at home with positive energy and love.

I was inspired to be positive, and gained confidence that I could do so, by reading *Grace and Grit,* philosopher Ken Wilber's book about the five years he and his wife, Treya, spent fighting her breast cancer in the mid-1980s, when so many women lost that battle.[1] They went through what Stephen and I were facing while remaining incredibly aware of their spiritual connection.

Ken and Treya's recognition of one another, as if from another lifetime, was so much like ours. It is a vivid confirmation of the powerful bond I have in my marriage and why I must be absolutely present and awake for Stephen. It is also an apt synchronicity that much of Treya's personal-growth work focused on being internally present in the moment rather than always feeling the need to do something external. I can certainly relate. Throughout my life I have felt more like a human doing than a human being. But the key in a situation like ours is to ask: Who are you being while you're doing?

The Benedictines taught that work can be prayer. "Doing" can be either holy or profane, depending on the consciousness with which it is conducted. I'm not "doing" much differently in terms of caring for Stephen compared with what I have always done—more, but not different. But my attitude is different. Laundry, grocery shopping, dusting, organizing can be either drudgery or a holy service; one depletes the doer, while the other renews. The facts are the same; the perspective makes all the difference.

Being a caregiver was a tricky business. I was constantly making adjustments in how I ministered to Stephen—and he was very sensitive to what worked for him and what didn't. For example, if my purpose was to extend love and make him more comfortable, that was fine. But if I fussed over him too much—actually trying to make myself feel better by making his pain go away—that was an interference.

August 22, 2004
Stephen's illness is so serious that the only way to deal with it is to go deep into Spirit. To listen as never before. To simplify and love.

Above all else, to love. This is not an experience in fighting cancer. This is an experience in finding the Higher Self through surrender to the love and forgiveness and purpose that have always existed. We work, and we pray only to dissolve the blocks to our union with the Divine Presence within our own hearts. Any other motive is delusional and small. The universe's assignments are plenty grand, and the stage upon which we perform our greatest roles will be the right one for us—if we but listen and obey.

August 27, 2004

I'm getting better at obeying, not resisting. I try to answer Stephen's requests with love and alacrity. Can a terrible disease be the best thing to happen to a couple? Is it wrong to thank someone for getting cancer? I'm grateful for this time of trial, because it so clarifies how mindful I must remain and how full of joy and love and light I must be to care for Stephen. And it is likewise disturbing to see how tenuous a hold I have on that awareness. Of course, the whole idea of "holding" is not right, because that's grasping and clinging out of fear. It needs to become a perfect flow of powerful energy (what the Chinese call "chi") that I float on, never sinking below a certain frequency.

It is, indeed, surfing the waves of change. I thought of that metaphor and then read it in *Grace and Grit,* where Ken Wilber describes the personal-growth work we do in life as "surfing."[2] We can only pray for strength and patience while riding the waves—especially when coping with the ups and downs of cancer and being a caregiver.

In the second week of October, Stephen began six weeks of daily radiation coupled with weekly chemo. He had done amazingly well in the first chemo treatments, thanks to his strong physical constitution and equally strong will to persevere. Before we launched into this next cycle, we had a wonderful reading and meditation time on Sunday morning.

October 10, 2004

Try to remember the feeling of peace and comfort from today—and how important Stephen is to me. He's the love of my life—my other half, my soul friend. I need him so much. I think I can get along without him and then find that I don't do at all well when we are apart. I must stay grounded in the present. Be aware. Be alive. Forgive. Love. Extend. Care. Be kind—and, above all, honor the divinity within and do not live in regret or remorse for what has gone before.

These things must be uncovered and accepted and allowed to move on. My friend Pat has a favorite saying that she attributes to death and dying expert Elisabeth Kübler-Ross: "I'm not okay; you're not okay. And that's okay." To be free from paralyzing perfectionism: that is a vital key to surviving all of this pain. It's impossible to be perfect, and it's unkind to expect anyone else to be so.

Throughout the chemo-radiation-chemo cycles, Stephen went to work nearly every day. The last two weeks of radiation-plus-chemo were cruelly debilitating, and he was forced to use some sick leave. But otherwise, on the day after a weekly chemo treatment, he would get up, get dressed, and drive himself to work. "It gives me something to think about other than how terrible I feel," he explained.

We were also getting better at working with the inevitable side effects of the drugs that were busy killing fast-growing cells, good ones as well as the bad ones. Cells in the brain, mouth, stomach, and hair all fell victim to the onslaught. "I've got chemo-brain today," Stephen would often say ruefully the day after an infusion. It was his way of alerting me that I was going to have to do the clear thinking for both of us that day—definitely a role switch in our relationship.

As much as possible throughout this first year of treatment, we acted like normal people. We did not identify with the "sick" people at the chemo clinic. We took my laptop to the appointments, plugged in two sets of headphones on a splitter, and watched movies or listened to music while Stephen got his infusions. We were not sick—we were just dealing with cancer. Otherwise, we were well and healthy in our approach to life and each other. It helped that Stephen rarely looked ill.

And he encouraged me to keep advancing in my business career—even when it meant my traveling on Tuesday after he had chemo on Monday. He was delighted with my progress as a professional development trainer—because I liked the work and because he knew I would be able to support myself if necessary.

My autumn was consumed with another session of the leadership academy I was running for the community college system. Stephen's weekdays were punctuated by radiation treatments. The first few weeks were inconsequential. But radiation builds up. It essentially fries the tissue that receives the highly targeted rays, so that by the fourth week, the area is inflamed and raw. For Stephen, this meant that a bowel movement was absolute torture.

I had never felt so helpless. Stephen bore his pain with great dignity. But I can still hear his cries every time he had to eliminate. There was nothing to do but endure, which he did with unbelievable courage. We celebrated his birthday a few days late, after the final radiation session on November 17. But we still weren't finished.

November 22, 2004

How Stephen suffers these days. The radiation treatments are over, but the effects last for weeks, continuing to cause terrible cramping. His moans just tear me apart as it sounds like the pain is doing to him. I wish I could hold him and comfort him, but he doesn't want to be touched. Plus, I've had a cold and I don't want to make him sick because his immune system is very weak right now.

We've still got weeks of chemo to go—and then life will be a matter of how to live fully with the ever-present threat of recurrence and the knowledge that, if the cancer comes back, it will be worse. Pat and her husband lived with his cancer for over twenty-five years. What an endurance test. You simply cannot fathom it in another person's life until it touches your own.

It seems so unreal and so impossible. I won't say "unfair" because what is "unfair"? These things just happen. Are they a call to be more mindful of the frailties of the flesh? To be more present in the body as a barometer of our mental and spiritual health? Who knows? Some say the mind creates the body. We talk of mind over matter. But what if matter doesn't mind and goes off creating its own reality—or unreality?

What will life bring? More than we expect. Less than we dream, if we dream amiss. Just as much as we can handle and no less than we deserve. The only limit is what we think we are capable of and how much heart we bring to each day.

I am amazed at how full the heart can be—and how wise—if given only half a chance. And in its fullness the heart is strong in its convictions—able to empty itself, and fill again, and overflow, and give, and give, in an endless stream of love and service. Truly, it is only fear that stops the heart, makes it catch in the throat and die unused. A tragic end, should we opt for fear instead of love.

So, like mountain men of old, bundled up against the cold, heads down, pushing against strong winds and snowstorms, we trudged through November, December, and January. We lived one day at a time, one chemo session per week. We tried our best to be kind and gentle with one another, succeeding better on some days than others. I was over-scheduled and under-slept, traveling and teaching, wishing I could stay home, even as my career opportunities continued to multiply. Stephen went deeper and deeper within, still managing to go to work every day.

"I'm sorry I'm not more fun," he apologized one day. But, honestly, what else could the man do? It's hard to be jolly when you're fighting for your life.

I often thought about how different our experience would be if I were the one who had cancer. I process my thoughts and feelings through writing, but even more so through conversation. I like to discover the truth and meaning of life experience in discussion with other people. It's one reason I loved our Sunday morning sessions so much. Often we would read a particularly deep line of poetry or philosophy over and over, asking each other questions about its meaning. Or sometimes we would sit quietly for a few moments, letting a passage resonate in our hearts before talking about how it might relate to us personally.

Stephen was quite forthcoming about his thoughts when we read together, but he guarded his feelings about being ill, about the level of discomfort he was experiencing. He tended to keep his deepest fears and concerns to himself—except for one really lovely practice: he wrote poems that sprang from his meditations and he was usually eager to share them with me. Somehow the act of putting these tender feelings on paper allowed him to clue me in to his state of awareness without having to engage in the strong emotions I know he feared might overwhelm him. It gave me a unique window into the mind and heart of this very private man as he worked to build a bridge from his human consciousness to the Divine.

December 18, 2004

Every hour I wait
For your love.
Now am I to wait no longer?

Do not disappoint
We are very close.

My manhood—
Your divine nature.

Listen carefully.
Stay awhile.
I have time to burn.

Oh, consume me.
I am yours—
At last.

You've been here
So long.
Why would I bid you good-bye?

January 6, 2005

As this cold winter day
    turns in the afternoon sun
    my house creaks.

The sudden sound of snow falling
    from the trees above
    momentarily dissipates the tension.

Oh, the joy from falling snow
    from the faith that the end is nearing
    that the future is full of life.

And that soon I will again feel
    the fullness of your fire.

Eleven

PUTTING CANCER BEHIND US

Thanks to the human heart by which we live,
Thanks to its tenderness, its joys, and fears,
To me the meanest flower that blows can give
Thoughts that do often lie too deep for tears.

—William Wordsworth

February 11, 2005

Hallelujah! Stephen made it. We made it. With any luck, he will never have to go through chemo again. I cannot even imagine what he has endured in his body. He's very tired tonight—finally letting down, I suppose, after having to summon so much will power just to keep going for these many, awful months. Six months of treatment, but nine months since the first diagnosis.

Now we must focus on being really positive, eating well, exercising, and not being afraid. I hope I can help; I'm so very tired too. I can't forget how tied to Stephen I am mentally, emotionally, spiritually—and how this last year has just ground away at us. Regardless, I feel that we've come through this hellish journey better than we were when we started.

In a word, Stephen and I had become more Wordsworthian—a term we used (after the great Romantic poet William Wordsworth) to describe a state of awareness that accepts life as so much more than the petty problems of daily existence. We wrote more poetry than we used to, and I think we were kinder, more understanding, and more grateful that we still had each other.

We were both working hard, keeping up with professional responsibilities. But there were instances now—and not just on Sunday mornings—when together we would find ourselves slipping more easily into those exquisite moments of contemplation that literally lifted us out of time and sorrow into a place of otherworldly awareness, where the soul feels as if it has been caressed by the gentle hand of God or touched by the delicate brush of an angel's wing.

The CAT scans and blood tests were clear in March of 2005, so we put cancer behind us. Stephen regained his strength and returned to his beloved woodworking projects—although not without difficulty. The chemo had caused severe neuropathy in his hands and feet, which meant he had to be especially careful when working with power saws and other potentially dangerous equipment. He exercised in his home gym, rode his bike, and even played some golf when the weather warmed up.

I dove into my career with renewed enthusiasm. I helped develop a course on assertiveness skills, frequently traveled to teach, and made a lot of progress on my book about doing great work in any occupation.

We intensified our readings together, expanding into wider exploration of Ken Wilber's philosophy, even attending a weekend workshop on his system of personal transformation called Integral Life Practice.[3] During one of the sessions on authentic communication, Stephen surprised me by telling the couple we were practicing with, "I want you to know that I am a cancer patient." I had never heard him make such a blunt confession of his condition. Why make the declaration now? Was it finally safe because he was in remission? Or did he want to make sure I never forgot that we weren't out of danger yet?

Whatever had been on Stephen's mind that day, we were thriving once again. Life was good. The monthly blood tests stayed clean. We relished our weekends. Sometimes we would just hop in the car and go for a drive, seeking out new parts of Colorado to explore. And we made the most of just staying home, enjoying being together, even while working on separate projects.

We rented movies to watch on the new television set we had purchased to grace the beautiful Arts-and-Crafts-style entertainment center that Stephen designed from a photo in a Stickley catalogue and built out of natural cherry wood. I noticed that he took frequent breaks while completing it and did even more planning than he had on previous projects, but the results were gorgeous.

We usually had a couple of home-improvement items on our shopping list, so Saturdays were often spent "hunting" for the perfect piece to buy. I was learning to enjoy the hunt more than the actual purchase, which was one of Stephen's great lessons to me: Enjoy the process at least as much as the final result; it lasts longer and you learn more that way. Stephen was back to his playful, teasing self—and we felt free to enjoy being in love, now with the deep appreciation that only comes from having weathered a frightening crisis together.

Stephen continued getting blood tests every month, which reminded us that the doctors were still keeping a close watch on his condition. He was scheduled for a routine follow-up CAT scan in June 2006, but there seemed to be no reason for concern. He appeared robust and healthy; and, except for the nagging neuropathy in his hands and feet, he felt really well. We were so grateful not to be thinking about cancer and how it had nearly derailed us.

Then, around the middle of March 2006—three months early— the oncologist noticed something unusual in the latest blood test and called him in for the CAT scan.

Twelve

A TWO-PART MISSION

Who can decide offhand which is better,
to live or understand life?

—William James

March 31, 2006

I am starting this new journal tonight because I want to capture the entire experience of whatever may be coming. These words—the story of our life together—may be all of Stephen I will have left. And this is the only way I can really come to terms with what is happening. If I write it, it's more real—easier to think through and find a way to act appropriately.

March 31 was Friday, a week before my birthday and the end of Stephen's spring break—one of the many benefits of his working for Denver Public Schools. It had been a gorgeous, warm day—perfect for a yummy lunch at one of our favorite patio restaurants and a stroll through the shops and art galleries of Cherry Creek. We rarely bought anything at their high-end prices, but the merchandise was always beautiful, which never failed to give us a lift. We both took a little nap after we got home and then I popped out to the grocery store to pick up a few things for the weekend. When I returned half an hour later, Stephen sat me down at the breakfast table.

"I just got a call from the oncologist about the CAT scan," he began. "It isn't good. I have three or four tumors on my liver. They're talking more chemo, maybe surgery. I have three to five years, maybe eight—but eight's pushing it."

"To *live?!*" I gasped, breaking into tears of utter disbelief. It was too horrible to conceive—the thought of Stephen having to endure that terrible poison in his body again, of his beautiful body being consumed with that deadly, wasting disease.

"We're supposed to see the oncologist on Monday after he's had a chance to review the CAT scans in more detail," Stephen went on. "He apologized for calling with incomplete information, but he wanted to give us a chance to deal with the news. The only thing he said for sure is that the cancer is treatable, but not curable."

Not curable. It stuns the mind. It's like a bad dream. Surely we'll wake up in the morning and all will be well. Maybe the tumors are benign. The mind grasps for any scenario other than "not curable"—clutching at any other possibility. But we both know this is it.

We talked a little about finances. We'll be okay. Thanks to Stephen's planning and the excellent benefits he receives through work, we are not in dire straits. There is a social worker to talk to about disability.

"I'm probably better prepared for this news than you are," Stephen said. My body felt numb as I sat there looking at him.

"Perhaps," I replied. "Except somehow I guess I've always known it would come to this. I just didn't think it would happen so quickly. I know we can deal with this." I was doing my best to reassure him. "I'm just concerned about how difficult it will be for our families." He nodded.

Suddenly we were both utterly exhausted, so we moved to the living room that is so full of his beautiful handiwork. Stephen was sitting next to me, as he rarely does, and suddenly buried his head in my lap. "I'm so sorry," he sobbed. We were both crying now. And I was so terribly sorry for him.

The thought of losing Stephen is just too terrible. The year he was sick was awful, but we came out at the end together. This will be worse. We'll be brave and loving and kind to one another, but I will end the journey alone . . .alone . . .alone.

And I'll bet we don't have three or five or eight years. Three or four tumors have grown in less than a year. Stephen has some kind of growth in his left breast that he didn't mention until now, and the oncologist said there might be something in his lungs. If that is the case, this cancer is moving fast.

"I may decide not to do any more chemo," Stephen said later in the evening. "It depends on what the prognosis is." Will chemo really help? Could a cancer this aggressive go into remission? What's the use of clinging to life if it's a medical hell? I think some people just live, and others don't. Some people get aggressive cancers, and others don't.

Things have been so good this past year. I feel more like myself than ever before. I know who I am now. I look in the mirror and I see myself—not a person pretending to be something she is not. I go into a classroom and I know I can deliver. I can make a difference in people's lives—not only because I have internalized the course content, but because I can tune in to their hearts. I trust my intuition to help me say the right thing at the right time to illustrate the material in a way that is especially meaningful to that particular group. This isn't just teaching, it's facilitation: making the way forward easier for other people to grow personally and professionally. Truly this is my life's work and I am thrilled with the process.

Stephen and I really are two halves of one whole. I will be losing half of myself and yet I will have gained all of myself because of him. He is the greatest gift of my life. He has given me my life. It will be my challenge to carry his love with me forever and to stay on the path we are still walking together.

Stephen's job is to forge his union with Spirit as deeply as possible. Mine is to try to keep up with his great soul. These things we do for one another. But, honestly, what a terrible birthday present. My face hurts from crying so much.

We woke up the next morning, April 1, still in shock, wishing somebody would yell "April Fool!" and make it all go away. We spent a long time sitting in bed, just holding each other.

"I'm so afraid I'm hurting you," Stephen said tenderly. He was still as weepy as I was.

"No," I assured him, "you will break my heart by leaving me, but you will not hurt me. I will be okay, but I won't have you to share the rest of my life with."

But I knew the reality was that I would be lost without Stephen. His strength and balance and love were what had made it possible for me to find my career and my authentic, soulful self. He was my rock. I floundered before I met him and I feared I would flounder when he was gone.

April 1, 2006

We tried to be normal today. Stephen worked in his wood shop, and I worked in my office until late afternoon. Then we had a gin-and-tonic and I made dinner—like two normal people who expect to spend another thirty years together.

The odd thing is that there is no fight in us today. No attacking the disease—a strange capitulation. I think we both are feeling that this cancer is really aggressive and that he may have less than a year to live. Maybe we're trying to kill him off in our minds, to just get it over with—to avoid the suffering and the pain. Or perhaps it's just shock from being blindsided; we can hardly speak. We just want to spend whatever time we have left in love and peace. The medical battle is too gruesome and, in the end, probably futile.

I pray that our beliefs in the continuity of consciousness after death are well founded. No, actually, I cannot pray at all. I believe and accept, but I do not pray. There is no bargaining: "Spare him, Lord, and I'll do thus-and-such." The only prayer is to be in tune with our own souls, with the stream that flows forth in love. If we can catch that stream, we will not be lost to one another.

Neither of us slept well that night. I was awake at 2:30 a.m., feeling isolated and abandoned at the thought of being in the house alone. The feeling was utterly desolate. Stephen was awake too, so we snuggled for a while until his light snores told me he could sleep for a few more hours. When we got up later, a glorious Sunday morning streamed through the house.

"Let's go to breakfast and do our reading out," Stephen suggested. But when we drove up to the café where we wanted to eat, we found it didn"t open until 10:00 a.m. So we parked the car on top of a hill overlooking the Platte River Valley with the whole cloudless Front Range of the Rocky Mountains stretched before us. It was a perspective we hadn't seen before.

We started our reading. As Stephen read his section, I looked over the scene. My eyes reached out to Boulder and Longs Peak in the north and suddenly the scene changed in an instant of understanding.

"Bunny," I exclaimed. "I can see what it is that we're doing. We have a mission together and it will go on, even when you're no longer here. Your part is to go up to Spirit; my part is to go out to many people and places. I'm not sure exactly what I'll be saying to them, but there are huge crowds—not just classrooms. I'll be doing the teaching, but you will be my inspiration. And this will be our work together—forever."

I had been looking out at the mountains, but in my mind's eye I saw myself standing in front of large audiences in auditoriums, even as I felt Stephen present with me, standing just to my right as I spoke. As the image faded, I turned back to him. He was smiling, but his eyes were filled with tears. He whispered, "That's beautiful, Bun. I'm so happy."

Thirteen

WHY NOT US?

When all is done, say not my day is o'er,
And that thro' night I seek a dimmer shore:
Say rather that my morn has just begun—

—Paul Laurence Dunbar

NOW THAT WE UNDERSTOOD we were working on a shared mission that would not end when Stephen's life did, we entered into the fray with renewed energy and purpose. We could not defeat cancer, but we could claim our purpose in life. Going back into chemo treatments could be worth the unavoidable discomfort if doing so could slow down the cancer and give us more time to prepare for our individual parts.

We were fighting for time—time for Stephen to deepen his meditation and for me become more proficient as a facilitator for the workshops, speeches, and other activities that would be part of my work after he was gone. We were determined to spend every available hour together, because this would be all we had for a long time. We could not say "forever."

These months—or years, if we were fortunate—would be the precious final moments of oneness in the physical world that would have to carry us both for many years to come. Would we one day be reunited on the Other Side? We simply had to believe so.

Gradually, we broke the news to family and friends. Even with faith in a spiritual mission to support us, telling others that this was the beginning of the end was like walking through fire. Every conversation or e-mail made the situation more concrete. Each time we had to explain what was happening, our own minds were forced to come to terms a little more with the fact that Stephen wasn't going to make it.

Explaining to his parents and siblings that they were going to lose their precious son and brother were the most heart-wrenching of those conversations. The words simply choked us. There was no way to soften the blow of "terminal."

"We thought you were doing so well," his father said incredulously.

"So did we," I said. "That's what makes this so difficult."

My mother and stepfather took the news just as hard. They loved Stephen as their own son and simply could not accept that his illness was incurable.

On April 3, we met with our oncologist and agreed to a regime of tests and treatment that began with a PET scan, oral chemo, and then biweekly chemo infusions. As I had feared, he gave Stephen only three to six months without chemo, double or triple that with treatment. It was discouraging to put ourselves back into the hands of the cancer establishment, but we agreed that we would give chemo one more chance to slow down the cancer and buy us some more time—which I believe it did.

April 5, 2006

Meanwhile, my heart is cracking wide open. I feel like I'm having a heart attack—a very long, slow, wrenching, stake-in-the-heart pain that cuts to the very center of my chest. My heart is weeping dry tears.

My friend Pat says we start grieving the loss, even before our loved one dies. What's lost is hope, and that is what so much of life is built upon—hope and trust. We hope for a better future and trust it will come.

The remedy, of course, is to stop dwelling on the future, to pull back to the present. Right now, today, in this moment, everything is fine.

It is far too easy in these situations to just check out, dissociate from life, try to escape the agony. But throughout the centuries, great spiritual masters have demonstrated that the way through pain is straight into it, not around it. So whenever I felt myself shooting into the future, either a better one or a worse one, I declared: "Everything is all right *now*. Everything is all right *now*. Everything is all right *now*." Most of the time, it was. And when it wasn't, I had the energy to walk right into the situation with Stephen and get through whatever was happening in that moment.

Around this time we found ourselves adopting an unusual attitude. Rather than asking: "Why us?" we started asking, "Why not us?"

"If anybody can handle this situation, it's us, isn't it?" I remarked to Stephen one day, and he agreed. Sometimes bad things happen to good people to make them better. Perhaps this was happening to us so we could demonstrate to others how embracing life in the worst of times can actually lead to a better life. We didn't say it could also lead to a better death, but I know we were both thinking it.

The month of April was very busy. Having lots to do helped keep the sadness at bay. Stephen went back on oral chemo (which almost immediately aggravated his peripheral neuropathy), and I resumed traveling and teaching. Every absence was an agony, but my career was getting some big boosts and Stephen insisted that I follow them. We got our wills and finances in order and came up with a plan for completing as many home-remodeling projects as possible while he still felt like working on them.

April 7, 2006

We think we want to know what's coming, but it's really much easier to be brave when we don't. We venture forth into challenges

with hope and optimism, using those feelings as life preservers when
the going gets tough. If we have endured once on the high seas of
adversity, we have that success to use as a life raft when the next trials
present themselves—especially if those trials are more of the same.

The second round of chemo is more difficult than the first. Not
only is the body likely to be weaker, but now we know what we're in
for. This is where we either collapse into fear and despair or plunge
deeper into Spirit for sustenance and courage—the wisdom of the
heart that carries us through hell to transformation.

It was easier to take one day at a time when I was actually with
Stephen. When we were together, there was no time. When we were
apart, there was the time since we'd been together and the time until
we would be close again. When we were together, there was only the
present; and the present was perfect. We were whole, complete—one
unit moving through time and space, united. We were clinging to
one another as never before.

April 17, 2006

I've had this thought before; but, still, it is really strange: gratitude.
How can someone feel gratitude for watching her husband die? And
yet, right now, my heart swells with love of God and gratitude for the
opportunity to assist a great soul in his passing. This is an honor and a
blessing. It is a promise we made and a promise we will keep: to walk
this journey together and to drink the full cup of sorrow and of joy.
As these thoughts penetrate my heart, the Divine Presence burns into
my awareness.

*Seek Truth and all will be well. Seek God, and Stephen will be spared
much suffering. His heart burns with the fire of his own divinity. Focus
on the fire, not the sorrow. The fire of Spirit is what consumes death. Not
substances or treatments. It is the fire that directs life, not ego, not fear,
not tasks, or lists. Let your actions flow from fire and fear not.*

A dear friend said she was speechless in the face of our courage,
which we find a bit embarrassing. We feel we have no choice but to
be courageous and follow through with the path and the love we

have worked so hard for. And, of course, I am reminded that courage is not an absence of fear. It means feeling the fear and moving ahead anyway.

The miracle is not the cure; it's the exit done with consciousness and love. The body will bear such awareness if the mind stretches up to Spirit. That is the true healing—attaining such hunger for eternity that the Divine Presence reaches across and pulls us to its own great heart.

That is the mission and the message: that two hearts should so beat as one that one may go and the other stay, but still as one. Can Stephen reach across the divide and tell me what he sees? Can I capture those eyes and see them looking back at me, across death into life? I will write what I see, to be sure.

The works of Wordsworth often gave Stephen context for his own meditations. We both felt that the great poet's childhood visions had given him true insight into the workings of the soul and its relationship with the Creator. Wordsworth had also experienced profound loss in his life when his brother John died at sea and two of his children died at ages three and six. And yet he had retained a strong belief in a benevolent universe, reflected in a poignancy that spoke directly to Stephen's heart. In a poem Stephen wrote in May, he included lines from *The Prelude* and *Tintern Abbey*.

Love Pays

When I'm dealing with the pain of losing you,
I sometimes think that it would be easier
   without love.
   Not that I'm afraid of being without you.
I would gladly accept it
   if you went first—gladly.

It's the thought that without me,
Because of me, your innocence,
Your joy—will be compromised.

But even this has recompense.
I am forced into the faith that
"A gracious spirit o'er this earth presides."
It's this giving over that restores me.

But even more recompense is the vision, that despite:
    "Evil tongues, rash judgments
    Sneers of selfish men, greetings
    Where no kindness is, the
    Dreariness of daily life"—

Despite all this ultimately you
Will face that portion of God
That dwells within you
And be given the opportunity
To walk
    into the fullness
    of that eternal embrace.

Can there be any greater joy for me?

May and June were up-and-down months, with lots of tears on my part, especially when I was traveling. Stephen resumed chemo infusions, with a central line that had to be surgically implanted in his shoulder to make the biweekly hookups easier and a chemo pump to extend the infusions over forty-eight hours. That meant flushing the line and changing the dressing at home. The drugs were rough, the nausea unrelenting. Only weekly acupuncture treatments seemed to ease the discomfort.

June 18, 2006

    Father's Day with Stephen's family. We told the kids that "Uncle Stephen is taking some medicine" so they won't be freaked out by the chemo pump he is wearing today. His fortitude is astounding and he still doesn't look sick. He goes to work every day, except for the day of treatment. His boss is a compassionate woman and, fortunately, his work does not require a lot of interaction with other people. So he can keep working, building up sick leave and vacation time for when he will need it even more than now.

The CAT scan in late June showed that some of the tumors had shrunk, which gave us a bit of hope that we were making progress—that we were, indeed, buying some time for life, for love, for more of whatever we could share. I tried not to act desperate, but it is really difficult not to grasp after your beloved when you feel him slipping away.

We did our best to live a normal life. Stephen's younger brother remarried in July, and we were able to attend the ceremony. Photos from that day show Stephen with less hair, but otherwise appearing healthy. In August we celebrated our sixteenth wedding anniversary—a precious milestone and a wonderful day of rest. A poem was all I could give my husband that really mattered.

Loving Stephen

My best days begin and end with you.
Your shower wakes me.
Your "good night" sends me off to sleep.
And all the intervening hours
I reference you.

I measure my responses by your honor.
I ask questions now because you do it so naturally.
I'm brave with the courage you lent me.
And I think a thousand times
How incomplete life was before we met.

Souls expand and hearts go deep in love.
And love grows from an act into a state of being
That carries us along the path it carves
By its own power.

I am in love—I love.
I live in loving Stephen.
And knowing that—
I live in peace and hope and faith
That loving never ends.

By September the chemo treatments were taking an awful toll on Stephen, with only minimal effectiveness. There appeared to be no new growth, but as is often the case with cancer in the liver, these tumors were proving to be very resistant to chemo. It was becoming clear that Stephen couldn't continue to endure so much poison in his system. A blood test—one I wish we had known about months earlier—revealed a genetic condition, known as Gilbert's syndrome, which actually hindered his body from processing the chemo. So we took a break from cancer drugs.

For the next few months, we concentrated on diet, mild exercise, acupuncture, Chinese herbs, and love to combat the disease. We spent lots of time together and, in October, we launched into having the kitchen remodeled. Stephen was no longer able to take on big projects by himself, but he had a dramatic vision for the kitchen and we found a contractor who helped us actualize his beautiful plan.

A CAT scan in early December showed the tumors picking up steam again. Some of them had doubled in size since September, and new ones had appeared. Stephen continued to feel well, but the images of his liver were appalling.

December 15, 2006

I'm teaching in New York and I just learned that my dear friend and fellow instructor Dave died suddenly last night in London. He was teaching at the education center and had gone to dinner with another instructor, appearing to be in good spirits. He didn't show up for work the next morning and was found dead in his hotel room, still wearing his dinner clothes.

What a tragedy and such a terrible loss for his wife, Leslie. He was the love of her life and she of his. It was a second marriage for them both, and they doted on one another. I wonder if Dave had any warning or premonition—some sense of the end that would take him in an instant. I try to think that one door closes and another opens, but some doors just close.

Leslie was devastated, but also comforted in knowing that, as she told me, "there was nothing unsaid" between her and Dave. She described their relationship as being open, honest, loving, and immediate. He left home to go teach that one last time with no regrets—except, perhaps, for working so hard to get all his work done in time for the round-the-world cruise they were going to take in a couple of weeks. Even so, I'm sure that Dave had only love in his heart. And not just for Leslie but, seemingly, for all of humanity.

Dave's memorial service was an explosion of testimony to the great heart of this man who lived every day of his life in service to the development of others. It was impossible not to feel brilliant in his presence. I was privileged to work with this amazing human being, and I vowed to carry on his belief that everybody has genius that only needs to be nurtured. His was a legacy of hope and achievement for countless others, including his wife. That legacy gave her much comfort in the months that followed.

December 29, 2006

What will be our legacy? I want mine to be something I have written—a book, perhaps, or some poems. Words do last if they are written down. I'm still ambitious; I want to make an impression and a difference. Stephen speaks of his legacy differently. He is not ambitious, except, perhaps, to convert those he loves to a spiritual perspective.

"How do we know what the truth is, except what we live in our hearts?" he mused to me last night. "There is no real certainty, no way of knowing on this side, except for our personal experience of Spirit."

I believe Stephen's legacy will be that he shone as a bright light to all he met. The shame is that so few have had a chance to really know him. I could tell his story, but he has kept so much to himself. So what, indeed, will be our legacy? Certainly that we loved each other.

Hopefully that we were kind, forgiving, harmonious, always striving to be better—and that we were content in our marriage.

In many ways, I am Stephen's legacy. He has shaped and tamed me without breaking me. He has pointed me up to the Divine and in to my own heart. He has planted himself in me, and that part of the story I know.

As we walked through these days of love and heartache, I became terrified by the prospect of living alone in the house after Stephen was gone. I was overwhelmed at the thought of my own grief and that of other people. I worried that I would not be able to handle what was surely coming upon us—possibly as early as next October.

But then, as I wrote in my journal, the voice of the Divine Presence would come through my writing, speaking to me of comfort and courage, assuring me that I was not alone, that I would be able to summon the strength I needed for both of us. And it always seemed to leave me with the sense that, when the time came, I would be able to walk with Stephen right up to the door of death. I was counting on that feeling to prove true.

Part Three

MIDWIFE TO
THE SOUL

Love seeketh not itself to please,
Nor for itself hath any care,
But for another gives its ease
And builds a heaven in hell's despair.

—William Blake

Fourteen

A YEAR OF LASTS, 1

*The distance we have gone is less important
than the direction in which we are going.*

—Leo Tolstoy

COLORADO WEATHER IS FICKLE at the end of March, but it was spring break and we were driving south—dodging snow showers over Raton Pass at the Colorado border, then safely across miles of high desert to the secluded valley where the village of Taos, New Mexico, sits at the foot of the Sangre de Cristo Mountains. There is something crystalline about northern New Mexico, and we always felt ourselves relax in the clean air and brilliant blue skies.

It was so good to act like two normal people on a little vacation, because the first three months of 2007 had been very intense. We were still under the impression that Stephen might live only until October, and he was beginning to have fairly consistent pain in his side, which was a bad sign. But we were determined to enjoy ourselves as much as possible—just the two of us, alone in the car, watching the scenery slip by, relishing the closeness that was so much a part of the soul connection we felt whenever we were together like this.

Owing to the bad report from December's CAT scan, Stephen had started the first of three rounds of oral chemo immediately after New Year's. Fortunately, there was a pill he could take that meant he could continue working and with lower levels of "chemo" brain.

Mentally, I had been in a weird place in January. On one hand, I wanted time to accelerate because the first floor of our townhome was still torn up from the kitchen remodel. This had been going on since October and I was getting sick of the chaos. On the other hand, I wanted time to stand still because Stephen had been home for his two-week Christmas vacation. It had always been tough to see him go back to work after the New Year; this year was worse because his condition was worse. If I could hold back time, said the crazy voice in my head, I could keep Stephen with me longer.

I was burdened on many levels. Some weeks earlier I had realized that journaling was no longer sufficient to process all the pain and confusion I was feeling. I needed help, so I started seeing a psychological counselor who became a valued advocate and sounding board. It really helped to have this person in my life who could remind me that feeling crazy is part of the deal while reassuring me that I was relatively okay, that I could endure, and that she would intervene if I actually start losing my grip. It was good to have unconditional permission to bring up all the conflicting thoughts and feelings that go with being a caregiver, so I was beginning to relax into living with uncertainty when my professional life suddenly took off again.

January 11, 2007

After seeing my counselor, I was looking forward to a quiet, introspective couple of hours at a coffee shop but was prompted to go directly home instead. Good thing I listened. My product manager called from the training company to ask that I write a new course on conflict resolution. My immediate response was to decline, but she reminded me that my colleague Dave (who just passed away in December) had frequently said I should be a course author. I hesitated, but Stephen encouraged me to go for it. Another good friend, also an instructor and an experienced course author, assured me I could do it. So I agreed—and now my mind is whirling with ideas for what to include in the content. It feels like the universe is stepping on the gas again.

I was thrilled to be paid for writing, but the timelines were tight and the expectations high. The compressed production schedule forced me to penetrate the mysteries of my creative process as never before. I often worked late into the night when Stephen was asleep—wondering how I could ever endure living alone and yet relishing the stillness that nurtured my thoughts. Being deeply creative was to me a holy process that seemed to open my mind and heart to heavenly forces.

January 20, 2007

It's late and I'm finishing course work for the night. I've been thinking about what it means to have a friendship with the Divine. How interesting to write that and then immediately feel the acknowledgement of "friend" come back to me. And as I write, here is what my friend says to me:

You will never be alone. You have never been alone. Only in your mind were you ever abandoned. The angels are always here. You may feel their touch. You are protected and loved. Life is unfolding as it should. Be strong. Have faith. You and Stephen reside in the palm of Spirit's hand. Rest there and be of good cheer. Stephen goes to his Divine Father and Mother. You are here as midwife to his soul. Help deliver him on his way and the heavens will open to you as well.

By February, the kitchen remodel was finished and the house put back together. We both breathed a sigh of relief and enjoyed cooking a wonderful Valentine's Day dinner in our gorgeous new kitchen that perfectly matched Stephen's woodwork in the living room.

He continued with oral chemo and seemed to be holding steady. Monthly CAT scans showed the cancer still growing, but not immediately life-threatening. The acupuncturist saw signs of strength in Stephen's immune system and overall condition, and he continued to look really well—so well, in fact, that one evening I suggested, "Maybe you won't have to go away after all." He wrinkled his nose at me and said nothing. He was so wary of false hope.

He made little mention of how he felt day to day, but even oral chemo has side effects. The neuropathy in his hands and feet was irksomely painful, and he was very tired at the end of each workday. I was writing like crazy on the new course, so we connected very little except on weekends, when we could focus on remodeling projects or just hanging out at home. Being together for two full days was always strengthening to both of us and seemed to unlock a special kind of creativity. We continued to write each other poems as a way to express in verse what was so hard to say out loud.

We were both growing a lot during this period, but it was more separate than shared. We each had so much to sort out about who we were as individuals—not just as a couple—because at some point we would have to un-couple and to do that was going to require a strong sense of self-identity. We didn't talk about it, but that is what we were preparing to do.

Driving vacations had always been our favorite, especially traversing the dramatically barren vastness of the Southwest. We often listened to an entire audio book as we drove, but this time we were talking about how different our lives had been from those of our families. Having grown up during the Great Depression, my parents had nurtured high hopes for me to do well in life. They had reared me with a strong church influence, but they had never imagined my joining a religious community that they thought offered no professional future or long-term financial stability.

Stephen's parents were not so concerned about his spiritual choices, but his financial ones gave them pause. His father had retired from Kodak as a distribution center manager, and his brothers were both doing well in computer-related professions. It puzzled them that Stephen had so little interest in material success.

"My spiritual path has always gotten in the way of whatever career path I followed," said Stephen somewhat ruefully. He was surely recalling how he had resigned from a prominent commodities trading firm in Chicago to move to our teacher's community in Montana—only months after achieving a huge success that would have guaranteed his future in the trading industry. Immediately before the market crash on Black Monday in October 1987 (which all the trading companies knew was coming), he and another employee had worked all weekend to implement a computer program they had been developing to identify any dangerous financial positions their clients might be holding. It worked perfectly, saving the company millions of dollars.

Stephen was a hero. The firm gave him a big bonus that year and was ready to accelerate his move up the corporate ladder. Instead, he turned his back on the rat race he foresaw in that life and moved to Montana to work for a $65-per-month stipend. On accepting Stephen's resignation, his boss had said to him, "I respect your choice, but I *do not* understand it."

"I've never wanted to be owned by a job," Stephen explained to me, "and that's what I felt would happen if I stayed in the financial world."

"I know what you mean," I agreed. "My career has always taken a back seat to my spiritual life, too. It's as if my soul has had its own agenda—always restless and hungry for something more—for a more spiritual life."

"So I guess that was really what we wanted to do all along, wasn't it?" Stephen concluded with a smile.

May 15, 2007

I feel myself disconnecting from Stephen as he goes more deeply within. I suppose it's self-protection. One way to ease the pain of losing your husband is to not need him. Make him irrelevant. Even decide that life would be easier without him. I have no idea what's going on in his mind (except that he's proud of my writing the conflict course), and he has no idea of what's going on in mine (except that I want to get a dog, which he's not crazy about). I have decided I won't be afraid to be in the house without him if there is a furry being here that already calls this home. A nice big dog would do that.

We did the best we could, one day at a time. There were the inevitable aggravations and obstacles to getting my conflict course off the ground—such as a new editor changing all of my graphics just days before the class was to run. Most problems were resolved with minimal fury on my part, so in early June I was on my way to Washington, D.C., for an initial test class with volunteer attendees. On the cab ride from the airport to my hotel, I called into Stephen's oncology appointment to get the results from his latest CAT scan. The news was not good.

June 4, 2007
The CAT scan shows two more tumors, with some of the old ones growing a full centimeter in three months. The next phase begins just like that—with no real chemo options. There is a new drug we could try, but it would mean transfusions and no real benefit. We had already decided not to conduct any more chemistry experiments on Stephen's poor body right now, so we're through with that, thank goodness. Stephen looks so well—it is unfathomable that he could be dying. I pray he feels no pain—that all he has endured will count for grace.

I flew home Friday evening, utterly exhausted after one of the most difficult weeks yet. I felt an additional burden of responsibility for Stephen's well-being, with actual weight being transferred to me—a physical energy I struggled to carry.

For a long time now I had felt as if Stephen and I were both carrying backpacks up a mountain. At certain points along the way, he would stop and hand me part of his load. The latest bad test results created another one of those transfer points. All week I had been adjusting to the extra weight while willing myself through the test run of my conflict-resolution course. I have no idea how I made it—we just do what we have to do.

After the poor test results, Stephen's acupuncturist got nervous about treating somebody who was going to die and recommended we see his teacher—the best change we could have made. Dr. C., who readily accepted Stephen as a patient, had spent years in the East studying Chinese medicine, and he followed a spiritual tradition that made him the perfect practitioner for both of us. I went with Stephen for his first appointment and was immediately impressed with Dr. C.'s obvious skill and gently intuitive demeanor.

"I felt better the minute he took my pulses," said Stephen as we drove home. (Chinese medicine identifies pulses for all of the major organs, not just the heart.) He was pleased with Dr. C.'s regimen of Chinese herbs, homeopathy, and dietary improvements that would support his body so it could fight the cancer on its own and keep the symptoms to a minimum—although throughout the summer he continued to get twinges of pain in his side. If I said anything to him about getting better, he just looked at me and shook his head.

I think in some ways it was easier for Stephen when I was traveling. He wasn't really feeling sick. In fact, Dr. C.'s treatments were giving him more energy, so there wasn't a lot I could do for him on a daily basis. Of course, I did his laundry and kept house, and I always cooked a week's worth of meals before leaving for a business trip, so food wasn't an issue. But I'm quite sure that being home alone in the evenings was a relief.

"My meditations are getting so much deeper," Stephen remarked one weekend morning while we were having breakfast. "Often now my heart center begins to spin as soon as I close my eyes. I can't tell you how important this is to me."

I had never been able to do sitting meditation like Stephen, but I felt my journaling and the poems that arose from writing were my own powerful communion with Spirit. I also considered listening for inner promptings to be a spiritual practice. For both of us, our ways of connecting with higher levels of awareness were becoming more critical as we did our best to embrace a positive present without dreading an awful future.

∞

Throughout the summer, Stephen felt well enough to push through on some of the remaining home-remodeling projects. Soon it was September—time for another CAT scan.

The cancer was still growing, but not as fast as before. It appeared that Dr. C's treatments were working to help Stephen's body fight back by eliminating toxins in his system and lowering the heat that chemo and radiation had caused throughout his body. Blood and stool tests had revealed numerous food allergies, so we had eliminated gluten, soy, and dairy from his diet. "These food sensitivities can kill you," said Dr. C, remarking that years of gluten reactivity weaken the colon and could actually have caused the cancer.

"We're not doing any more chemo," Stephen told our oncologist firmly at our September appointment. It had long since become "we" and "us" when it came to these decisions. Anything that happened to one of us happened to both of us. I felt Stephen's pain and he felt mine.

There was something triumphant about declaring that we were officially taking back control of Stephen's life, but there was also something terribly final about it. The difficulty of these decisions cannot be overstated. If I had been the one with cancer, I would have reached this conclusion much sooner, because I know I could not have withstood the toxicity as long as Stephen did. His strong constitution and amazing willpower had allowed him to persevere with oral chemo through May, but he simply could not face getting back on that toxic roller coaster.

Fifteen

A YEAR OF LASTS, 2

*In the most painful corners of our experience,
something alive is always waiting to emerge.*

—John Welwood

STEPHEN AND I BOTH LOVED AUTUMN, and we really wanted to enjoy it this year. I was scheduled to teach my new conflict course in London in October, so in late September we went to the mountains for a week.

We had a feeling this might be our last real vacation because of the constant discomfort Stephen was feeling in his right side. Many of our bodies' organs don't actually have nerves in them that directly register pain, but the surrounding tissue does. The liver didn't hurt, but the fact that it was enlarged by the tumors was making it press on other vital areas that were complaining about the intrusion.

But we were not dwelling on pain as we slipped into the sleek silver Mustang convertible we had rented for the trip—because Stephen had always wanted to own a Mustang. With the XM radio tuned to our favorite oldies, we zipped off to the historic old mining town of Telluride, with stops along the way to look at standard poodle puppies and to visit some friends.

Stephen was not enthused about introducing a dog into our already stressed lives, but he could see my point about needing a companion when he was gone, so he had agreed to at least check out some litters with me. We both liked big dogs and had decided on a standard poodle because the breed is smart and does not shed. But this particular puppy excursion was a disaster.

When we walked into the breeder's cluttered house there were poodles everywhere. Two adult show dogs stood on grooming tables on the front porch. The new mommy dog still had her sausage-sized babies in the whelping nest. An older male poodle immediately glommed onto Stephen—literally pinning him on the couch—while three half-grown siblings from an earlier litter raced around in constant motion, creating chaos at every turn.

Poor Stephen turned ashen in the noise and mess, especially when he noticed the chewed-up wooden rocking chair in the living room. This was not a good way to convince him we needed a dog! Mangled furniture was one of his greatest fears about owning a puppy. We got out of there fast and drove on to our friends' house without another word about dog ownership.

The next morning, we put the top down on the Mustang and set off for Telluride, driving over Monarch Pass, which rises over 11,000 feet above sea level. By the time we got to the summit, the temperature had dropped at least twenty degrees, but we were determined not to put the top up. This was an adventure and we were not going to wimp out!

Telluride's setting is breathtaking—massive peaks that rise abruptly from a horseshoe-shaped valley covered in aspen and pine forests. The accommodations were perfect for our favorite vacation pastimes—hot stone massages and great food—and we drove through the surrounding mountains with the Mustang's top down, taking our time to enjoy every moment of sun and wind that just blew away our cares. It was easy to forget our troubles in the rarified air of the high Rocky Mountains. Or so it seemed until we went for a walk around town on our second evening, after an early dinner, through the shops and galleries that were still open.

I tend to walk briskly, especially if I'm excited about something. As I got caught up in the beautiful artwork and handcrafted designer clothing and leatherwork we were seeing, my pace quickened. Leaving one shop, I was quickly starting off to the next one when Stephen said sharply, "Slow down! You have got to walk at my pace or I can't do this."

I stopped in my tracks. "I'm so sorry, Bunny," I said as tears sprang into my eyes. "I forgot you were sick."

"I know," he said with resignation in his voice. "Just stay with me, okay?" I felt instantly deflated and we both sagged wearily, with barely the energy to walk back to the hotel. We flopped into bed without discussing what had happened. The rest of the vacation was lovely. But after this experience, I tried not to forget that Stephen was getting weaker, even while doing my best not to treat him as if he were dying. It was a delicate balance.

October 12, 2007

Stephen has already survived longer than we anticipated eighteen months earlier. Unfortunately, nothing is clear about how long he could actually continue to live. Sometimes he seems to be doing so well that I believe we still have a chance to beat the cancer. At other times I am afraid he won't last the year.

I am remembering what an astrologer friend said in 2005 when I asked if she could see anything in Stephen's chart that would indicate how long he would survive. I don't live my life by portents in the stars, but over the years I have found some benefit in being aware of impending trends or cycles. Of course, a reputable astrologer will never predict death; my friend would only say that she saw "liberation" in Stephen's chart starting in October of 2008.

"Whatever is going on with him will be finished by then," she said.

I hope we will have more time than that, but—just in case—I must assume we do not.

Life was very strange for me these days. I was living in two such different worlds: one at home, doing everything I could think of to help

Stephen feel better; the other in the business arena, working very hard to improve my skill and confidence as an instructor and facilitator.

I was also breaking up deep psychological patterns of self-doubt, self-criticism, and self-limitation. It wasn't so much that I was conscious of breaking them; it was more that, in order to deal with life as it was presented to me each day, I had to listen for inner guidance as I had never listened before. I continued to deepen my intuitive sense of what to say and when to say it in the classroom, and that carried over into my life with Stephen. I learned to trust that Spirit would direct me and that I would know what to do as the illness worsened. As the healing voice of inner guidance grew stronger, the nasty voice of the inner critic grew silent. I don't know when it went away, but it did.

October 30, 2007

We know the body is afraid to die, and that's not a bad thing. We want the body to fight to live. But what we are really fighting for is life everlasting for the soul. And not just Stephen's soul that will go on to eternity, but my soul that will stay here for a season longer—and must have faith and resiliency to continue our mission.

Stephen's illness has so highly focused our attention on the preciousness of life. It has given us the courage to dispense with attitudes, habits, and patterns of behavior that do not serve our current situation. You simply cannot face imminent death without making a choice: What of yourself will you fight to save? I am so grateful for that awareness.

Soon it was mid-November and we were steeling ourselves for the holidays, believing these would probably be our last family celebrations with Stephen among us. Then, as so often happened to us, things took a positive turn that would have long-lasting consequences. Stephen's condition did not improve, but our lives did—with a new addition.

November 12, 2007

Stephen's fifty-fifth (and possibly final) birthday. I had given up on finding a standard poodle puppy, deciding it was too much work and a frivolous desire, based more on my fear of being alone than on my perennial love of all things doggie. But then serendipity struck.

Yesterday I discovered a newspaper ad for what I thought was an adult standard poodle. Turns out it was a "fire sale" for four puppies remaining from a litter of eight. I was hesitant to see them until I learned that the sire was one of the top poodles in the state and part of the breeding line I liked for their soft eyes and sweet dispositions. So, off we went this morning to see puppies.

It was love at first sight. The mommy dog was the most beautiful solid-black standard poodle we had ever seen. As we walked into the breeder's (clean!) breakfast room, four curly black puppies lined up along the patio door like perfect little statues. As the breeder opened the sliding door, in they bounded to greet us. Puppy #1 went right to Stephen and didn't leave.

After a very few minutes of playing with his new little buddy, Stephen said to the breeder, "We'll take this one." I was shocked. Stephen Eckl had never made a major purchase of any kind without thinking about it for at least a day.

"Are you sure?" I didn't believe my ears.

"Yes, write her a check."

So just like that, we had our puppy. I was leaving town the next day to teach, so it wasn't until Saturday that we could take possession of thirteen-week-old Bentley—named by Stephen—who became the source of love, laughter, and lightness we sorely needed in our lives.

November 17, 2007

Today we were like new parents, outfitting the nursery—only we did our shopping at PetSmart—filling the back of the van with a doggie bed, crate, bowls, toys, and puppy food. Stephen held on to Bentley in the van while I completed the paperwork in the house with the breeder. When I came out, those two boys were already bonded.

"He's so sweet," said Stephen, cradling an armful of timid black fluff. "Let's get him home so he knows where he lives now."

Getting a new puppy when your days are numbered may not be the most practical idea in the world, but the sheer joy of this bouncy little being that literally leapt into our lives was worth every inconvenience. Stephen was transformed: laughing, rolling around on the floor with Bentley, taking him for walks, teaching him to sit and answer to his name. The whole experience lifted our hearts as nothing else had done for a very long time.

Stephen's co-workers also noticed the change. They told me what a proud papa he was and how amazing it was to see the normally taciturn Stephen become absolutely gabby when they asked about Bentley. Even though Stephen had resisted my desire to get a dog, clearly this was one of the best therapies we could have devised for him.

December brought with it very bad news indeed—another turning point and more physical/psychic weight for me to carry. The cancer had grown, with some tumors changing only 25 percent but others as much as 40 percent. This really was the beginning of the end, and we both knew it.

Each discouraging CAT scan report had put us through emotional changes and realities to adjust to; this one was breathtakingly final in its impact. It was not an absolute death sentence, but it marked the end of a certain mindset we had been sustaining that had allowed us to push back against the idea of death. From this point forward, we had to embrace the inevitable. Now there were plans to make and work to do for the next set of challenges that would take us ever deeper into the unknowns that surround the end of life.

We had managed to get through Thanksgiving in pretty good shape. Unlike last year, I now had a beautiful, working kitchen; so I gladly fixed the traditional family dinner, as I had ever since we'd moved into our townhome in 1998. It was a very happy occasion.

My mother and stepfather and Stephen's parents were there, along with his younger brother, Rick, and Rick's wife and their children. Stephen did not look at all sick, and other than the constant pain in his side, he was feeling well enough to really enjoy the day. Nobody said anything about cancer; all was light until we went around the table after dinner, taking turns saying what we were grateful for. When Stephen said, "I'm grateful for Cheryl," I could not hold back the tears.

Now it was Christmastime. We put up a huge live tree and gaily decorated the house. I sent out Christmas cards with photos from our Taos and Telluride vacations and new pictures of Bentley looking adorable. But despite these outward signs of holiday spirit, we could not face trying to be cheery for anybody in person.

Stephen's family was spending Christmas week at Rick's ski condo near Winter Park, and my folks were surrounded with friends at their senior-living center. So we excused ourselves from their gatherings and celebrated our last Christmas and New Year's alone—just the two of us together with our little Bentley. It was simply the best we could do.

Sixteen

A PROMISE TO KEEP

For those who understand it, death is a highly creative force.
The highest spiritual values of life can originate
from the thought and study of death.

—Elisabeth Kübler-Ross

January 6, 2008

Last night I dreamt of myself as a devotee of the Hindu goddess Kali, devourer of time and death. She appeared as I had seen her years ago in a poster, with dark skin, several arms—one of which held a sword—a fierce expression on her face, wearing a necklace of skulls, sitting on bodies of the dead. She is a fearsome creature, but she is also the Mother figure to whom many of the world's great Hindu saints, such as Sri Ramakrishna, have turned for solace.

In the dream I saw myself as a person who sits with the dying to help them tell their story and move on. People need to tell their stories. It's a kind of life review, a confession—and an opportunity to identify how much they have actually contributed to life. Kali swallows up the shadow self, the grasping energy of ego, so the soul that is liberated can rise from the ashes of disappointment and despair and soar to the heights of union with the Divine. Here is what I heard her say:

I am present at the moment of death. I am witness to the transfigura-
tion. I take on the battle for the soul. I am the midwife of rebirth and
I facilitate the journey over to the Other Side. I preach the message of
self-awareness. I call souls to their true mission. I open them to possibil-
ity and show them how to take steps to God's heart.

Early January was a busy time. Bentley was enrolled in puppy
obedience school, which was not going well. The poor dog was so
confused. He was thirteen weeks old when we got him and had had
practically no training from his breeders, who had never bred a litter
of puppies before.

Because it was a week before Thanksgiving, new-puppy classes
were not starting until after the New Year. So to get him started, I
hired a woman who worked for a dog-training franchise, only to
discover she didn't know how to handle a precocious male standard-
poodle pup. She frightened Bentley with her briefcase and things
went downhill from there. We parted ways in a couple of weeks, but
not before the puppy had suffered another setback in his training.

By the time Bentley and I started junior obedience class in
January—he was now too old for beginners—he had a lot of bad
habits, the worst being not coming when called. He was more
interested in playing with the other dogs than in obeying, which
meant my spending most of the class trying to get his attention.
Standard poodles are really smart, so he had quickly figured out I
was a total pushover; but, of course, he would obey Stephen, who
was learning simple obedience techniques from *The Dog Whisperer*
on television. Stephen was very good at establishing a hierarchy and
making clear who was the "alpha dog." Bentley was not allowed to
invade his space (for that matter, humans weren't either), and the
puppy had to be calm on the lead when they were out for walks.

In addition to taking Bentley to puppy school and running the
household, I was also completing more revisions on the conflict
course and resting after a bad fall on the ice. One day right after

Christmas, Stephen, Bentley, and I had been out for a walk before lunch. We were crossing an icy patch of road when my feet suddenly flew out from under me and I landed flat on my back, hitting my head sharply on the rock-hard pavement.

Bentley scampered over and stuck his nose in my face, apparently thinking this was some kind of game. I pushed him away and started to cry. I wasn't really in pain, but I was shocked and frightened by how severely I had whacked my head. After the serious concussion I'd sustained in the 1997 car accident, any threat to my head terrified me. It had taken me two years and multiple migraines before I fully recovered. The first thought that went through my mind now was, *I can't get hurt! Stephen needs me. Please, God, don't let me have a concussion.*

But my head did feel slightly concussed. Stephen was very concerned and watched me intently for several hours, not letting me doze off, even though I was tired and shaken. When it appeared that I had not actually sustained a serious injury, he let me go to sleep that night; and the next day I went to our acupuncturist, who had a regime to help the brain heal after a concussion. I went for several treatments and, in a few days, felt back to normal. I was okay—a huge relief to both of us. I simply could not be out of commission right now.

I'm sure Stephen was worried about what it might have meant had I been seriously hurt. I know he remembered what a mess I had been after the car accident. He was always the stoic patient, but I needed a lot of emotional support if I was in pain—something he had never been very good at providing and which he was particularly ill equipped to offer these days.

January 15, 2008

Stephen keeps giving me pointers about taking care of the house and finances and all the things that will need watching out for when he's gone. It's as if he's training me to be a widow, and I don't want to hear it. I may just lose my mind. It's hard not to want to die, too—to just go with Stephen when he leaves, for the two of us to disappear together and not have to deal with the grief and anxiety of our families and friends.

I keep telling myself not to wallow in hopelessness. That's the perfect way *not* to make progress. There is always hope, but we do have to choose whether or not to embrace it. My friend Pat reminded me that you can't push the river; it will go where and when its force takes it. The choice is to go with the flow or drown resisting it.

By late spring it was time for decisions requiring sensitivity and tenderness, even as we moved forward to make room for what came next. We sold Stephen's band saw, his exercise equipment, and my treadmill. We created an office space for him in the loft. We spent more time reading together and focused on being normal. Stephen still did not look terribly sick, but he was clearly weakening.

"You're going to have to find somebody to take care of Bentley the next time you travel," he said abruptly one day in early June.

"Why?" I asked, greatly puzzled. I thought we had a very workable system in place. Until now, whenever I traveled—which had been frequently in recent months—Stephen would drop Bentley off at doggie day care on his way to work. It was a solution that Bentley loved and that made him pleasantly calm in the evening.

"It's just too much for me now to drop him off in the morning and pick him up after work. Plus, he still needs to be fed and taken out at least once to potty before bed," Stephen explained. "It's just too much, Bun. I can't do it."

"Of course, I'll figure something out," I said, realizing he must have really struggled the last time I was away to teach. I knew how hard he pushed himself to be "normal"; admitting he couldn't do something meant it was causing him tremendous pain and fatigue.

However, as he felt his strength ebbing, selling exercise equipment and taking care of the dog were the least of Stephen's worries. His greatest concern was leaving me. He was genuinely doubtful that I could handle his household responsibilities as well as my own, and I know he worried that I might not keep up financially—that I might actually lose the house he had poured so much of his creative soul into.

I had not realized how seriously he doubted my ability to carry on without him until one evening before bed. He was in his room reading and I was in mine doing the same. We had long ago begun sleeping in separate rooms because I was working late into the night on the conflict course and he had to get up early in the morning for work. It had also been much easier for him not to share a bed while he was undergoing chemotherapy treatments.

I had been rereading Ken Wilber's *Grace and Grit* and was intrigued by his description of a meditation technique called *tonglen*—a practice of "taking in and sending out" from the Tibetan Buddhist tradition whose focus is on extending compassion to all living beings. I decided to try it because Wilber said it had become an essential practice for him and his wife, Treya, during the last few years of her battle with breast cancer.

To begin, I seated myself for meditation, back straight, breathing naturally, noticing the breath going in and out until I felt myself enter a state of calm awareness. The next step was to visualize a loved one who was in pain—in this case, of course, Stephen. As I breathed in, I imagined all of his suffering in the form of a dark, heavy substance flowing into my body and traveling down to my heart.

The basic instruction is to rest briefly with that suffering in your heart, where you feel it being consumed. Then on the out-breath, you visualize all your own positive qualities of loving-kindness, compassion, and health being released out to the one in pain as rays of love, light, and healing energy. You try to see the other person as being released from his or her suffering, now surrounded in joy and a sense of well-being. You can repeat the process for several breaths in a formal meditation practice or, as Buddhist nun and teacher Pema Chödrön says, you can do *tonglen* on the spot for people who happen to cross your path. You simply breathe in their pain and send them comfort. You can also extend this blessing to groups, cities, nations, or continents—even to the entire world.[4]

I have to admit to being a bit concerned—as are most people who try this technique for the first time—that willingly taking in the negative energy of another person's illness or anxiety would make me sick. Apparently, this doesn't happen. Instead, you stop recoiling from suffering—your own as well as that of others. You learn how to enter into pain, allowing it to flow into and through your heart, where it is transformed into compassion for all those who suffer and blessing for the one who is willing to hold that attitude for the entire human condition.

I did not attain such lofty awareness that night, but as soon as I felt the energy of Stephen's suffering enter my heart, I knew its deepest cause: he did not suffer for himself, he suffered for me. His greatest burden in leaving me was the fear that I might flounder as he had seen me do so often, that my faith would be destroyed, and that I would be vulnerable without him to protect me.

I immediately got up and went into his room, where he was still awake. Sitting next to him on the bed, I touched his arm and said, "Is leaving me what concerns you most?"

"Yes," he said, his eyes filling with tears. "I know how much you depend on me and I worry that you won't be okay."

"I will be, I promise," I said and kissed him on the forehead. "I promise." I went back to my room and cried myself to sleep.

It actually made sense that Stephen would be worried about me. Because he was so strong and in charge of our relationship and our home, I didn't have to be. The people I had worked with in Montana would have had no doubt of my ability to handle projects and crises because that's what they had seen me doing for years. But Stephen and I had never worked together, except on our home-improvement projects. And, during those times, his physical strength and problem-solving genius had so outshone mine that, to him, I must have appeared weak and confused. It now became critical for me to convince him I would be able to carry on without him. And it wasn't long before I got an opportunity to prove it.

∞

June 3, 2008

Lightning strikes! Yes, literally. I was upstairs at home, working on my laptop, with a thunderstorm going on outside. I noticed some lightning, but it didn't seem that close. Suddenly, without warning, there was a colossal *Boom!* that shook the house like a bomb going off. I thought the tree outside the window had been struck, because I saw leaves and branches flying. I ran outside to discover that our house had actually taken a direct hit that blew off shingles and siding and smashed a giant hole in the apex of the roof. I immediately called our insurance company to report the claim and then realized I had better call the fire department too, because we had a wooden shake-shingle roof that could be on fire!

In less than ten minutes the fire department showed up with their ladder truck and five firemen in full regalia. Fortunately, there was no fire, but the lightning surge had burned an electrical outlet and fried Stephen's office equipment in the loft. It also destroyed the furnace, air conditioner, and garage-door opener and fused the 220 wiring from the stove onto a water pipe that ran next to it in the ceiling of my office in the basement.

Talk about divine intervention! Somebody was really looking out for us that day. The strike was more remarkable for what did *not* happen than for what did: the only appliances or systems that were destroyed were dangerous (the faulty wiring), inadequate for the future (Stephen's too-small computer), or old and ready to fail (everything else).

It took a couple of months to get everything repaired, but I handled all of the coordination and even got a job offer from the disaster-recovery company to be a project coordinator. Stephen was visibly relieved to see I could think clearly in a crisis and deal with whatever might come my way. I believe this was when he finally accepted that he could leave me.

Seventeen

ACCEPTING WHAT IS

*These roses under my window make no reference
to former roses or to better ones; they are for
what they are; they exist with God to-day.*

—Ralph Waldo Emerson

IN LATE JUNE, I TAUGHT my final business course before going on leave from work and preparing to stay home for as long as Stephen should live. He was getting weaker, too nauseated to eat much for meals, and in a great deal more pain. The liver was pressing on his diaphragm, which made it hard for him to breathe lying down. Tylenol was no longer enough, so we got him some stronger pain meds, which helped; but time was running out.

"I don't think I'm going to make it through the winter," Stephen admitted to me one day. "Each day is getting more difficult."

One day our friend Kathleen stopped by while I was out. She and Stephen spoke for nearly an hour, for what they both assumed would be the last time. Later she told me, "He looked beatific. He was thinner, but serene and obviously at peace. There was really nothing left for us to say at the end of that visit, and I was okay with that. I knew who he was and he knew who I was. That was enough."

July 23, 2008

Two days ago we got the results of the latest CAT scan. The liver is just covered with cancer—more cancer than healthy tissue now. It's got one huge lesion of 10 cm. It's hard to imagine how the liver is functioning at all.

I felt so sorry for our oncologist. After reviewing the images, he asked what we wanted to do—because there really is nothing left to do. There is one more chemo drug we could try, but the most it could give Stephen would be another six weeks and that is under the best of circumstances. Sadly, Stephen has always been on the "worst of circumstances" side of the chemo-effectiveness statistics.

We answered that we had already decided not to spoil the quality of whatever life Stephen had remaining by giving him more chemo. The doctor has always respected our treatment decisions and agreed that he really wouldn't recommend the treatment.

"It's just something I feel obligated to offer," he said. "Some people want treatment until the very end."

"Thank you for everything," I said as we shook hands with him for the last time. We all knew this was good-bye.

"You're just breaking my heart," he said as we left the examining room where the three of us had worked so hard to make Stephen well. We all had tears in our eyes and his voice cracked as he said, "I really wanted you to do better." He is such a tender man; I don't know how he has done this job for nearly thirty years.

Stephen and I weren't surprised at the CAT scan results, but it was still a shock to see them. I could barely move when we got home. My body hurt everywhere. I wrote an e-mail to a few close friends, asking for prayers, and felt them take some of the burden.

On Tuesday night, we called Stephen's parents. That was so hard. He could hardly get the words out to tell them we're out of options. They were just in shock—especially his dad.

"Isn't there something you can do?" he asked incredulously.

"No, there really isn't." I had to step in because Stephen couldn't talk. "There is one more chemo drug we could try, but that would just be torturing him for no reason. We're going to give him the best quality of life we can now with acupuncture and Chinese medicine. That will at least support his body to fight as long as it can without adding poison to his system."

We've really downplayed the seriousness of Stephen's condition to his parents—especially since he was feeling and looking so well until about March—so it was hard for them to accept bad news. They could tell he was declining when we saw them last, on July 4, but they were still holding out hope.

By now, Stephen and I were feeling a profound sense of holiness about this journey into the Great Unknown. Years before we met and married, we had each committed ourselves to the idea of soul liberation, or union with the Divine. The fact that achieving such a union probably meant leaving embodiment had not really meant much to us at the time. But now that we had finally ruled out any remaining treatment options, we recognized that our current circumstance—difficult as it might be—was exactly what we had signed up for years ago. Of course, knowing that didn't make delivering terrible news any easier.

July 24, 2008

I'm gradually sending out word of Stephen's condition to friends and other family members. It's a hard message to send—and yet I want people to know that we're basically okay and to understand how we are dealing with this final stage. Last night I said something about "my poor Bunny" and Stephen said, "Don't use that word; I don't feel poor." Indeed, we are rich beyond words because we have a path and a deep, deep yearning that propels us to the Divine.

Since I was no longer working, I started cleaning out years of files in my office, trying to create physical and psychic space so I could be more available to Stephen. He was still pushing himself to go to work every day, but the pain in his side was increasing, his color was getting worse, and his voice was weakening. He was beginning to lose weight. Now that I was able to stay home, I got more rest and felt myself doing a better job of listening, being in touch with Stephen's needs and my own inner guidance. This was vital.

July 25, 2008

Bentley keeps us laughing with his playful antics, but it is clear that Stephen is dying. I'm so often at a loss for what to feed him or what to say to him. Trying to treat him normally is difficult, but necessary; he doesn't want me hovering over him.

Just as I had earlier become an expert on metastatic colon cancer and its treatment, in July I became an expert on the sick leave, vacation benefits, and disability retirement that Stephen had accrued at work. He wanted to make absolutely certain he would have sufficient paid leave before he quit working. I was quite sure he had more than enough.

July 29, 2008

Last night we talked about "bucket lists"—the desperate dash to do all the things you wish you had done before you die. "I don't have a list," Stephen said thoughtfully. "When you've done your best to live according to God's will, you're satisfied with your life. You don't need to throw off the shackles of the prison you have made of your life, because you've been free all along."

It pained me to see him struggle off to work, but I could not beg him to stop. It had to be his decision because it was such a final one. He would be going home to die; and that was a terrible admission— not of defeat, but of entering into the final phase of his life and our life together.

August 11, 2008

What a relief! Stephen has finally decided to stop working. Friday will be his last day.

"I hope we can enjoy some of the time we have together now that you won't be working," I offered tonight. Stephen gave me an incredulous look and said, "I hope you don't think this retirement is going to be some kind of Elysian Fields." His comment stung me; he could be razor-sharp in his response to what he considered human nonsense. Of course, I know this is not going to be a picnic; it's the beginning of a very difficult time. But Stephen is not actively dying just yet, and I don't want to treat him as if he is. Life will be a delicate balance as pain and disease progress. I'm just trying to get ready.

"I think we should have a visit from hospice next week so they can explain our options," I said somewhat tentatively. I hated bringing this up, because I don't want Stephen to feel like I'm pushing him out the door. I just want us to be prepared. I think he read my expression of reticence and softened noticeably.

"You're right," he said. "Thanks for thinking ahead."

"You're welcome," I answered gratefully. "And let's spend more time reading next week, like we do on Sundays. That's a way we can have more quality time together, don't you think?"

Stephen nodded. He has always loved our Sundays because we connect so deeply during our readings. It's when we have the most meaningful conversations and when I find out more about what he's thinking. We communicate authentically in these sessions. It's the essence of our relationship—the part I will miss the most.

August 12, 2008

Today is our wedding anniversary and we know it's the last one. Eighteen years—the same length of time I was on staff in the community. Actually, that was eighteen years and two months, and then I passed through death in that car accident. Two months from today is Columbus Day, October 12, and we may meet death again. Perhaps I'm being a little too superstitious here, but I have to assume it's all the time we have remaining.

It's hard to say how long we actually have left—and it will depend on what Stephen wants to do. There is so much we have already resolved. There really are no issues remaining between us that I can see. The only reason for prolonging his passing is to help our families come to terms with his death. It actually may be better for him to make a timely exit and let me tend to the family. Saying that feels like I'm being more selfish than generous. I really don't want to share him, and I don't want him to be intruded upon. So I'll have to let him decide how to handle saying good-bye.

Knowing when to be the gatekeeper and when to keep it open to the person who is dying is one of the more difficult dilemmas for a caregiver. Those decisions about phone calls and visitors are best left up to the patient for as long as he or she can make them. Stephen has always been a very private person and is becoming more so as his health deteriorates. And yet he is so generous with our families. He has never wanted to cause other people pain or sorrow. I'm sure it tears him up to know how devastated they are to lose him.

On Sunday, August 17, we had brunch with Stephen's family to celebrate our combined wedding anniversaries. It was an odd gathering, because nobody said anything about how much thinner he looked. Of course, Rick's middle-school-age children were there, which would naturally stifle any mention of actual symptoms. But it was like the conspiracy of silence the hospice books talk about. It's a form of denial, a way to protect ourselves from the unbearable: *If we don't talk about it, it won't happen*—or so goes the thinking.

For several months now I had been reading books by hospice experts. My favorites were *Dying Well* by Ira Byock, M.D., and *Final Gifts* by Maggie Callanan and Patricia Kelley, both hospice nurses.[5] From these and other resources I was beginning to get an idea of what actually happens at the end of life. It was important for me to understand what Stephen might be experiencing, and I definitely wanted to know what I was going to deal with.

I was also trying to put myself in the shoes of Stephen's family. We lived an hour away from them, so we didn't see them very often—which must have been hard for them. I knew they were having trouble coming to terms with the fact that his illness was terminal. Yet I must admit to being surprised when, over brunch, his dad asked if we were going to travel now that Stephen was no longer working.

"Go to Italy," he urged. I'm sure he was remembering the wonderful trip he and Stephen's mom had taken several years earlier.

"Dad," I explained as gently as I could manage, "Stephen is way beyond able to do any kind of traveling." I was incredulous. Could he not see how diminished Stephen was? I wanted to yell out, "Can't you see he's dying?" But I didn't. It serves no purpose to get angry at people who are doing their best to cope with the greatest sorrow of their lives.

Thankfully, Rick called me after we got home. Watching us walk from the restaurant back to our car, with Stephen somewhat unsteady on his feet, he had known something was up.

"I'm wondering if you and Stephen would like to come up to the condo for Labor Day," he suggested.

"Rick, Stephen can't make any more trips to the mountains," I blurted out.

"That's kind of what I thought," he said, "but I wanted to be sure. And I need to know what to tell John"—their brother—"because he's thinking about coming out from New York with his kids for Columbus Day in October. And our cousins also want to know if they should come out."

"If they wait that long, they'll be too late." I was astonished to hear myself be so blunt. "Stephen is really sick, and I think this is going to go very fast now that he's not working. If John and the cousins want to see him, they need to get here sooner rather than later."

"Okay," said Rick. "Thanks for telling me the truth. I'll let everybody else know."

Wow! This is tough, I thought as I hung up the phone. I didn't want to be an alarmist, but the date of October 12 was so firm in my mind that I simply had to go with my intuition and plan accordingly. I knew it was the right thing to do for Stephen—so he didn't have to plan anything himself. I could not imagine how difficult it must have been for him to soldier on that last month feeling his life force ebb away, watching himself become irrelevant. He had always been so strong; to become so weak was a horrible indignity.

August 18, 2008
  Stephen's older brother, John, just called from New York City and wants to come out right away with Scott and Jaime (his children,

ages eighteen and twenty-seven). I'm glad I've got the house in good shape after the lightning strike. Things are going to start popping around here.

I spent the next few days finalizing details of Stephen's sick leave and vacation time and setting up hospice care. We immediately got the hospice team on board to help us do a better job of managing Stephen's pain and other symptoms. At the first nurse visit, I learned that Stephen had been in much more discomfort than he had let on. I could understand his not wanting to give in to the pain and give up on being able to work, but it grieved me that we hadn't gotten busy on serious pain management sooner. Of course, the medication gave him nightmares and interfered with his meditation; so it was, understandably, a tough choice for him to make.

As Stephen was winding down at work, he had begun an e-mail correspondence with his niece Jaime, John's daughter, a young attorney just starting her career in New York. These few exchanges were precious to Stephen, and they gave Jaime a way to process getting reacquainted with her uncle and then almost immediately losing him. These notes also provide a unique look into Stephen's thinking as he stood on the threshold of his last two months.

Jaime wrote to him saying she was sorry that they had not kept up with each other over the years, and then again asking about his condition. He wrote back:

July 30, 2008
Jaime, please don't regret that our relationship got put on hold. It was largely a matter of circumstance anyway. When I first got diagnosed I started to regret things here and there; it's maddening. Consider it tuition for one of life's lessons. The following is a quote I believe to be true. It kind of applies: *You cannot perceive spiritual truth until you feelingly experience it, and many truths are not really felt except in adversity.*[6]

Besides, it's still not too late. If you want, I would very much like to correspond via e-mail. I will try my best to keep up. I'm really interested in your politics and your involvement with the ACLU.

Thanks for your support. I feel it and your love,

Stephen

August 11, 2008

Jaime, I was delighted to get your e-mail. Overall I'm doing fine. When I first got diagnosed (about four years ago), the battle was primarily in the mind. I had to let go of feeling guilty for not taking proper care of my body. The fact that colon cancer is hereditary did help. (Both Mom and Rick had precancerous symptoms.)

But there was still the sense that I could have prevented this. My acupuncturist's theory is that food allergies can cause tumors over a lifetime. As it turns out, I have a very high allergic reaction to soy as well as to dairy and gluten. So I don't know the specific cause and effect. I stopped going down this line of thought. It is what it is.

The toughest fight, of course, is saying good-bye to Cheryl. The vision of her, sometime down the road—alone—was very painful for me. You almost wish you didn't love anybody: no relationships, no pain. Retrograde obviously, but still—how do you deal with the grief?

Well, I believe that life here on this planet is for the birth and growth of the soul and that I could use this event as a means of growing my soul (the ultimate treasure). That the only way to deal with it is to extend my time horizon beyond death, accept the fact that life contains adversity, and pray that Cheryl will likewise accept the challenge.

I have been very fortunate in my marriage. Cheryl has been a perfect complement: extrovert to my introvert, animated to my passion for an economy of motion, etc. She has been my partner and best friend, and now my hero. Recently she affirmed to me that dealing with my illness has made her a better person—and that she couldn't imagine being deprived of this experience. How liberating is that!

For the last several months the battle has become more physical. I can feel my body fighting harder to do normal tasks. Unfortunately, it's becoming harder for me to meditate. Throughout this whole process (chemo and radiation) my meditation periods had been getting stronger and stronger. Meditation is my daily reminder of who I am. I've been meditating in one form or another for about thirty years. I can't imagine living without this daily communion. Perhaps I could go on a spiritual retreat after I go on medical leave. I'm going to look into that.

Anyway, thanks again for the e-mail. Keep asking questions, if you don't mind.

Love,

Stephen

August 18, 2008

Hey, Uncle Stephen, I admire your strength and spirituality as you go through this hard time.

What you and Cheryl must be going through is so difficult to imagine, but at least you have each other. I bet it is hard thinking that you could have done something to control your illness, but you have to think that practically anything these days can cause you to be sick and get cancer. Most of the causes of cancer are even unknown. You could have done everything in your power to prevent this and it still could have happened.

I heard this morning that you are not doing well at all. I think my father and brother are going to see you this weekend. Unfortunately, I cannot go and will not be able to make it until September 12. I hope I will make it to see you.

I am really sorry about everything and I truly believe that you will be going to a better place where you will not be in any pain. I have been thinking a lot about death lately as I recently had a friend die a tragic death. I began to question people from work, my friends, my family, and asked everyone what they thought happened when you die. I came to the conclusion that we must all go to a better place where we are always happy, never sad, and we are reunited with the loved ones that we lost. What are your beliefs?

So I heard you ended work on Friday. How was that? How was the weekend? I miss you, and you and Aunt Cheryl are in my thoughts and prayers. I love you very much.

Write back when you can,

Jaime

August 26, 2008

Wow, what a difficult question to try to answer. First, I think we should make a distinction between the "Place" and the "You" after death.

As for the "Place": I believe that God has set up an incredible system for our self-realization that extends far beyond our mortal life, even to eternity. It only makes sense that the physical forms of the next world would also advance.

As for the "You": I think we remain exactly the same intellectually and spiritually. We face a real dichotomy in our makeup. We have evolved out of an animal form and yet we have been given a small piece of divinity to indwell our mind. The body makes demands on us physiologically based on all the inherited instincts that have allowed it to survive in the animal world. The spirit world is completely the opposite. The animal world binds us. The spiritual or inner world can, if we choose, liberate us from our animal nature, which is basically selfish.

When we pass through death, we get a new body, which is a little less animal-like. Spiritually and intellectually, however, we are exactly the same. If you look at life as if it is a journey to know God through self-creation, the idea that death could magically, instantaneously, make us perfect seems a little naive. Besides, why would you want to miss out on your self-creation? So I don't think we are happy all the time and just like here, there are some trials we must still pass through; but the tools are sharper and the teachers infinitely more capable.

I understand you have been in touch with Cheryl regarding your upcoming visit. I'm looking forward to it.

Love,

Stephen

John and his son, Scott, arrived on Friday, August 22, for a long weekend, which proved to be an important visit for everyone. John promised to return a couple of weeks later with Jaime. The family was finally able to talk openly about Stephen's condition. He answered questions, laughed and talked, especially enjoying his conversations with Scott about the New York Yankees. They were both huge fans.

At the end of their visit, we drove them to the airport—an official "bon voyage" ritual that was very important to Stephen. When he returned home, Scott wrote his college application essay about his uncle as a person who had greatly inspired him. Fortunately, I was able to read Scott's words to Stephen while he could still appreciate what a difference he had made in the life of this young man.

Essay by Scott Eckl

Death is defined as the permanent termination of all life functions of an organism. It is the end of life. Everything I know in this world will end when I die. Death is everywhere and is unavoidable. Everyone knows they will die, but many push the thought out of their mind and go on with their daily lives.

But for my uncle Stephen, my dad's brother, death is more a part of his life than life itself. In July of this past summer my uncle, who had been diagnosed with cancer four years ago, was given a few months to live. While everyone around him was enjoying the warm, lively summer days, he had to realize that in just a few months everything he knew would end. This came as a shock to my family, who thought that the cancer had somehow been in remission. When my dad and I visited him in August, we comforted him in every way we could, but none of us had ever encountered this situation. As I witnessed my uncle go through his experience, I learned so many things that I could not have learned anywhere else.

My uncle Stephen is a very thoughtful and spiritual man. Every Christmas, while I got DVDs and video games from my other relatives, he gave me books. When I was younger, I moaned and threw them in the back of my bookcase. Now I realize that all he wanted to do was stimulate my mind and open my imagination. I love talking with him because he never really answers questions; he always asks another question that causes me to think in different ways.

My uncle lives in Colorado and I live in New York, so I don't get to see him much. When I went to see him in August, probably for the last time, it didn't seem to me as if he were dying. He was just the same person, except for the effect of the cancer. Death is something that tests everyone's mind and spirit. And the way he has handled it has taught me many things, not just about death but about life as well.

When I was younger I remember reading a novel called *Tuesdays with Morrie* by Mitch Albom and I remember thinking about death and the life lessons that it teaches others. This situation with my uncle is very similar to Morrie's situation in the novel. I don't know what I would do if I were in their situation. I would only hope to be like them. If Morrie is like my uncle, I consider myself like Mitch in the fact that we both learned so many important lessons from listening to people like Morrie and my uncle and their experience with death.

What I have taken out of this experience is that life is a privilege and should not be taken for granted. I have to notice that there is so much beauty in life. I overlook it in my busy lifestyle. I learned that you realize what you have only when you lose it. I think my uncle looks at things differently, almost as a child would. A child looks at the world and is amazed by its beauty and wonder. My uncle looks at it the same way because he is seeing it for the last time. I want to look at the world as he has every day so I can really value the opportunities life brings.

I'm sure my uncle Stephen's final struggle with death has been the biggest challenge in his life. His perseverance and strength have shown me that I can overcome any obstacle in life because no obstacle is as large as death. I hope I can be like him as I encounter other struggles in my life, as he has done with his upcoming death. I will miss my uncle's wisdom, willingness to listen, and ability to stimulate my mind. I value what his experience has taught me and thank him for revealing to me so many things I would never have noticed without him.

Eighteen

RUNNING THE RACE

Bring me my Bow of burning gold:
Bring me my Arrows of desire:
Bring me my Spear: O clouds unfold!
Bring me my Chariot of fire.

—William Blake

August 28, 2008

"Toiler, is thy heart fearful or exultant when before thee lies eternity?"[7] Stephen had agreed to meet our hospice social worker and amazed her by beginning their conversation with this question.

Clearly, he is pondering this matter for himself—can he actually embrace the experience of dying? He wants to experience death from the inside out—not with an outer show or expectations from others. My first inclination would be to make it all a ritual, an opportunity for connection, personal growth, sharing—very interpersonal. For Stephen, this experience is intensely personal, but that's it—he wants it to be clean, private, quiet, spare. No hand-holding, no sympathy, no drama.

"I think too much emotion is detrimental to spiritual progress," he said to me some months ago during one of our Sunday readings. He's making sure I remember that now.

I feel myself getting in his way today. It's time for me to let him be undisturbed. I also want to be undisturbed. I would like to simply vanish with Stephen. He agrees. "I just want to disappear into a cave," he said with a melancholy smile, "but people keep knocking on the door." And then he added matter-of-factly, "This is service."

Getting the hospice team involved was a turning point. I finally had people to answer my questions: What was going to happen? When would it happen? What supplies or training would I need? They assured me I would be able to take care of Stephen and that he wouldn't end up in the hospital, even if he should fall out of bed. They had ways of dealing with most any eventuality. That was a huge comfort.

I was going into a state of mind I can only describe as a martial-arts stance—vigilant and aware while grounded, clear, and relaxed. My days became a kind of waking meditation in which I was both acting and observing myself in action. I was acutely aware of Stephen's needs, while also paying attention to my own, so that unresolved emotions did not cloud my ability to be present for whatever he needed at any moment.

I gave myself permission to acknowledge both positive and negative emotions, to process whatever was arising, and then to move on. It was vitally important not to let frustration or impatience or resentment take hold. I knew it was only human to have all kinds of crazy thoughts about the dying: wishing they would hurry up and die, wishing they would stay forever, wishing you had never met them, wishing they could give you the affection they were no longer capable of extending. I was determined not to feel guilty about these thoughts, but I was also determined not to let them take up residence in my mind.

I did not feel needy, but sometimes I was very sad. One night I got down on the floor in my bedroom and just sobbed my heart out for a couple of minutes. And then I was done. It was like releasing the pressure on a garden hose with a kink in it. The water gushes out and then goes back to a normal flow. The release was highly therapeutic, and it usually lasted for a couple of days.

I craved silence. I wanted to retreat from too much "busy-ness." Journaling became crucial for collecting my thoughts. Stephen was resting a lot, so I did the same. I was like a long-distance runner— pacing myself so I could make it to the finish line, which I believed was not very far ahead.

August 29, 2008

So the challenge now is to not let cancer define us in this final push. During the last four years, we have done a really good job of putting our attention elsewhere. It is clear that Stephen wants to continue doing so. Now that we've got his pain more or less under control, he wants as few nurse visits as possible and no hovering. This may mean I get less information about how he is feeling, but it also means my focus is on life, not death.

We are at peace about where he is going. We know I have a mission that will continue to unfold. So let's just be together every day we have. It's as simple as that. And with that attitude we can extend these weeks to months if necessary and not be anxious to get it over with.

On Labor Day weekend, Rick, and his wife, Jackie, came over for dinner and to watch a football game between the University of Colorado and Colorado State. It was a very good evening. At dinner, Rick and Stephen told funny stories about their childhood in Rochester, vacations at their German-immigrant grandparents' inn at Saranac Lake in the Adirondacks, and going to a Yankees game with their other grandfather, who was a Mets fan.

After the football game, the conversation turned to the purpose of life, death, and the afterlife. Stephen waxed poetic about some of his beliefs, repeating much of what he had written to Jaime in his e-mails. He really wanted his family to understand where he was coming from and where he believed he was going. It was a great connection with Rick and Jackie. We agreed to have another evening like this, but we never did. There were so few opportunities left, and the proverbial sands were pouring through the hourglass faster than anybody realized.

September 6, 2008

I find myself wanting to make more changes in the physical, as if moving furniture is going to help. Actually, somehow, it does help. I keep my mind occupied by imagining I'm purchasing and rearranging furniture—trying to create the perfect physical matrix. I need to keep breaking up old, worn-out patterns, making way for fresh energy, cleaning out cobwebs and inertia. Because many days—like today—I can hardly move. I think it's because Stephen is dying. It feels like I'm feeding him energy, which makes me so tired.

I'm continuing to clean out clutter, mostly in the basement, converting my office to a guest room for the upcoming visits by Stephen's cousins—sons of his mom's sister. I feel so overwhelmed by junk, as if my possessions own me. I have to lighten up the physical to deal with the transformation that is taking place in our minds and hearts. I want all aspects of the environment to support Stephen as he etherealizes.

He has lost about ten pounds in less than a month. He continues to get weaker and more fatigued. We continue reading and discussing inspirational works—creating more "Sundays." Unfortunately, it is becoming more and more difficult for Stephen to focus his mind or even read.

September 11, 2008

"I'm not going to fight the weight loss any longer," Stephen said today. Each decision is an admittance that death is taking over, but I agree with him. The weight loss is inevitable and forcing him to eat seems cruel. There is no point in his taking another drug to increase his appetite if it's just going to cause more side effects. We have a regime that is working right now, that we can handle without additional interference.

The hospice books say that not eating is natural and actually makes dying a lot easier. The body seems to know when to stop taking in food. It is not uncomfortable—in fact, not eating means the body doesn't have to work so hard to process food. Many caregivers are reluctant to stop offering food because it's how we show affection—by feeding the ones we love. It was hard for Stephen's mom when he stopped eating much. She was a wonderful cook who had always nurtured her family with delicious food, but for a long time there had been nothing she could bring us because Stephen could eat so little.

September 13, 2008

What a wonderful two days we just had. Stephen's cousins—Harry, Bob, and Jim—arrived from the East Coast on Thursday evening. Rick and Jackie joined us for a great day on Friday, just hanging around the house, eating, drinking beer, playing board games, talking, telling stories, and howling with laughter—with Bentley always in the middle of the fun. He is such a social doggie.

This morning Stephen's mom and dad and Rick's children joined us for brunch, and then the cousins had to fly home. They are all very busy people with families and hefty job responsibilities. It was a short but very moving visit. It's too bad John couldn't have been here. The six boys have always had so much fun together. Stephen is exhausted, but this was fabulous therapy for him.

September 15, 2008

My goal for the coming week is to spend more quiet time with Stephen and less time running around. He was very appreciative when I told him I was going to sit still and just "be" with him. He has always been so much better at sitting still than I have.

Today I also decided to make a change in Stephen's hospice team. The nurse who had been assigned to us was very competent, but not a good fit in terms of personality. She was very sympathetic, which is probably what a lot of hospice patients and their families need. I could tell that hospice workers are well trained in drawing people out, getting them to talk. But we had different needs, so I asked for a change.

Asking to change nurses might not seem like a big deal, but at the time, it was. This was all uncharted territory for me, and I was determined to follow my intuition—which said to get somebody who was direct and down-to-earth. Fortunately, the hospice supervisors were completely open to my request; they said they made changes all the time. Nobody's feelings were hurt, and we got the perfect nurse, who took up less of Stephen's energy when she visited. She also gave me a crash course in what to do when things got worse. Sometimes this meant not "doing" much of anything.

Stephen and I both came from very task-oriented families. Our parents and ancestors were "make it happen" people who rolled up their sleeves and tackled any challenge that came their way. This can-do spirit was admirable and, in most cases, useful—but not now—because at this point in our lives there was very little for doers to do.

Being present was what I felt most called to do for him. There was actually a lot going on during this period, but it was all happening inside Stephen. What he needed most was for people to simply direct love and peace to him through their thoughts and prayers so he could work out his own inner balance between being "fearful or exultant when faced with eternity."

It is so difficult for the one who is dying, especially somebody as sensitive as Stephen. He was coming to grips with the fact that he really was not going to make it. Even for someone who is not afraid of death, the body's demise is still a wrestling match. The mind may be at peace, but the body puts up a serious fight to stay alive. This is as it should be; but it puts the dying under great stress that they probably cannot articulate to anyone else because they are in the midst of it—living it, working it.

Dying is not romantic, except perhaps in the aftermath. Even when you have faith and support, it is a brutal journey to get to the release. It is tiring and sad and also, in our case, oddly tranquil—at least as long as Stephen wasn't in pain. This was a time for prayer and forgiveness because everybody had to find their own way of learning not to push the river.

I started doing less and less, napping whenever Stephen slept. Despite our need for privacy, I tried very hard to be kind to everybody. It was difficult for me to articulate what was really happening, but I think, in their own way, others understood.

September 16, 2008

Slipping into the great joy. At first I thought of writing "void," but it is joy into which we are slipping. Of course, it is more difficult for Stephen because he is struggling to keep hold of his conscious connection with Spirit. The drugs and the disease are affecting his ability to think clearly or to meditate. But I can read to him—and as I do, I am lifted up to the joy he will dissolve into. What an incredible experience. This is "near death" and it is extraordinary.

As Stephen struggles with his physical body's decline, I get to experience a touch of his destination. At some point we will flip. He will shoot over to the Other Side—into this joy—and my struggles will become more physical. But I will have been touched by eternity.

September 18, 2008

Last night before bed, I took Bentley out to pee. As I was standing in the cool grass, I suddenly had the sense of a spiritual being right next to me. Just a presence, comforting, attending; letting me know it is good that I am listening.

Tonight Stephen and I read about prayer. True prayer asks for wisdom and understanding while the one who prays does everything possible to solve daily problems. True prayer changes the one who prays. Magic does not; it tries to change God and get goodies. This is my prayer: for wisdom and understanding and guidance.

Stephen's most profound and constant prayer was to *want* to do the will of God, which he believed meant becoming entwined in the joyful activity of the Divine—desiring to share the inner life with God. So often "the will of God" is held over your head like Damocles' sword, just waiting to strike if you get out of line. Stephen and I felt otherwise, preferring instead an ancient Aramaic definition we had once heard: "The will of God is the harmonious cooperation of movement that includes discipline." Discipline can also be thought of as *discipleship*. More than two years earlier, he had written a simple poem that clearly captured that sentiment.

The Will of God
May 23, 2006

I so want
To want
The will of God
So that when or where
It will
It will be so

September 20, 2008

Tonight Stephen and I watched the movie *Chariots of Fire* on television. The movie was about achieving inner peace. "I do feel peace," Stephen said as the movie ended. "It is why I pray." It was a very tender moment for him. He was deeply moved—actually to tears.

"Do you want to talk about it?" I asked as gently as I could.

"No," he said, waving me off. "Maybe tomorrow, but not tonight."

I had to leave him alone to collect himself. I went upstairs, closed the bedroom door, and sobbed. I have to give myself up to these primal tears when they come. This is grief that turns me inside out. I literally feel like I'm crying my heart out. I'm crying so hard from the very depth of my gut, I'm surprised my heart doesn't just lurch out of my chest onto the floor in front of me.

September 21, 2008

A rough day. The pain got ahead of Stephen in the morning and the meds didn't catch up until evening. I read to him and then he was ready to discuss *Chariots of Fire*.

"It's about running the race for God," he explained.

The main character, Eric Liddell, was a Scottish missionary who was also an incredibly fast runner. Only his good friend understood when he said, "When I run, I feel God's pleasure." Other runners recognized him as a "gut runner"—one who ran for something bigger than himself or his country. Someone who dug deep to win, and who was willing to put it all on the line to avoid running on Sunday. That was a principle he was not willing to violate, even for the Prince of Wales. Before the race, an American competitor gave him a note that said, "He who honors God, will God honor." Liddell's reward was peace and a sense of divine communion the other winners did not experience.

So with tears in his eyes, Stephen said, "I have always run the race for God and nobody has ever understood me." It was like hearing a cry from his soul that he had lived as a stranger in a strange land for most of his life.

"Our friends do," I suggested.

"Yes, our people from the community do," he agreed, "but my family has never understood me."

Of course they didn't, though they loved him and he loved them; my family didn't understand me, either. We had each chosen a different path than they would have chosen for us. Fortunately, we found each other and the mutual understanding that had been one of the greatest gifts of our marriage.

September 23, 2008

Tonight I read Stephen *The Little Prince by* Antoine de Saint-Exupéry.[8] For some reason I had never read this book that was one of his favorites—especially for those famous lines about how the heart actually sees what is important in life, spoken by a wise fox the Little Prince has tamed with love. Earlier in the story, the Little Prince had been growing a single rose on his tiny planet, and he was concerned about her. The little fox explained that he was still responsible for the rose because he had tamed her.

"Oh, my God," I exclaimed, my eyes welling up with tears. "That's what we did, isn't it? We tamed one another."

"Yes," said Stephen, smiling through his own tears of realization that all remaining barriers between us had simply vanished.

The image I have in my mind of that moment is of a waist-high stone wall—representing all vestiges of fear or mistrust or differences in style—dropping silently into the ground, leaving only our two hearts united in absolute devotion to one another. In that stunning moment of recognition, we saw each other purely and completely.

We are one another's rose. We have pruned and watered and nurtured each other so that now we are free to bloom. This has been the essence of our marriage—to transform the human foibles in one another and let the Divine emerge.

Stephen taught me how to channel my fiery nature. I opened him up emotionally and gave him space to express his own banked fire. I let him be himself, and he showed me who I really am. And now at last we are completely in love—no boundaries, no separation. Just trust and love and tears because when you have been tamed, you are both vulnerable and strong.

The ego defenses are erased; and in their place is openness, forgiveness, happiness, and grief—grief because such sublime vulnerability cannot last in this world. You are given a glimpse of what can be in the next world. You are given tokens and memories with which to recall your encounter with the Divine.

The one who has tamed you—the one who has given you both himself and your self—must go on. But never again are you the mewling ego, sniveling one moment and snarling the next. You have become more real, more stable, more trustworthy—perhaps even more divine—because your beloved has loved you enough to release you from the bondage of fear and to show you how to be brave and true—and finally alone. And Saint-Exupéry says that being tamed can lead to sorrow. But the tears are a sign of the presence of true love. Who would not risk such pain for such enduring joy?

"I'm wearing out, Bunny," Stephen said quietly after our reading, looking me intently in the eye. And today I clearly see it. He is growing weary of fighting the pain, of trying to keep his body going. He is so weak and tired; he barely gets out of bed now.

Nineteen

APPROACHING DEATH

While with an eye made quiet by the power
Of harmony, and the deep power of joy,
We see into the life of things.

—William Wordsworth

SEPTEMBER 30 WAS A RECOVERY DAY after having company over the weekend—moving furniture around in the master bedroom to create more of a hospital setup, including putting the computer on a rolling table so we could watch movies together in bed. Stephen had moved back into the master bedroom when John and Scott came to visit, so that we could use his room as a guest room, and he stayed from then on.

John and Jaime had flown in from New York the previous Thursday and stayed with us for five days. It was a good visit that allowed all of Stephen's family more time with him. He was too weak to make the hour-long car trip to and from Rick's house in Boulder, so on Saturday we had held a combined birthday party for his dad and his niece Lauren at our house.

Jaime was a doll to help with Bentley and the kids so I could play hostess. It seemed like she had always been here, and I told her I would adopt her in a minute—never mind that she had a boyfriend and a job in New York.

Years ago, Stephen had had a vision of Jaime in a dream—before her parents knew they were pregnant with her. In the dream, Jaime had made Stephen promise to give her spiritual guidance; now he was able to make good on that promise. They spent many hours together—just the two of them—with Jaime sitting next to Stephen's bed so he could talk without getting up. He asked her many questions about her work and her life; she asked him about his beliefs and his approaching death. They had been exchanging e-mails, and now they had an opportunity to really get to know each other. This was a private, priceless time between them.

On Monday we drove John and Jaime to the airport—which just about ruined all of us, especially Stephen. He was in so much pain, so overheated, and so nauseated, I wasn't sure he was going to survive the ride home. But he had insisted on seeing them off in person.

"I have to say good-bye at the airport," he had said emphatically. Stephen was still in charge.

Everybody was crying and hugging, not wanting to let go for what would be the last time. "I don't want to leave," sobbed Jaime, weeping bitterly. Tears were streaming down John's face as he put his arm around her and led her off to the concourse. My heart just ached for all of us.

October 2, 2008

Last night we were discussing the movie *Sideways*. I have always loved Miles's speech about the Pinot grape because he was really describing himself: thin-skinned, temperamental, needing constant care and attention—not a survivor. And, of course, his love interest, Maya, was the persistent, patient, tender gardener who would help him express the fullness of his potential—just as he said the Pinot grape required.

"How is that being the Buddha or a Christ figure?" Stephen asked, harking back to one of his favorite topics. He loved Jesus's teachings on the brotherhood of man and believed that following in the footsteps of Christ or the Buddha was how to best serve our fellow human beings. He was always quizzing me on what I thought such a person would do with life's challenges—even those presented in a popular movie.

"I think helping others reach their full potential is what the truly self-actualized person does," I said. "I believe somebody who is Buddha-like has so completely realized the self's divine potential that in his or her presence the other person is also free to be real. The Buddha projects no obstacles, so there is nothing for the other person's false self to stick to."

"Some people treat the Christ as a magician," added Stephen. "He or she is not, although the transformation that can happen in the presence of such a person can seem sudden and magical. Instead, I see the Christ as the master facilitator—one who removes barriers while allowing the other person do the personal growth work that is the individual's responsibility."

"That's certainly what you've done for me," I said. Stephen smiled.

October 4, 2008

We won't be taking Stephen to any more acupuncture appointments. Yesterday's treatment was painful for him and he got really nauseated on the way home. We've increased his time-release pain meds, which helps both of us make it through the night. When he stirs, I wake up; and Bentley whines to make sure I do.

It's a strange time. Stephen is still Stephen—but he is getting weaker and more confused by the day. Part of the confusion is the morphine and part of it is the liver cancer. He's not seeing dead people yet, but he is not quite all here either.

"Are the police involved in our situation?" he asked last night.

"No," I replied. I try not to be judgmental of anything he says.

"Good." He was clearly relieved. "I have this constant dream going on in my head, so I can't tell for sure what's real and what's not."

I can tell it really bothers him to feel himself declining. I am happy to observe that I don't love or respect him any less because he is so frail or befuddled. It's not a matter of feeling love at this point. It's a matter of *being* love. To attend. To just be present. To sit with him. To hold a space of safety that protects his ability to process his experience without interference. To be close and not offended by the deterioration of the flesh.

It gets more difficult as we slip deeper into death's grasp. Somehow I didn't think Stephen would linger like this—I thought that, given the severity of the cancer, he would be gone without this slow wasting away. At this point, he is not ready to go and I'm not ready to let him. Although as I write this, I realize we are getting closer.

October 5, 2008

Stephen is now too weak to bathe without help and nauseated to the point of actually vomiting.

"Do you feel yourself slipping away?" I asked.

"Do you mean: Am I dying?" he said. "I don't know; I don't know what it's like. I've never done this before. I'm very tired. I guess that's not a bad way to go—to just go to sleep."

He barely made it upstairs after we watched a movie in the living room. "In a couple of days I won't even be able to walk to the bathroom," he said wearily while holding on to my shoulders as I led him up to bed.

The nurse comes tomorrow—and none too soon. We'll have her come twice this week. I honestly think this week is all we have. October 12 is next Sunday—18 years and two months since our wedding. So little time.

October 5, 2008, later that night

Okay, God, please talk to me. Help me do this. I am letting go. I have to let go because Stephen is dying. Tonight, while walking Bentley, I did get the sense that I can let go of Stephen. Death becomes inevitable. It's the only logical next step when the body just starts shutting down. It's going to happen, with you or without you. So you may as well go with the flow. Stephen is barely here. I would not be surprised if he just slipped away tonight. I could deal with it if he did. But I really need him to make it a little longer.

As it turned out, Stephen was to last another ten days. I did not yet know what the real "approaching death" looked like. Besides, there were still visits that needed to happen and chances for closure with family members.

October 6, 2008

A jolly visit from Stephen's aunt and uncle from Virginia, who came over with his mom and dad. Thank goodness for Bentley to act as a positive topic of conversation. He certainly does lighten up the room with his antics and general adorableness.

In fact, having Bentley around made these visits much easier for Stephen. I think one reason people have such a hard time visiting someone who is dying is that they don't know what to say. The question on everybody's mind is: "Gee, what's it like to be dying?" But, of course, that's usually not appropriate; and for the person who is dying, making conversation can be really awkward. Stephen had always disliked being the topic of conversation; now the idea was especially repugnant to him. So having Bentley as the center of attention was ideal. It was no secret that Stephen was on his way out, but we didn't have to dwell on it.

We also had a visit today from our new, no-nonsense nurse, who made a lot of changes. It was clear to her that Stephen was about to enter the next phase of his dying process, and she wanted to be sure we were both prepared.

She pegged Stephen for the stoic he is, and pushed him to take more pain relief to help both of us. He reluctantly agreed, allowing her to increase the meds to prevent breakthrough pain. This means he will actually need less medication overall and will stay more consistently pain-free. She also got him to accept an anti-nausea drug and ordered a hospital bed, side table, and bedside commode. All of these items should help make him more comfortable.

We'll move the queen bed over so I can sleep on a bed instead of the floor. (I have been sleeping on a mat adjacent to our bed because we disturb each other if either of us moves abruptly.) Being next to Stephen, but in a different bed, will also make it easier for me to keep an eye on him without waking him up.

"How long do we really have?" I asked as I walked our nurse to her car.

"Possibly two weeks—but that's just an estimate," she said. The nurses were careful not to make predictions. "Once Stephen stops eating, it should be about a week. But nothing is for sure."

I just wanted somebody to tell me what was going to happen, which, of course, they couldn't do. And here is another reason why it is difficult to set a timeline on the dying process. As it turned out, Stephen continued to take in some nourishment until about thirty-six hours before he passed away. So watching for specific signs of impending death is a tricky business. These physical signs vary considerably from person to person.

Tonight Stephen got more protein down and ate some applesauce as a way to help him take his pills. As I was feeding him, Stephen suggested, "Why don't you create a spreadsheet to keep track of all my meds?"

"I don't need a spreadsheet," I resisted. "I know what to do."

"Of course," he said. "I was just thinking about what I would need to do on my own."

"But you've got me," I reminded him. "Is it hard to let me do everything for you?"

"Yes—and you'll find it difficult, too, when it's your turn to go— Little Miss Have-to-Be-in-Control-of-Everything." A very astute observation, made with that teasing smile. At least now I'll be more able to trust hospice, or perhaps have my own nurse. It's something I'll remember to set up in advance. Don't wait too long to get help.

The caregiver's work is tough, but watching Stephen slip away was strangely easier than I expected. Wanting your spouse to be released from pain and suffering is a sure way to let him go more readily. And so much of Stephen was already gone. He was no longer mine. He was gathering unto himself and unto Spirit.

October 7, 2008

Stephen slept through the night until 6:30 a.m. and during the day didn't need any of the liquid morphine he calls "flash." He also ate more and felt better. We were able to read and talk more about the Other Side, and we got into that sublime state of communion where we are truly ourselves. The loss of that communion will be my greatest sorrow, because I believe it takes two people to create it—and I don't know anybody who thinks quite like we do.

October 8, 2008

The challenges are mounting. Finding food that works for Stephen gets more and more difficult. The applesauce that worked yesterday made him sick today. There are still some family visits to work in. I find myself being irritated with people's sympathy; today I rejected the suggestion from an elderly neighbor (whom Stephen barely knows) that she come over for a visit.

My mom stopped by with some beautiful roses and to say good-bye. She loves Stephen as her own son. Seeing him so ill just breaks her heart, although she said that realizing how sick he is makes it easier to let him go. It is hard for me to see her so sad, and I know she feels the same about me.

Stephen and I had a lovely reading this afternoon, finishing a section in *The Urantia Book* that corresponds to what our teacher called the universities of the Spirit—arenas of action in which the soul continues to gain spiritual mastery, even after death. Many esoteric teachings speak of progressive levels of consciousness through which the soul rises on its journey to Paradise. This book called them the mansion worlds, after Jesus' statement, "In my Father's house are many mansions."[9]

The thought of engaging in an eternity of learning never failed to thrill Stephen. "I feel really content with where I'm going," he said with amazing serenity. "There should be nothing to fear from here on out." And then he wondered aloud, "Do you think we slowed down or sped up in our spiritual development after leaving Montana?"

"Oh, it has definitely been a speeding up for me," I answered without hesitation. "Our lives have become such a deepening of understanding and faith and an amazing experience in learning to live mindfully."

"I think we eventually would have gotten to this same place if we had had another thirty years together, don't you?" smiled Stephen. "You know, like those couples who have been married for decades who are so much alike. Instead, I think the cancer has been a gift of acceleration so we could make up for the time we wouldn't have."

So Stephen will be on his way to a beautiful existence. When we read about the experiences he can expect upon reaching the mansion worlds, I felt jealous of the people who will get to be with him. Will I be able to catch up once I get to the Other Side?

I cried when I read aloud that he will not forget me and that I will be a large part of him as he goes on. We have surely grown into one another, and I'm sure that in coming weeks and months I'll find many ways in which I have internalized him. I certainly hope so—especially the way he always brings me back to center.

Will I ever remember to ask so many questions? Will I have the patience to enjoy the process as well as the results? Will I have his eye for beauty and his ear for what is good? Will I have the courage to push through to the truth in my life? In so many situations, I would have settled for a mediocre outcome, except for Stephen's guidance. Now I have to do it myself. I must listen more intently for his guidance within me.

Later that evening, Stephen felt strong enough to bathe with me helping. He was still able to hold on to the shower rod and stand for me to towel him off. As I knelt to dry his feet and legs, I was reminded of a ritual we used to perform in our community to commemorate Jesus's washing the feet of his disciples. Suddenly the image of his body became numinous. I wasn't just ministering to my husband—for an instant I felt that if I looked up, I would see the face of Jesus. These were legs of the Master himself. This was the body of Christ, and I felt that my service would be a holy one if I could maintain that awareness.

October 9, 2008

I think Stephen may be slipping into a coma. He was up every three hours last night. The pain meds cause such persistent constipation—just something else to deal with in the comfort department. This morning he was able to swallow his time-release pills, but didn't take any food. He's been asleep since 8:00 a.m., and now it's nearly 1:00 p.m.

Our friends Ann and Henry were supposed to come over, but I called and explained that Stephen couldn't do it. They understood, but Ann said she was sorry she hadn't listened to her own prompting a few weeks earlier to buy Stephen a "bon voyage" card, wishing him well on his journey—not into the sunset, but into the sunrise. He would have loved that!

The nurse is supposed to come this afternoon, so I'm not sounding any alarms. My intention at this point is to disturb Stephen as little as possible, to maintain an atmosphere of absolute peace. I'm not going to alert his family until the last minute because it's likely to cause quite a bit of anxiety. Better to let them enjoy their visit with Stephen's aunt and uncle, who are flying back to Virginia today, and let him be at peace.

We had our wonderful connection yesterday. It was a sense of absolute oneness, and he was so pleased that we are on the same wavelength. We have said what we need to say. We know we are inextricably part of one another. So the bond is sealed. The death process has most likely begun, and I expect it to be complete on October 14—next Tuesday.

The hospice nurse visited in the evening and confirmed that Stephen was definitely starting his transition. He admitted to her that he was seeing people we can't see—at the moment, people he didn't know. He had many other symptoms of body functions shutting down and was taking only a minimum of liquids.

We got Stephen set up with a catheter. We have to turn him to avoid bedsores (which are starting). I got full instructions on how to administer pain meds if he can no longer swallow. Also, what to do to avoid pneumonia as his blood pressure decreases, how to adjust the meds, how to help him in case he gets agitated, and to expect him to go through a phase where nothing I do is right. I guess we've already experienced a bit of that with various foods he couldn't eat. Anyway, this is a lot more "nursing" than I was anticipating.

After our wonderful nurse left, I felt overwhelmed and abandoned. She's leaving on vacation on Saturday and won't be back until the following Monday. Our next-door neighbor is also leaving tomorrow night for the weekend. Today I broke down and begged her not to go—not really appropriate—then called her on her cell phone to apologize as she was walking Bentley for me. I had to pull myself together, realizing I could call any one of several other friends if I needed them in the next couple of days.

It is so hard to know what to do about family because Stephen doesn't want to see anybody. The hospice team emphasized that it was my responsibility to take care of him first, me next, and then the family; but I don't want anybody to feel left out.

Just let go, I keep reminding myself. *Stop worrying. Just be with what Stephen needs and go from there.* I'm lying in our bed, pushed up right next to his, with Bentley as the sleeping guard at the foot of them both. I pray God will give me strength.

October 10, 2008

Oh my God! What a night we had last night—diarrhea, diapers, and disinfectant. Now I understand why you don't find "details of dying" on the Internet. This is not the picture of my beloved I wanted to record—except to document that I could get through the poop, that Stephen could rally to get into the shower, and that we could manage to get him cleaned up for another day.

Today he has rested well and was even quite alert around lunchtime so I could get his thoughts on how to help his family through the ending. Even in his weakened state, he was able to give me excellent guidance to be proactive, which was the perfect approach when I called his mom and Rick. We agreed that they will come over this weekend to say good-bye, and after that will help out only if I need assistance giving meds every few hours. I think this is actually a relief to them. Seeing Stephen like this is probably just too hard for them to bear.

Stephen realizes he's dying and, now that we have settled on how to help his family say their good-byes, he seems to be relaxing into it. We read a little this afternoon and he listened to Alex Jennings reading *The Psalms*.[10] So beautiful. "The Lord Is My Shepherd."

"Sometimes I feel like there's somebody else in the room," he admitted today. I expect it's his guardian seraphim, who, he believes, will guide him on his transition to other dimensions. We are not alone on this journey.

Part Four

THE OPEN
DOOR

Thus alone can we attain
To those turrets, where the eye
Sees the world as one vast plain,
And one boundless reach of sky.

—Henry Wadsworth Longfellow

Twenty

IN HIS OWN WAY

*The history of a relationship
and family is transformed when
the story of two persons ends well.*

—Ira Byock, M.D.

CANCER PLAYS CRUEL HAVOC with everyone it touches. Stephen was enduring pain on all levels: physical, emotional, spiritual, psychological. He was losing everything—physical strength, mental acuity, personal dignity—and I'm sure his faith was being tested. He worried about me and his family and grieved over the loss of the future he would not live to see. I was losing my husband long before he actually died. The strong man I knew was wasting away. Now I must be the strong one. And both of our families were in shock, not knowing what to do or how to be of assistance, not wanting to believe that nothing could be done.

I considered myself fortunate to be Stephen's sole caregiver because I was able to be with him every step of the way, but it was horrible to watch him suffer. For over four years it had been frustrating when I could not ease his pain, especially during the early radiation and chemo treatments that had been so torturous. But at least I was able to feed him, comfort him, read to him, and, in the end, be with him as he made his transition to another world.

Stephen did not want any other caregivers. "I don't want a lot of nurse visits," he had said emphatically when the hospice team came on board. "I don't need a social worker and I don't need a chaplain. Just control my pain and I'm fine." He wanted to be left alone to meditate, listen to music and poetry recordings, and prepare himself for his transition. So as his condition worsened, his family was only partly aware of how quickly the end would come.

Throughout his illness, Stephen had been determined to minimize emotional reactions from anybody and everybody. I'm sure his co-workers had known for a long time that he was very ill because of his weight loss and the jaundice that had been creeping over his complexion. They hadn't said anything to him, but he had noticed a change in their attitude toward him.

"They look at me like I'm already dead," he remarked ruefully one evening several weeks before he stopped working. He had been ethically bound to confide his condition to his boss but had sworn her to secrecy. Nevertheless, for months before he decided to quit working, she had been transferring some of his responsibilities to other people. It bothered him that he was already being replaced—long before he was actually gone.

"Are you going to say anything on your last day at work?" I asked.

"No way," he declared. "Can you imagine having to say good-bye to thirty crying people?"

I couldn't have done that either. In fact, I probably would have done as he did—bringing home a few personal items at a time, even leaving behind the little mini-refrigerator he kept under his desk so he wouldn't call attention to the fact that he was clearing out his office. On August 15, his last day at work, he stayed late after everyone else had gone home and slipped away without anybody telling him good-bye.

Stephen was a stoic—bearing, with scarcely a comment, pain that would have flattened most of us. He was also a contemplative, which meant he was highly sensitive to levels of emotion that would not seem extreme to others. I tried to be attuned to his feelings; but I often had to dial back, especially if I was trying to find out how he was really feeling, which he didn't like to talk about—even to me.

So, Stephen's death was particularly hard on those who had to watch and wonder from afar. Everybody did their best not to seem desperate or give way to feelings of remorse or regret; but as the situation worsened, desperation crept in.

October 10, 2008

A bizarre turn of events. John called from New York to ask how Stephen was doing and ask if he should come back out to see him again. This surprised me because John had already flown out twice in the preceding months, once with his son, Scott, and again with his daughter, Jaime. Both visits were profoundly moving to everyone, but the good-byes at the airport were really difficult, especially the last one. And I knew that, in Stephen's mind, he had said farewell to his brother and did not plan to see him again. Saying good-bye a third time would be too much.

"There's really no need for you to come now," I said. "Stephen is stable and could last for quite a while." John seemed okay with that explanation, even though I didn't quite believe it myself. What I didn't want to say was that Stephen actually didn't want him to come back. "I don't want him here until after I'm dead," he had said firmly when I whispered to him that John was on the phone.

Rick called a bit later and I told him about the conversation with John. He was also rather surprised. Around 10:00 p.m. the phone rang and it was John again, announcing that he was coming out—and that he was going to stay with us, as he had on the previous two visits.

"John, you can't come out and you can't stay with us," I said—probably more forcefully than was necessary. But I was getting really worried that we might end up with an emotional scene at our house when Stephen needed it to be most peaceful.

"Why?" he asked, obviously surprised.

"Because Stephen doesn't want you to come," I explained.

"But why?" John was getting upset and I didn't know what to do. I took the phone into Stephen's bedroom and quickly explained to him what was going on. Even with one foot practically in the grave, he was still the master problem-solver.

"Give me the phone," he said in the hoarse whisper that was now the best he could do for speech. "Bro, don't come," he croaked to John. "You'll shorten my life. It's making me sick just trying to talk to you." He fell back on his pillows and handed me the phone. I was in tears.

"John, please do as your brother asks," I pleaded. "Don't come. Promise me you won't."

"Okay," he acquiesced. "I'll cancel my flight."

October 11, 2008

I'm beside myself. Rick just called to say that John is coming after all. *What am I going to do?* I thought as I hung up. Then the phone rang again and it was John. This time we came to an understanding that he needed to be with his family now. I realized that he had unfinished emotional business with Stephen and that at least being in Colorado would help him.

"But you can't come to the house," I said firmly, "because Stephen can't handle seeing you again after he's said good-bye. It would just be too much."

"Okay," John said. "I get it. You're in charge, Sis."

I was so glad he called me "Sis." That meant we were not fighting, which I absolutely did not want. Families have fallen out at just such times over much less, and I didn't want that to happen. I felt like such a "meanie"—but I knew my first responsibility was to uphold Stephen's wishes. And just to make sure there were no problems, I made it clear to the rest of the family that he would not see John again—not for lack of love, but because of too much feeling.

I may have overreacted; but, at the time, Stephen was really unnerved at the thought of having to deal with anybody who was overly emotional about his passing. Thankfully, everybody kept their composure, and we scheduled time for Rick and Jackie and then Stephen's mom and dad to come over to the house to say their own good-byes. John would be with his family, which he and they needed; and Stephen would have the peace and quiet he needed for his final days.

October 12, 2008

Today, Stephen spent most of the day with his eyes closed, but he was conscious enough to have a wonderful visit with his mom and dad. It was difficult for him to stay awake, but he did participate—amazingly so—and he really connected with them. His deep love for them was tangible to me and I think they felt it too.

Stephen's parents were very brave. They laughed with him and told him how much they loved him. And his dad said the most important thing he could have said: "I'm proud of all my sons."

Now that they have gone home, there is nothing for us to do except to witness Stephen's transition. He has been looking quite blissful and does not seem to be in any pain. He's becoming like a sweet child—so loving. Today, as I was putting a pillow under his knees, he said to his parents, "Isn't she beautiful?" That means more to me than almost anything because he has never been much for compliments. He said it with such love and purity—it just locked into my heart.

After his parents left, I said to Stephen, "You've said good-bye to everybody else. Please don't leave without saying good-bye to me." He opened those big blue-green eyes and said, "Is this a joke?"

Classic Stephen! He would always bring me back to earth whenever I got too sentimental. And, of course, he was going to say good-bye—in his own way.

Twenty-one

WHAT DO THE SIGNS SAY?

Sunshine cannot bleach the snow,
Nor time unmake what poets know.

—Ralph Waldo Emerson

As I HUGGED STEPHEN'S PARENTS and closed the front door behind them, I felt a profound sense of completion drop around me. All of the physical good-byes that could be said had been said. We were entering the last days of Stephen's dying process and now it was just him and me—making our way around the last bend on the path we had walked together for nearly two decades.

I went back upstairs to sit with him, feeling a calm, solid readiness for this final stage. I also felt gratitude for the hospice nurses who were making it possible for his leave-taking to unfold as we had both wanted it: at home, in peace and love, with minimal interference but maximum support.

If there is such a thing as angels in embodiment, I believe they work with hospice. Most people I know who have met these selfless servants have been deeply touched by their kindness, compassion, and gentle focus on the patient, not the disease.

"We don't treat the numbers, we treat the pain," Stephen's hospice nurse had said to us when encouraging him to accept enough medication to prevent breakthrough pain. "Our job is to keep you comfortable, not to rigidly adhere to a certain protocol."

Of course, hospice care is administered under very careful guidelines. But the emphasis is on the patient and his or her loved ones, not on the actual cause of death, whatever that may be. I knew this from reading several wonderful books written by hospice professionals, but the experience of being attended with such compassionate expertise was an enormous blessing to both Stephen and me in this delicate period during which the dying person gradually tips over from this world to the next.

In this phase, patients clearly have a foot in both worlds. They are in and out of a dream state, and their language is often metaphorical. They may talk about departed loved ones, angels, spiritual masters, unseen visitors, or the idea of going home—which they seem to find especially comforting and attractive.

The problem here is that the patient's deeply personal "in and out" expressions can be very confusing to loved ones. This is especially true if loved ones are not emotionally prepared to let the dying person go on—or if they simply do not understand that what is not logical to those still living in the physical is profoundly real to those who are leaving it.

The authors of *Final Gifts,* two hospice nurses, encourage caregivers and loved ones not to make the common (yet perfectly understandable) mistake of contradicting the person who is dying when he or she says something that doesn't make sense.[11] Even if it's well-intentioned, insisting that their visions of heavenly visitors are not real can cause painful stress and confusion for those who are passing over. Holding a loving space of acceptance for whatever arises in the awareness of the dying is the greatest expression of compassion in these moments.

I was grateful to have had this understanding well in mind before Stephen entered this phase of his transition because it prepared me for the wonderful dream conversations we had over several hours late on Sunday night.

October 12, 2008

Stephen was very restless tonight. Even with anti-anxiety medication, he was up and down, sitting on the side of the bed and talking to me intently. At one point, he said, "Did we win?"

I thought perhaps he meant the Denver Broncos, who had played earlier in the day. "No, the Broncos lost."

"No, did *we* win?" he insisted.

"Do you mean did you and I win? Yes, we won big. In fact, I think we completed all our assignments."

"How can you tell?"

"I don't know; it just feels complete." Ever since Stephen's parents had left that afternoon, I really did feel that all the doors had closed.

"Okay," he said, and settled back into bed.

Later on, Stephen had more questions—and I'm so glad I was ready to play along. "Are we going back to the USA now?" he asked.

"Yes, we're going home," I offered.

"Are we flying?" he asked, a bit eagerly.

"Yes." It was easy to imagine being airborne.

"Are we free?"

"Yes, we're free."

"Did we do anything wrong?" He seemed concerned that we were somehow in trouble. A couple of days earlier, he had asked if the police were involved. At that point, he was conscious of being in two worlds and just needed clarification. Tonight, he was fully in the dream world.

"No, we did everything right," I assured him. "That's why we're free."

"Do we have an escort?"

"Yes, they're called Blue Angels. They're F-16 fighter planes." I was out on a limb here, but that's the first thing that popped into my head; so I went with it.

"That's a hell of an escort."

"Honey, it was a hell of a battle." I was not exaggerating!

That explanation seemed to satisfy Stephen, and he went back to sleep for a couple of hours. Around 4:00 a.m. he sat up again. I was sleeping with our bed pushed over right next to his hospital bed so we could snuggle if he wanted to be touched, and so I could easily check to see if he was breathing. But when he decided to swing his legs out of bed, I had to leap out on the other side and run around to where he was sitting so he didn't fall on the floor. This time his questioning was more insistent:

"What do the signs say?"

I really was at a loss here, so I said, "I can't see them, but I think they say: 'Home' or perhaps 'This way to Paradise.'"

Then he said, "Dance with me." He was trying to hold me and stand up. Now, this was comical, because the only other time we had danced in eighteen years of marriage was at our wedding. Stephen was many things, but he was not a dancer.

"Let me just hold you and we'll dance right here," I said, swaying back and forth with him sitting on the bed.

"No, turn around. Tell me what the signs say." He took my shoulders and with amazing force turned me around so I was facing in the same direction as he was. But, of course, I still couldn't see any signs.

"Honey, I can't tell, but I'm almost sure they say something about 'Home.'" I felt bad that he was so frustrated. For some time, he had not been able to read with his physical eyes. Now his dream eyes were failing him as well, and he needed help that I could not give. I had been reading to him from his favorite books, which he loved; but now, when there was an important message for him from the Other Side, I didn't have access to it. I tried to reassure him, but I felt sad that I was failing him at this critical time.

Somewhat reluctantly, he agreed to go back to sleep, so I tucked him in and went back to my side of the bed. As soon as my head hit the pillow and I closed my eyes—I saw the signs! Dozens of them, held up like placards by all kinds of smiling people: young, old, large, small, and—judging by the motley appearance of their clothes—from different periods in history. In big, bold, black letters the signs said:

WELCOME
STEPHEN ECKL!

"Honey! I see the signs! They say 'Welcome, Stephen Eckl!' They know you and they have the welcome committee out for you!"

"You mean like Ellis Island?"

"Yes, but this is better than Ellis Island. It's much more beautiful, and here they know your name. And they're all ready to welcome you."

That seemed to be the answer he was looking for. He immediately settled down and slept soundly until morning, and he rested peacefully throughout the day on Monday. How interesting, I thought as I nestled back into bed that night, that Stephen would follow the metaphor of going to the USA, the land of freedom, with a stop at Ellis Island, the reception station for people coming to the New World—exactly where he was going!

Twenty-two

THROUGH THE DOORWAY

We die well because we have lived well,
and we live well because we know that we will die.

—Virginia Morris

STEPHEN'S FINAL HOURS were a bit like our wedding day. We had done our best to put everything in order, to be conscious and loving. But somehow when the long-anticipated day arrived, it was hard to believe the event was actually happening.

Maybe it's from watching too many movies. When the dramatic moment begins, we expect background music with soaring violins and piano glissandos, or perhaps a voiceover narrating our thoughts and feelings. Instead it was just us—Stephen and me—quietly going about the business of him passing over to the other side of life, leaving me behind, as we knew he eventually would have to do.

October 13, 2008

Yesterday, when Stephen's mom commented on how fortunate he was to have me, he replied, "It is a blessing that Cheryl had no agenda." I hope that has been true. I must be mindful to continue that way. His transition may take as long or as short a time as he needs. It is my job to protect his passing, not to influence it.

And I did get my good-bye. Last night Stephen rolled over toward me, lowered his head and said, "I bow before my wife." I barely heard it and could be mistaken that that is what he said—but somehow I think it is. He also said, "Be strong." And just a little while ago he kissed me and said, "You're the sweetest thing on the earth. I don't know how I ever could have . . .and I really mean it." I couldn't hear every word because he's been whispering everything. Yet I felt his gratitude—and it means the world to know that I really did help him in his hour of greatest need.

It's 10:00 p.m. and he's been very restless again, with some pain. Earlier this evening he decided to sleep with his head at the foot of the bed. He said there were "friendly guys" coming up the path, one standing by the table, and a little girl whom he didn't know. "Where did we get her?" he asked. I finally got him turned right side up in bed, and he looks like he can rest now.

October 14, 2008

What a terrible night last night! The worst we've had for pain and restlessness. It took a lot of liquid morphine to get on top of the pain—something I didn't realize would happen once Stephen was no longer able to swallow the time-release pills. I knew I had permission to give him as much liquid as he needed; but I wasn't sure how much to give him at once, or how frequently. I called the hospice hotline and got through to the nurse, who gave me a dosage guideline to follow.

I finally got Stephen settled down around 3:30 a.m., and after that he was no longer consciously responsive. He did not wake up, even when the nurse's aide came later this morning to bathe and shave him and change all of his bedding. He looked so clean and fresh and peaceful after she left. In fact, I thought his skin looked almost luminescent. After the discomfort of last night, I was surprised to see a slight smile about his mouth and a little crinkle of happiness around his eyes.

The "floater" nurse I really liked was on duty today. What a blessing! She recommended a subcutaneous pump to deliver a constant dose of morphine and better anti-anxiety medicine that would help Stephen (and me) sleep through the night. These measures will keep him comfortable for as long as it takes his body to give up.

The problem is that Stephen is young with a strong heart and kidneys, which means his body still has some fight in it. The nurse said that getting him settled down with pain control and no anxiety will help his body relax, stop fighting, and actually give up sooner.

He could still last until the weekend. I pray not, although I *can* endure if necessary—especially if we don't have any more midnight crises. I wish we had hooked up the pump earlier, but I suspect it would have knocked him out and we might not have had the beautiful conversations that came amidst the restlessness of Sunday night.

One awful thing is that Stephen's skin is starting to break down all along his back. The nurse says it's because he's not eating anything. That's another reason to help him go quickly. I got a kiss last night and he was so tender before he started having such awful pain. At least he's going to be more comfortable now and he won't be trying to get up. Knowing I'll be able to sleep tonight, I've cleaned house, done laundry, and even washed my hair. If Stephen should happen to go tonight, I want things in good order.

All kinds of thoughts have been racing through my head today—such as wishing Stephen would pass on so I can get on with my life; I have social events I could attend starting on Saturday. How incredibly petty to prefer my social life to having a couple more days with Stephen! Yet in many ways he's already gone. I can still touch him, but I can't reach him—and that's really hard.

This was just one of those thoughts I noticed and let go. It's natural for the human mind to want the suffering to be over for its own selfish reasons. And I felt caught on the threshold between the end of my life with Stephen and the beginning of my life without him. Despite my efforts to focus on the spiritual, I was still a human being in the midst of a heart-wrenching situation that was often surreal.

The nurse returned later in the afternoon to install the subcutaneous pump and was amazed at how different Stephen looked after only a few hours. She checked his back and discovered he was mottling—a sign that the blood was being withdrawn from the extremities. The color in his face seemed to be worsening—the jaundice a particular feature of his horribly burdened liver. His breathing was shallower than earlier in the day. He was more peaceful, and the nurse said he might actually go during the night.

I believed the general admonition that patients who are in a coma can still hear, so throughout the day I played CDs of classical music and spiritual teachings in Stephen's room. After the nurse left, I put on Alex Jennings's readings of *The Psalms*. This man's voice sounds like the late Richard Burton's, and the recording was one of Stephen's favorites that he listened to over and over when he had trouble meditating.

After I had some dinner, I started reading aloud to him—this time focusing on passages about the seraphim that shepherd souls from one world to the next, literally gathering them under their pinions of light for the journey out of time and space. I had felt their presence from time to time in recent days, and reading about them now was like narrating what I was sure they were doing for my beloved husband.

In the "Bardo" teachings of Tibetan Buddhism,[12] reading to the departed (and departing) is believed to assist the soul in traversing the nether world and aiming for the rainbow light that signifies higher levels of consciousness. I believe that any prayer said for the dying is useful—particularly if they are afraid to die or do not have a strong belief in where they are going. And most especially if they ask for prayer support to help them on their journey to the arms of the Divine.

In Stephen's case, I had no concern that he might get sidetracked on his way to heaven. His belief in his destiny and his years of preparation had set him on an unwavering course to higher realms. I actually felt, as my friend Kathleen said she had felt at her mother's passing, that my poor prayers were hardly needed to intercede for a soul with rocket launchers in his back pocket.

Still, I knew Stephen delighted in words of Scripture, and he loved to hear the story of the seraphim and their unfailing love for the souls they tend for eternity. As he lay there, breathing hard but otherwise at peace, I read for a couple of hours—often with tears in my eyes as I witnessed the final hours of one who loved God with all his heart and who waited with patience for the angels to take him.

When I tired of reading, I put on Handel's *Messiah* and once again took up my journal.

October 14, 2008—8:00 p.m.

I feel like a child on Christmas Eve—too excited to go to sleep, lest I miss Santa's arrival. Of course, Santa never comes if you're looking. You must be asleep, or at least in a state of peaceful being.

This journal has been an incredible tool of self-reflection and also an assurance that I will not forget the events of these many weeks. As I told Stephen's mom today, doing this much journaling has enabled me to track every thought and feeling that has arisen, examine it, root out the useless, keep that of enduring value, and move on.

If we're too full of our own stuff, we simply cannot respond when called upon—especially if the response requires utter devotion and selflessness, which, to my mind, is the definition of caregiving. It takes absolutely all the strength you can summon. But if you can free yourself of distractions and embrace unwavering service to another human being as the highest purpose of life, the pain translates to bliss; and heaven truly showers you with blessings and love. I really do believe that.

My heart aches. My mind reels in disbelief that my precious Stephen is about to leave me forever. Each labored breath takes him closer to his Creator and one more step away from me. I am already alone. Except that this house feels so different—somehow filled with love and possibility.

My heart is in ecstasy for both of us. I pray I can retain what Stephen has taught me. He always brought me back to center. He kept me sane and always gave me a new perspective. He was patient and kind and steady at the helm—always solid, eagle-eyed, and brave beyond words. He has lived humbly according to his principles, without fanfare, and with an unwavering devotion to all that is good, true, and beautiful.

How many of God's children lie dying this night? How many of them are alone, in fear, terrified that they are sinners about to face a negative, vengeful deity? And how many are simply working out their final hours on earth, resting in sure faith in the Creator's perfect mercy and the magnificent plan that awaits the soul who has truly loved the Divine? I believe this is what Stephen is doing. His breathing appears to take tremendous effort, but he is not restless. His face almost bears a smile—and he is beautiful to me.

I was never once repulsed by his body, even as the pounds dropped off and he became pitifully thin. He never stopped being my knight in shining armor, even when he became too weak to stand. Even in his final days, he was instructing me, admonishing me to be strong, and reminding me to be wise, patient, and (please!) not impulsive.

So my path is devotion to the Divine Presence, a listening ear, a willing heart, and a determination to live the remainder of my life in loving service that knows when to do and when to just be. This is the legacy Stephen has left me—a home filled with his handiwork, a spiritual path, a belief in my ability to become more of my authentic self, and the memory of a love so powerful that (I believe) it will transcend death.

It's 9:00 p.m. The moon is full tonight. I'll finish listening to *Messiah* and then try to sleep. I wonder if I will feel this blissful once Stephen is actually gone?

Around 10:00 p.m., I decided that Stephen might indeed last through the night. I was tired, and, confident that the morphine pump was managing his pain, I went to bed next to my sweetheart. Around 12:30 a.m., I awoke suddenly, hearing someone call: "Cheryl!" I looked over to see that Stephen was still breathing. I got up and checked him out, seeing no sign that his breathing was any shallower than earlier or that his color was any worse.

I moistened his mouth with a swab, gave him a bolus from the morphine pump, and lay back down, watching him for any sign of change. I imagine Stephen knew I was watching him and waited for me to doze off before silently slipping away—just as I had suspected he might. It must have been the silence that woke me this time, because when I looked at the clock—1:11 a.m.—and then looked at Stephen, he was gone.

There was no audible fanfare. No roll of drums or sounding of trumpets—at least none to be heard with human ears. Stephen was simply no longer there. His body was still. I put my head to his chest, where I had rested it so many times for comfort, now hearing only silence.

I had envisioned walking to death's door with Stephen, kissing him good-bye, and sending him on his way. Instead, he just left.

"You're gone, aren't you, baby?" I said, and stroked his forehead. I tried to shut his mouth, but couldn't. I sat with him for just a few minutes, trying to absorb the actual moment for which we had so long prepared—somehow trying to grasp the fact that we had come to the fork in the road. Our solo journeys had begun.

I called hospice to report the death and then called Stephen's family to let them know he was gone. It came as a shock to them, because the last I had said was that he might linger another day. I had decided not to say more for a couple of reasons: first, I wasn't sure what was happening; and, second, I didn't want them to feel obligated to stand watch during the night. I knew Stephen wanted a quiet exit and felt he would do better without any of us watching as he breathed his last.

These decisions are difficult and personal. Not everyone is as solitary as Stephen. Many do want their final breath attended by loved ones, with prayers and songs and the comfort of physical touch—although hospice books are replete with stories of the dying slipping away only when loved ones have briefly stepped out of the room. In Stephen's case, he had wanted me with him but even pushed me away from time to time if I became disruptive in my caregiving, which happened if I watched him too closely or hovered like a nervous mother hen. He didn't like being clucked over.

My nature is to want everybody to be happy, so it was hard for me to ask the family to restrict their visits or, in the case of this last morning, to wait until the hospice nurse had finished his routine examination and legal procedures that document the death and dispense with unused morphine. Fortunately, the timing worked out perfectly, and Stephen's family drove out to see him once more.

Stephen's younger brother, Rick, decided not to come; his mom and dad and older brother, John, did. Electing to view the deceased is also a very personal decision—and one that I was glad to honor, either way. Rick wanted to remember Stephen's last words to him after the Colorado–Colorado State football game (Go Buffs!), and John wanted to say one more good-bye. This was a very important moment of closure for him; I'm so glad he got to experience it.

For Stephen's parents to have one last farewell with their son was very important to help them accept that he was really gone. The enormity of the loss stuns the mind. You just can't wrap your brain around the completeness of the absence. So when you have trouble conceiving that he is not coming back, sometimes you need to be able to say to yourself, *Yes, he is gone. I saw him with my own eyes—and he is dead.*

So the family stayed with Stephen for half an hour. Then we went downstairs and sat around the dining table with coffee and muffins, telling "Stephen stories" and letting the tears flow freely. After they went home, I went back upstairs to see my darling one more time. Colorado law allows up to twenty-four hours to keep the body at home, which can be very helpful if you have any sense that the departing soul is having trouble letting go of its physical form. Many people plan rituals or additional prayers for this time of transition.

In Stephen's case, I knew he would suffer no lingering attachment to the form that had ceased to serve him. I had a sense that he zoomed out of his body as soon as his breath had stopped and was well on his way to higher spheres. His body now looked profoundly lifeless and the skin on his face was becoming more haggard and drawn, so I decided to call the funeral home to pick him up.

If you are the caregiver, this is a time to have the company of somebody who does not need your emotional support. Thankfully, my next-door neighbor, Dottie, came over to take care of me and my dog. I was in a state akin to autopilot, which I think is probably the only reasonable response in the moments immediately following the death. I was doing everything that needed to be done. I was going through my mental checklist. I wasn't crying. I was holding it together for everybody else. I was making sure that Stephen's body was being treated with tender dignity and that Bentley was being cared for. The loss had not yet sunk in, so I was doing "fine." However, everything would have been much harder if not for Dottie's reassuring presence and watchful eye.

Two men from the funeral home arrived in about an hour. I must have expected young paramedics, because when a slight older man and his younger, burly assistant appeared at my door, dressed in their funereal black suits, I was stunned and actually a bit amused. This was October 15—two weeks before Halloween—and somehow it was like trick-or-treat, or something from the old *Addams Family* television show.

My obviously addled reaction aside, they were sensitive and performed their duties with great kindness—asking permission to move Stephen's body before placing it on the gurney, explaining what they would be doing and where he would be taken to await cremation. They came with a simple gray shroud and laid it over him. Then they allowed me to have a final moment with his body before they covered his face and moved the gurney into their van.

October 15, 2008

So Stephen went away and I will never see him again. I can't feel him at all—and do not expect to. How I wish he could send me a postcard from the Other Side, telling me what he is seeing. Actually, I do not expect he will see anything until he has been safely transported and allowed to orient himself to his new surroundings.

I have to orient myself as well. Everything looks the same and yet nothing is the same. The hospital bed where Stephen lay just a few hours ago is still in place, with my bed right next to it. All of his clothes are still in the closet. His towel is still hanging by the shower in his bathroom. His favorite books are still on the nightstand. Nothing has been disturbed, and yet my entire world has been rocked to its foundation. Stephen is gone and his absence is stunning.

At the end of a day filled with phone calls from family and friends, I went to bed exhausted and alone—except for my big, sweet Bentley. "It's just you and me now, kiddo," I said as I hugged my wooly boy-dog. "It's our first night alone in the house, just as I expected. And I'm very glad you're here."

Twenty-three

THE GENUINE HEART OF JOY

The image of the deathbed frightens us . . . .
Yet some people instinctively reach into
the heart of the event and extract the treasure.

—John O'Donohue

YEARS AGO, WHILE DRIVING TO my father's memorial service in Sun City, Arizona, I was struck with a powerful image of him literally skipping around heaven—delighted at being free of his poor, sick body and thrilled to discover celestial halls of learning where he could spend all of eternity exploring the workings of the universe. My father had been a lifelong learner, so he was exuberant to find that heaven was—among many things—a schoolroom in the mind of God.

Having had such an experience, I should not have been surprised that I awoke the day after Stephen's passing with the words *There is joy in heaven* singing out from my heart.

October 16, 2008

I am ecstatic in the joy of Stephen's liberation. Surely all of heaven celebrates his victory! I am enfolded in his happiness and love as his gratitude comes flooding back to me from just beyond the veil. I feel

my heart opening with an energy that is both in me and around me—
buoying me up, reconnecting me to Stephen's heart. I am full to overflowing in the exultation of my beloved. He has made it to the Other
Side and now sends me back a taste of his new world.

I called our friend Kathleen, blissfully exclaiming that I wanted
to throw Stephen a party to celebrate his liberation. Thankfully, she
brought me back to earth. "Be careful," she warned. "You're still in the
clouds with Stephen. Take a step back before you rush into a service.
You don't want to blow people away. You have to lead them to joy, not
force them into it."

Kathleen was right, and her good advice grounded me a bit, so I
could get started on the long list of errands that had to be done.

I spent two hours at the funeral home today, going over details of
the cremation and exploring options for a service. I also told them
the "What do the signs say?" story. They were charmed and grateful
to hear about a positive experience. Their job gets pretty heavy sometimes. The family counselor encouraged me to write about Stephen.
She said, "You know what you have and not many people get that
experience." I appreciate that she put it in the present tense; the love
is still here, even if my husband is not.

Yesterday another friend remarked that Stephen and I had walked
directly into our challenges with open hearts. That is true. We did not
hold back. And in the end, I was showered with blessings. Stephen
completely opened his heart to me. He was no longer an enigma. He
said exactly what was on his mind and fully embraced me. He was so
sweet and tender—even as he barely had the strength to raise his head
from the pillow.

So I ran on a combination of adrenaline and joy. It was a glorious
October day—full of sun, crystal blue skies, and golden leaves. I was
busy "doing." Doing keeps you sane—at least until you run out of
energy. I started putting the house back together and got the ball
rolling on the memorial service that I knew both his family and

I needed to achieve a sense of closure. I decided to hold it on the Veteran's Day holiday because that had been an annual day off for Stephen, and we usually spent it relaxing and celebrating his birthday, which fell on November 12. Then, as I was sending out an e-mail announcing his passing and inviting people to the service, the dark reality hit me: I was writing the obituary of my marriage.

October 16, 2008—at night

I am announcing to the world that he is gone. That means it's real. That means he's not coming back. That means this isn't all a terrible dream from which I will awake. I am painfully awake; and now that I have some space from other people's thoughts and emotions, I can cry from the very depths of my soul.

Such grief feels absolutely primal. When these tears come, I do not just *feel* sorrow, I *am* sorrow—deep, wracking, howling sorrow—and pain that feels like my guts are tearing apart.

As long as Stephen was here—even a fragment still alive—we were still attached. Our very cells had grown together. But now that he's gone, those cells are dying. The "Stephen energy" in me is being amputated, wrenched away. The pain is excruciating.

There is something about being a wife, and then suddenly a widow, that is different from being a daughter, and then suddenly fatherless. It is part of the mystery of the marriage bond—the intimacy of man and wife, the joining of two human beings into a single unit that bleeds cruel tears when one half of that pair dies.

It is hard not to die too. Tonight I am cracked wide open. Tonight I am severed from my beloved. Tonight I am unspeakably, crushingly alone—and there is no remedy but time. So I remember my mother's courage in losing her husband of fifty-seven years, and I am not afraid to cry all of my tears—letting them purge me for whatever the universe wants me to do next.

This is agony I did not feel before, and I'm glad I did not. Stephen was still with me in the present, so the point was to not poison those precious moments with the darkness that would come all too soon. Now he's gone, and the moment of despair is here.

Now is the time to plunge into grief and be cleansed by it. Now it is a purging, a purification, and a release from the stress, fear, hopelessness, and unrelenting responsibility of being a caregiver. I know that part of the elation I felt today was simply relief at no longer bearing the full weight for both of us. For days I have been bent over, unable to stand up straight, and too tired to take Bentley for much of a walk. This morning I stood up, embraced the new day, and got the puppy back into his discipline.

In the days following Stephen's death, I processed a lot of grief by responding to wonderful notes of comfort and encouragement I received from family and friends. I also found myself comforting others, including a friend who wrote to me as his wife lay dying of breast cancer, saying, "Your message has given me renewed strength and appreciation for all the good that has come out of this journey as we become ever closer."

I also received some insightful counsel from friends who were deeply committed to the spiritual path, including this from a former mentor that crystallized grief's message for me:

Cheryl,

I loved the way Chögyam Trungpa spoke of grief. He spoke of a stage on our spiritual path as the "Genuine Heart of Sadness."[13] That in being willing to stay moment to moment with our felt sense of sadness, we go through a passage into authentic being where we are a grain of sand and the emperor of the universe at the same time.

The practice of staying in that fire has been one of my greatest teachers. I trust that your "path with fire" is a horrible gift, as mine has always been. I'm sorry for your loss. You are fortunate to have that kind of love.

Wayne

Dear Wayne,

I did not know of Chögyam Trungpa's teaching on grief, but it is absolutely in line with my experience right now. I had never entered this stage of the path before. Of course, I have had losses: the loss of my father, my community, my pride in many ways—the loss of attachments to things great and small. But the loss of Stephen is something entirely other than these—as I feel the cells of him that were part of me literally being pulled out—in large handfuls, it would seem. His love and the many lessons he taught me are sealed in my heart forever, but losing that physical presence that so grounded me just by being in the same house together—that is the loss that is so shockingly unrelenting.

But I am determined to walk into this grief and embrace its lessons just as surely as Stephen embraced the "horrible gift" of his cancer, and as I was able to embrace my role as caregiver. A couple of weeks ago he said he thought we would eventually have reached this point of oneness if we had stayed married for another thirty years. It's what you see of couples that have been together for decades. What we got instead was a gift of acceleration that allowed us to compress those thirty years into a few months. We didn't know that's what we were doing. We were simply focused on not poisoning today with the probable sadness of tomorrow. We lived each day as it came and, in so doing, were able to immerse ourselves in service to one another. It broke our hearts, and it broke us open in a way I don't believe mere time can do.

So for me the "path with fire" has both heat and pressure. It forces you to plunge into the deep places of the heart and mind where God lives—to find respite, inspiration, strength, courage, compassion, insight, and, eventually, consolation and peace. And to emerge from that fire as a diamond, a new person who either goes straight up to the arms of the Divine, as Stephen has done, or out to serve others, as I feel called to do.

We are truly forged in that flame. We are refined. I am finding that the knowledge of this path—the privilege of walking in the footsteps of mighty souls—gives perspective to a wider plan for each of us and helps me deal with the grief. When I find myself still in disbelief that Stephen is no longer here, the awareness of our path reminds me why he was not afraid to go—and then, amazingly, it is as if he did not leave. At that point, I feel that the "Genuine Heart of Sadness" becomes the "Genuine Heart of Joy"—albeit a joy that burns the heart, even as it causes the heart to sing.

Cheryl

Twenty-four

WITH SHEER DETERMINATION

I am not what happened to me.
I am what I choose to become.

—Carl Gustav Jung

THE DAYS IMMEDIATELY FOLLOWING Stephen's death were a roller coaster of emotion. I was still running on the adrenaline relief of no longer being a caregiver. It's hard not to feel guilty about being relieved; but it's natural to breathe easier, knowing that your loved one, who was in pain, is no longer burdened by a horribly sick body. Death is a kind of birth and the labor pains are agonizing, even in a beautiful death. It feels good when the pain stops. This was one of the emotions I gave myself permission to feel. I noted the possibility of guilt and let it go. I was grateful to begin moving on, even as I was desperately sad that Stephen wasn't there to move on with me.

I felt a tremendous need to get the house in order, to make the space mine so I could function, and to create some kind of structure that would help me discover exactly what "normal" was going to look like in the coming days, weeks, and months. I also had to convince myself that Stephen was gone. All of his belongings were still here; why wasn't he?

A neighbor advised me to make a few changes right away. I had already decided to buy the new bedroom furniture I had wanted for years. My mother and several friends agreed that doing something dramatic was probably a good thing. So I ordered a new bed, chests, and media center for the master bedroom. I got rid of the old furniture we had been using since our Montana days and rearranged most of the second floor, creating the space where my new life would unfold. And I grieved.

October 17, 2008

I don't ever want to forget Stephen, but it's so hard to hang on to that presence. I don't feel him at all. He has left me with relics of his life, but the grounding is gone. I'm tired of this experiment; I'm ready for him to come back. How can he possibly be dead? It is unfathomable. I'm utterly at a loss. No, I am the embodiment of loss. There is only emptiness, and I don't know how I will endure it.

Last night was freaky. The hospital bed had been picked up, so I moved our bed back to its regular place. This means I'm sleeping atop where Stephen was lying and I do feel the energy of him occupying the same space.

My e-mail about Stephen's passing was whipping around the country, so I was hearing from people I had lost track of a decade earlier. Most notes were filled with compassion and love, although I got one strange e-mail from a woman I didn't even know who decided to share her knowledge about alternative medicine, including an assertion that "for future reference, no one has to die of a degenerative disease."

What?! So I wouldn't accidentally kill my *next* husband? Outraged, I wrote back to her in a white heat that she could not possibly know what we had endured, nor could she be so certain why people die. Fortunately, she took the rebuke well and apologized; but now, I realized, amidst everything else, I had to expect that some people might be clumsy in how they responded to Stephen's passing. I frequently found myself trying to make others more comfortable with the fact of death, even as I was trying to wrap my head around the surreal fact that he wasn't coming back.

Many people, like one of my neighbors, admitted to not knowing what to say. He had seen the funeral home men taking Stephen's body away and had just frozen in place. Comforting him and others actually helped me because, to comfort them, I had to focus on the positive aspects of what I believed was Stephen's victory—which I strongly felt every time I started talking about it.

Yet I was having such an odd reaction to people: especially during the first couple of days, I found it painfully difficult to accept their condolences "for my loss." It's what we say in our culture, and we mean it; I had said it myself. But now it struck me differently and I sometimes had trouble hearing it if that's all that was said, especially by relative strangers. I was still partially in the clouds with Stephen, feeling his joy, while the rest of me was in such agony that their condolences almost made me angry. How could they even comment on the loss that was tearing me apart?

Friends tended to say things such as, "I'm so terribly sorry, I know how much you loved him." I appreciated that because to me it meant they were allowing themselves to be touched by the agony that was bursting out of me. People who had lost a spouse seemed to understand that I was going through psychic surgery even while walking around, pretending to be a regular person. Sometimes I felt normal and other times I was completely out of it. After a week or so, I was able to be more gracious and more appreciative of the fact that, as a culture, we are woefully ill prepared to deal with the shock of great loss. People just don't know what to say.

On Saturday, I attended my book group's annual October retreat— the event I had been hoping to attend while Stephen lay dying. We played a self-discovery game that was amazingly insightful, and I found the conversation comforting. Although I was exhausted that night, I wrote in my journal that I felt a power and strength I had never felt before—as if I were truly coming into my own.

That feeling continued to grow in the following days as I began work on my eulogy and the program for Stephen's memorial service. Many counselors use art, music, or poetry therapy as way to express grief. I found that writing gave me that creative outlet.

October 19, 2008

I had intended to do our regular morning reading on this, my first Sunday alone. Instead I awoke with the very clear direction that I was to get busy writing. So I wrote for most of the day and, to my great delight, discovered that writing about Stephen makes me feel as if he were not so far away.

I am amazed at the fullness I feel while writing. I think this is Stephen pushing me to get on with things. Don't mope around; he certainly isn't. I hope people don't think I'm insensitive—it's just that he and I both have things to do. He is the wind in my sails, and he's blowing with great force to move me along.

Several friends and family members had offered to accompany me to Stephen's cremation, but when the day arrived, I was glad I had decided to attend it alone. This was the final physical step I had promised him I would complete. It was my job to see his body safely into the flame.

October 24, 2008

I got to see Stephen's body one more time. They had dressed him in his suit, which fit so badly now. He looked like an old man—exactly as I suspect he would have appeared if we had been married for those extra thirty years he had imagined, making him eighty-five years old instead of fifty-five. His skin was ice-cold—he had been refrigerated (not embalmed) all this time. His eyelashes were still long. I stroked his forehead and said, "Good-bye."

Then they closed up the cardboard box and slid it into the furnace. Thank God I knew his spirit was not there; it was only a body he no longer needed. He was like a chick that had long since hatched into its new life, leaving behind only a useless shell. I sat for a while and meditated until I felt surrounded with light—and then I left. It takes several hours to complete the cremation. There was no need for me to stay.

For years Stephen and I had called each other "Bunny." As I was pulling out of the parking area, I saw a little cottontail rabbit in the grass. He wiggled his nose and then hopped out of sight. Perhaps this was a coincidence; perhaps not. Perhaps a gentle wink from the universe. Anyway, my precious Bunny is gone forever. There is nothing left of him now but a pile of ash with a metal tag in it to make sure I get his remains and not someone else's.

Imagine that I could be a widow for thirty years! I can't really see much benefit to living that long. I've had my true love, a successful career, and a rich inner path. What point is there to living longer, except to come up higher in awareness? Otherwise, it all seems a bit useless—just sticking around, trying to be reasonably happy. My opinion matters little here; you don't get to go until it's your turn.

Around this time, a dear friend gave me a powerful poem by the Spanish poet Pablo Neruda called "If I Die."[14] Stephen could have written it. As soon as I heard the opening lines, they seared themselves into my mind as a mandate from him to survive "with sheer determination," to paraphrase Neruda. I must not waver, lest my suffering cause him to die all over again.

So I summoned the will to keep going, even though I was beginning to need a break of some kind. Sitting in hot water at a spa for several days was sounding better and better. I started canceling on social events—just too tired and in need of peace and quiet. I found I could do only one thing a day—be it a little project such as rearranging furniture or eating a meal with friends or even having a long phone conversation. I would wake up in the morning with some energy, but any kind of human contact drained me immediately.

The following Sunday was a turning point. Sitting in what had been Stephen's room—now a simple guest room—I finally came back to myself and to his presence.

October 26, 2008

I have lost his body, but I have not lost his spirit. And when I am in this room, reading, meditating, and writing, I am one with my Stephen. I am in that holy place that he and I shared. I am comforted and I am whole. I am already in that eternity to which he has so joyfully gone—just a little ahead of the rest of us—to pull us up, to point the way, and, perhaps, to send back the occasional reminder that such a soul as his is meant to be the rule for us to follow, not the exception to marvel at and then forget. I want to do what Stephen did, in my own way—and I promise always to remember.

Twenty-five

THE POSTCARD FROM HEAVEN

'Tis said the life that gives one moment's joy
To one lone mortal is not lived in vain;
But lives like thine God grants as shining lights
That we in darkness Him aright may see.

—T. Ramakrishna

STEPHEN EXPECTED TO BE LONG GONE from the earth. "Don't try to find me," he had admonished. "I won't be here." He was very much opposed to attempts to contact the dead in any kind of séance or spiritualism practice. Instead, he anticipated moving immediately into the universities of the Spirit that he believed await every soul that chooses to continue its journey to eternity.

And it certainly felt as if he were well on his way. The feeling of his absence was breathtaking. I would find myself holding my heart, barely able to breathe from the crushing weight of my loneliness. Where once a part of Stephen had lived in me, now there was nothing. It was like the phantom pain of a now-missing limb. Except this was my heart—as if a portion of it had been carved out of me.

It was into this void that an essence of Stephen returned to take up his lodging once again. It was not the physical mutuality I had once experienced when we were standing side by side. Now it was more of a deep inner knowing that we would always be spiritually connected. Somehow the divine spark in me would always sense the Divine Presence with which Stephen was merging. And whenever I put my attention on that connection, I would feel him alive and present with me.

October 26, 2008—evening

I finally started going through photos, looking for special ones to use for the memorial service. I was okay until I found the one of Stephen and me sitting at the Maroon Bells—his spiritual jumping-off point and where one day I will take his ashes. Then I crumbled into tears again.

I found cards he had written me—even one he wrote a week after our wedding. And somehow, in a brand-new way, I truly internalized how much Stephen loved me. How could I not have realized? How could I have been so disconnected, so self-centered before he got sick—even doubting that he loved me? Do we ever really know what we have until it's gone?

I did love him. I loved him with all my heart—or at least as much as I was able to give. It took me a long time to trust him, and that must have hurt him. It took me ages to go where he wanted to take me—and that must have been hard for him. And yet he loved me, and I made him happy. In the end, I took care of him as no one else could have done; but in between I could have been kinder. I could have—what? I don't know—could I have begged him to stay?

I don't think so. It's more likely that I had to be somewhat detached so he could go without suffering a double agony. I had to stay busy so he could go where angels would take him. Yet, I wonder: did we have to put that much space between us (both of us continuing to work and me continuing to travel) so we could actually bear to let him die?

I found myself crying, demanding: "If you loved me so much, how could you leave me?" Perhaps I made it too easy for him to go. Maybe he would have fought harder if I had. Were we too laid-back? Some people might think so—but I had to follow his lead. I did what he wanted. Things happened by increments, so I didn't always notice the decline until change gathered the momentum of a freight train with death as its destination. Now I'm alone—and I don't want to be alone. I want my Stephen back. I have everything in life except the one person I truly want.

Looking at the photos from Montana and the years before he got sick, I am amazed to see him so robust, so full of ideas and projects and energy. He loved the process of creating something new, such as our storage barn, or the beautiful landscaping around our apartment building. It took me many years of working on projects with Stephen, but I did finally learn to love the process almost as much as the result. That made him very happy.

Several days earlier our friend and former neighbor, Marie Antoinette, had written me from Montana offering to do a pastel portrait of Stephen based on any photo of him I would like her to render. I knew she did exquisite work and had a deeply spiritual way of capturing her subjects' essence, so I immediately accepted this generous gift from her heart.[15]

Today, I found the perfect picture of Stephen to send to Marie Antoinette. It's from our vacation with my parents in San Diego in 1997—before we left Montana, before my car accident, before we moved to Denver, before my father died—and before cancer. There is that "Stephen" look: loving, penetrating, gentle, strong, centered, yet dynamic—absolutely real. All at once, completely himself. He seems to say, "This way. Follow me. I did it; so can you." All with a slight twinkle—dignified, gorgeous. The love of my life. I wish I had loved him better.

I spent most of several days going through photos and keepsakes—crying, remembering, finding images I had never seen of Stephen from childhood, college, his days in Chicago, and wonderful pictures of him with his family. All with that incredible smile so many people mentioned in their tributes to him. He was a happy man, and it showed.

November 1, 2008

By the end of the day I actually felt that I had locked the essence of Stephen into my heart. I'm no longer afraid I'll lose or forget him. This is a huge comfort. If he lives in my heart, I don't have to be lonely. When I write, he is there with me—all one.

At the same time I was poring over photos for the memorial service, my friend Marie Antoinette was creating her portrait. In just a couple of days she e-mailed me to say it was complete.

November 2, 2008
Dear Cheryl,

I finished the portrait of Stephen. He is wonderful. I have to say, whenever I draw people who have moved on to the Other Side, I do not run into the customary stumbling blocks and it is so much easier for me to capture them. I believe it is because they guide and inspire me and my hands as I keep my heart open to them. I felt that Stephen was doing that. He felt very alive to me and very eager to reach you. On his wavelength of light, I believe he was reaching out to me in his own reserved way, to reach you, to make you feel the continuity of who he is. I hope this portrait can serve as a reminder of that, and that you feel him touching your heart when you look at it. I sincerely hope it can serve as some sort of bridge to him, and from him to you.

Love,
Marie Antoinette

The portrait was like seeing Stephen peering back from heaven. There was such radiance about this portrait—as if Marie Antoinette had captured his soul's liberation. She had indeed painted a bridge to him—just as I had been feeling for the past twenty-four hours as I was going over photos from his life. Now, to have this picture of what I would identify as the resurrected Stephen left me breathless.

Even though he did not expect to contact me from the Other Side, I had jokingly asked him (should he find out that he could) to please send me a postcard. And, thanks to the artistry and attunement of our dear friend, he did. Several days after the memorial service, Marie Antoinette sent me more information about her experience while creating Stephen's heavenly portrait:

> I really believe you and Stephen still work as a team. I can feel it. When I drew Stephen, he was there, as I told you. There was more to it that I didn't want to say because it's sometimes inappropriate trying to describe an ethereal experience. However, after reading the eulogy you e-mailed, I feel that I should. If you don't mind, I feel that my boldness is prompted by Stephen. Here's what I felt the night that I completed the portrait:
>
> After putting the finishing touches on the portrait and conveying to you in the e-mail what I had felt during the creation of it, I put it away and went to bed. As I was falling asleep, I saw, in my mind's eye, Stephen in the pose of the portrait, except full-body, stretch out his hand and indicate I could come. You were with him, hand in hand, and moving into an inner world in a cosmic-dance-type energy. (I wonder if travel in the spirit is much like an energy dance.)
>
> He intends for you to be aware of what he has found, a new world that lives and breathes the mysteries of God he so avidly studies, a new domain of light, a dimension of color, with geometry in the air. He extended his hand to me to give me an opportunity to see also. In my soul I trust these experiences, so I accepted and came along; but after just a few split seconds of tuning in, I felt I should let go.
>
> There is such happiness between you two. While you wanted to include me, I felt I didn't belong. So a distance appeared and the opening in consciousness closed. However, the reality of it remains.

So Stephen did send me a postcard after all, and that portrait became an instant comfort to me. I immediately felt his presence radiating out through those eyes that seemed to follow me—encouraging me, offering advice, even admonition to slow down, take it easy, be logical, be organized, and be kind.

I believe Marie Antoinette witnessed in her meditation the open door through which Stephen walked to the next world. And the postcard from heaven shows him looking back through that doorway, beckoning each of us—for what one person has done others can also do.

Over the next few days, I worked very hard on Stephen's service. I wanted it to be inspiring for everyone and I felt it was important for Stephen to get a powerful sendoff, for his family to be comforted, for others to know him better, and for me to bear witness to the extraordinary life I had shared with this man of great heart. This was the closing of one cycle and the opening of a new one; we needed a ritual to mark the occasion.

Once the "postcard from heaven" portrait arrived from Marie Antoinette, the program and all the other preparations fell into place. I rented a professional sound system because my friends Kerry and Kathleen had agreed to provide live music for the service. Our friends Frank and Christina—whom we had all worked with in Montana—were flying in from Maryland, and everybody planned to stay at my house for a slumber party and reunion. I couldn't think of anything better than having some of my dearest friends there to support me and share "Stephen stories."

The day of Stephen's celebration was cloudy, but the event was transcendent. Even the wildlife was in tune—flocks of geese taking to the sky (as if on cue) as the service began and, again, while Stephen's mom delivered her eulogy, taking her theme from the story of Jonathan Livingston Seagull, the little gull who was determined to fly higher and faster than anyone else in his flock.

The service was conducted by our hospice chaplain, a remarkable woman who had met Stephen only once but had immediately recognized him as a contemplative and a kindred soul. Both she and her husband had spent over thirty years in religious orders of the Catholic Church, so she understood Stephen's commitment to his spiritual path—which she nevertheless found remarkable in a man who was not a monk or a priest.

Stephen's parents, his brothers, and I were able to deliver our eulogies with only a few stops for tears. It was not easy for any of us, but I had felt strongly that delivering individual eulogies would be a good way for each of us to handle some of our grief. My experience was that, in writing out what you intend to say, you have to dig deeply into your life, your love, and your emotion to pull out those essential memories that can then act as a bridge to consolation and closure. Weeks later, Stephen's mom and I still were receiving grateful comments from people who said how moved they had been by the service—especially the gorgeous music written, arranged, and performed by my dear, talented friends.

After the service, I was the last one to leave the funeral home. For a while, I sat in my car in the parking lot, eating a sandwich before driving to the reception, where I planned to circulate with the guests rather than eat. As I was sitting there, I saw Stephen in my mind's eye. "Good job," he said, and gave me a big thumbs-up.

Do we imagine these things? Perhaps. I really don't care. There are mysteries we cannot explain in this life about how our loved ones tend to us and communicate with us after they have walked through the door from this world to the next. I believe the good news is that they *do.*

The day ended with a glorious sunset—all orange and gold and purple with rays of light shooting out from behind the majestic Rocky Mountains. The day had been cloudy, which made the sunset all the more spectacular, breaking through, illuminating the clouds. It was as if the heavens were broadcasting the liberation of a most beloved son of God: Stephen Alan Eckl.

Twenty-six

TOUCHING BOTTOM

Where the last anguish deepens—there
The fire of beauty smites through pain.

—George William Russell

As anyone who has experienced profound loss knows, grief peels off in layers. Every so often we reach a plateau where we can rest a while, and then we plunge back into the abyss. The sense of loss never completely goes away. If we continue to let the process unfold within us, we do eventually get to a place where the clouds part and the sun breaks through to a new life and a new way through that life—but not without a lot of work and even some apparent setbacks.

January 6, 2009

Eleven years since my father passed away and nearly twelve weeks since Stephen has been gone—since Stephen died. I have to say "died," because it's still so difficult to accept that he really is gone, not just elsewhere.

As the days, weeks, and months go by, I make a reluctant peace with grief. I am less afraid to be alone than I expected. I am less sad at night than I thought I might be. I am increasingly able to be as brave and strong as Stephen wanted me to be. I have great faith in the future. Still, I purposely do not think too far ahead because I don't like the idea of being a widow for ten, twenty, thirty years. I'll be a widow just for today and that is enough.

I keep myself busy with projects, such as remodeling the upstairs bathrooms, which have needed a complete redo for years. ("I'll do the first floor," Stephen had promised. "The upstairs is yours to fix up as you wish.") Today I'm painting bathroom walls so the handymen I have hired can install toilets, lights, mirrors, and towel bars tomorrow. And I am staining what seems like miles of baseboards and cabinets before new carpet can be installed.

Having something physical to do, with a timeline for finishing, was very important these days. I needed reasons to get up and get going in the morning. Bentley was at board-and-train doggie school for three weeks, so he was out of the way, which was a good test for me. I missed his company less than I would have done in the first few weeks of Stephen's absence.

I do know how to be alone, but grief stuns me. I am surprised at what dissolves me into tears. A sad movie does it, of course. Talking to other people about Stephen's incredible passing does not. Telling stories about his courage and spiritual depth brings me great joy and lifts up my soul, while going to one of our favorite restaurants after a day of making decisions about bathroom fixtures and countertops makes me cry as I sit in the booth across from where he should be.

Tears come from nowhere. They rise and fall, seemingly of their own free will. It is a shock to realize how utterly helpless I feel in those moments.

January 25, 2009
Bentley came home from doggie boot camp yesterday, a much calmer and more obedient dog. He knows his commands and usually does them the first time he's asked. He seems happy not to obsessively

follow me around the house as he used to, and I'm glad to ignore him a bit, because everything else seems to be disintegrating.

I'm fighting a cold, which means the remodeling work is falling behind. The clock in the living room has stopped working and now the freezer has gone out. What else could go wrong? There is so much to take care of. It will probably take a year to complete all the projects. I guess that's just the kind of year it's going to be—laying new foundations, new roots.

I had also taken on providing daily housekeeping and care-giving services for my elderly mother and stepfather. This entailed my going to their apartment every morning except Sunday to do light clean-up chores, laundry, grocery shopping, chauffeuring them to medical appointments—basically whatever they needed. They were both nearly ninety years old and in failing health, but it made no sense for them to hire outside help to hang around their tiny apartment waiting for them to need something.

My becoming their part-time caregiver seemed like the only reasonable solution—at least for a few weeks; and they were paying me, so I didn't have to worry about going back to my training job any time soon. However, I was concerned I might have trouble handling the daily routine and emotional stress of being in the thick of their challenges as well as my own.

February 11, 2009

Okay, God, I need some resolutions, please—and fast. My body is telling me I need to be completely free of all obligations so I can heal and focus on my own creative work. But how do I accomplish that?

I'm also beginning to feel that Bentley needs a new home. I'm just not sure I can do this "alpha dog" stuff. And, as I feared, I don't think I can continue working for my mom, even though I know it helps her. I'm so tired; I feel like collapsing all the time.

I'm taking a Tai Chi class, and that seems to make me feel better; but I find I can do only one or two chores a day. The new carpet has been installed, and I've finished all the remodeling for now; but the basement is still a mess. I feel overwhelmed by my possessions, and I have yet to start sorting through Stephen's remaining clothing and the garage full of his woodworking equipment.

Today I told one of my business colleagues that, for the foreseeable future (maybe forever), I could not help him with any more consulting projects as I had done occasionally after going on leave of absence. I simply have no energy, no interest. That lifted a huge weight, but I feel like I'm carrying Stephen's backpack around again. I honestly don't know if I can keep going.

Spiritual teacher Matthew Fox says we must "bottom out" in our grief.[16] We must cry the deep tears of agony that cleanse our bodies and open our hearts. It is as if grief were a huge swimming pool of sadness. Unless we dive down to the very bottom of that pool, there is no solid foundation from which to kick back up to the surface for the air of life we need to renew ourselves and move on. Until then, we can paddle around in grief for years—nearly drowning, but never finding an end to the sorrow. We cannot heal if we resist the very emotions that will carry us through the pain to the bliss of grief's resolution.

I felt as if I were drowning in that pool. I was exhausted on every possible level—too tired to move, too weak to swim up or down in grief's dark waters. I hadn't really cried for a couple of weeks, but I was profoundly sad. I felt as low as I could go, but I had not yet touched bottom. It was my puppy who finally pushed me all the way down.

February 15, 2009

Today is Valentine's Day weekend and I am excruciatingly sad. Yesterday I met with my book group and we had a wonderful conversation. They were very supportive, but this lovers' holiday seems to be hitting me harder than Thanksgiving, Christmas, and New Year's combined.

This morning the sun was shining and I felt pretty good until I remembered that today was another milestone—four months since

Stephen's death. Today four months seems like four years, and I miss Stephen so bad my body hurts. I can hardly move, but I must. Bentley is going bonkers because he needs some exercise.

During the three weeks he had been home from obedience school, Bentley had started falling back into his old habits of trying to be in charge of me. It was my own fault. I'm just too much of a softie to be a good "alpha dog." You're supposed to make a dog work for rewards and affection, which I found hard to do—especially when I was sad and Bentley was acting cute. Although he weighed nearly fifty pounds, he was not quite eighteen months old and was still adorably puppyish in his behavior.

He had been doing well on his commands in the house, but he had trouble containing his exuberance outdoors. He hadn't been getting enough "romping and running exercise," because his trainers had banned him from the dog park. They said it just taught him to go crazy around other dogs and ignore me, which was true.

So even though I was very tired, I took Bentley out for what was supposed to be a nice long walk. We were doing fine until he decided to lunge after a couple of cats that looked like way more fun.

"Bentley! No!" I hollered. A strong leash correction did nothing. He was pulling so hard, I had to grab the scruff of his neck and give him a shake—the trainer's correction of last resort. He yelped sharply and spun around in disbelief.

"Oh, puppy, I'm so sorry," I said and then started to cry. I couldn't bear that I had just caused him pain when it was my fault he was being disobedient. I was not being a good dog owner and I knew it. I was going to have to find him a new home.

We rushed back to the house—me sobbing, him trotting along on the leash, looking up to see why I was making such a fuss. I dialed the dog academy where I had taken him for training, crying so hard I could barely read the phone number. A week earlier I had alerted the owner that I was having trouble, so he wasn't entirely surprised when I called.

"I need help with Bentley," I blubbered into the phone. "I'm ruining this dog. He's falling back into his old habits, and it's my fault. Can you help me?"

The owner was a champ. "Of course," he said. "If you can get him over here today, I won't charge you to board him, and we'll find him a home. As a matter of fact, I may already have the perfect situation for him. My wife's best friend and her husband have been wanting a standard poodle. Don't you worry about Bentley; I'll take care of him."

This was a huge relief, but there was no time to dawdle. It was 4:30 p.m. The dog academy closed at 6:00 p.m. on Sundays and it takes nearly an hour to get there. I had to hurry.

"I'd better not drive all the way across town by myself," I thought as I started tossing Bentley's belongings into the back of the car, still sobbing uncontrollably. "I have to call somebody to go with me." Thankfully, my friend and neighbor Evie answered her phone.

"Evie, I have to get rid of Bentley," I wailed. "The dog academy will take him if I can get him there fast. Can you go with me?"

"I'll be right there," she said without hesitation.

Bentley had been dancing around in the garage, very excited about going for a ride in the car with his bed and all of his toys. As soon as Evie arrived, he bounded into the back seat and off we went on our last trip together.

Having another person in the car helped me calm down, and we drove across town without incident. When we pulled up to the dog academy, one of the trainers was in the parking lot. He came around to the car. I opened the back door and Bentley leapt out, happy to see his trainer buddy again. Not looking back, he scampered off to the kennel he knew as a second home. I would never see him again.

Later that week I got a call from the dog academy, saying that the owner's friends were coming to meet Bentley on Saturday. They were both near retirement age, with a college-aged son who lived with them. This meant Bentley would have men in his life, which he had surely missed since his alpha dog (Stephen) had gone away. They had a big backyard and were seasoned big-dog owners, so my wooly boy would get the discipline and ongoing training he sorely needed.

February 21, 2009

It's Sunday and still no word that Bentley definitely has a new home. This concerns me, although I am beginning to feel that I can let him go. Actually, I guess I have to let him go emotionally so his new family can take him. Of course, I'm still hanging on—thinking he has to go to his new home first; but I have to trust the universe enough to let him go. That is the only way to freedom. Dropping him off at the dog academy was one thing; now I have to release him from my heart. He needs to move on and so do I.

It appears I have to make the first move; I thought it was the other way around. How interesting that in even the smallest aspect of life we have to step out in faith. We must willingly walk into what is unknown to us, trusting that the way through to the Other Side is known to the Divine. We have to turn everything over to God every day.

It doesn't count as surrender unless it hurts. It's not a sacrifice unless it's a real cutting loose—a stepping back from a situation you can't control or into a possibility you did not design. It only counts for grace when you truly let go. So right now, today, I am surrendering Bentley to the care of the universe.

I'm at rock bottom, God. I give up.

Part Five

PILGRIMAGE

Pilgrims are persons in motion—
passing through territories not their own—
seeking . . . a goal to which only the spirit's
compass points the way.

—Richard Niebuhr

THE MIDDLE PLACE

*The real inner life and freedom of man begin when
[the] inner dimension opens up and man lives
in communion with the unknown within him.*

—Thomas Merton

THIS IS HOW NEW LIFE BEGINS: with struggle and release. First Stephen had to go, then Bentley. I was beginning to understand why it was right to get Bentley in the first place and why now it was right to let him go. Certainly it was for both joy and tears. Having Bentley in our lives forced Stephen and me to let emotions in and out, as nothing else could have done in our months of sorrow and loss.

For Stephen, the laughter helped him love freely at a time when he was considering that it might be better not to love at all because losing love hurts so much. He adored Bentley and loved him openly. With Bentley around, we were a family; and we opened our hearts as parents to this wooly little being. Our love passed through him and back again. We sometimes talked through Bentley to each other when otherwise we might just have clammed up from sadness. Instead, we played and laughed when there really wasn't much to laugh about.

For me, loving Bentley—and then having to send him away for his own good—ripped the scab off the wound of letting Stephen go to a better place. In some ways, losing my dog was even harder than losing my husband, because Stephen understood what was happening and believed deeply in where he was going. I couldn't explain to Bentley why his human papa had disappeared and why his human mama was now sending him away. It just broke my heart, and this renewed grief was raw, primal, and overwhelming in its intensity.

With Bentley gone, I had lost the last physical comfort I had built up around myself. The emptiness was staggering. Yet, I had to admit that having a bouncy adolescent dog around the house had actually become a distraction from the deep grief work I knew I must do. Re-homing him was the right decision, but knowing that didn't make bearing the pain any easier.

February 28, 2009

I'm at an odd stage of transition—the ill-defined middle place that author William Bridges calls "The Neutral Zone."[17] I am not who I used to be and I am not yet the person I will become. Right now my life is all about creating new patterns. I'm finishing up the life that ended when Stephen died and exploring the one that began when I delivered my eulogy at his memorial service.

The ending has to do with grief—touching bottom so I can rise up and breathe the clean air of resolution and transformation. I'm still figuring out what it is I am beginning. I do know it depends on getting my health in order so I have the energy to move forward. My mandate now is self-care. I'm not expected to accomplish much. This means staying home, hibernating if necessary. I am patient now— perhaps for the first time in my life. The universe is telling me to stop, rest, listen, read, reflect, learn. It has been a while since I heard that special voice speaking to me; today it brings words of comfort and encouragement.

Don't worry about action. Pay attention. Wait. All things will come about in the fullness of time. Learn not to push; learn to flow. Learn balance and poise. Be kind, quiet, happy. Enjoy solitude and silence. Sit in the sun. Plant flowers. Learn to draw. Be the artist that you are. Write a poem—or not. Be still and collect your soul. Nourish all in you that is good and true and beautiful. Relish the warm wind blowing through your soul. This is one time when you can allow yourself to be blown along because all your hard work has put you firmly in God's jet stream. It is safe to be here. You will love where it takes you.

March 3, 2009

Many people ask me if I'm getting out. Am I seeing people? Am I doing anything social? And, yes, I am. But why does nobody ask if I'm going within? Am I communing with Spirit? Do I feel Stephen in my heart? Do I feel the continuity of his being whenever I think of him? Do I feel the fire of present and future purpose? The answer to all of these is yes—but only when I feel in touch with my own soul. Only when I write, as I have been doing for some time now. Only when I'm doing something creative, such as writing down my thoughts and feelings and memories about my life with Stephen. In those moments I find comfort; only then am I not alone.

March 6, 2009

My tears are much closer to the surface these days and, actually, I'm glad they are. I don't want to get over losing Stephen so soon. I don't want to crust over the wound before healing has an opportunity to do its work from the inside out. In order for true healing to take place, I must be willing to feel the pain and learn from it. It's okay to put a dressing on it, but the wound cannot be healed unless I understand what wounded me in the first place—and then work to heal the cause, not just the effect.

My wound is loss—and there is a "what" to it, not just "who." Of course, the "who" is Stephen. But what does losing him mean to me? That's what I need to know to really push up from the bottom of my grief. In order to build a new foundation for my life, I need to understand the old one.

So, what have I lost? Physical presence, to be sure. Sexual intimacy—although chemo and pain had killed that long before Stephen died. Love, care, comfort, partnership. A date on Saturday night. Warmth, creative input, a sounding board. There were many losses before he actually left.

Going deeper: In losing my husband, I lost my best friend and companion, my *anam ćara*, my psychological rock and spiritual guide, my menu planner (I still don't know what to feed myself!), my role model for peace, and his always reliable logic and reason. My traveling buddy is gone, taking with him his unique perspectives and fresh ideas. I have lost my protector—the person who truly loved me for myself, not for what I could do for him, and the one person I had eventually come to trust completely. The one who gave me space to be myself, and the one who settled for nothing less than my honest, soulful self. The one who did not budge when I complained, and the one who would not leave until he knew I would be okay.

Now consider: Is there anything gone I am glad to have lost? Yes. First of all, Stephen's suffering. Next, the inner critic. Then, fear of many things: certainly the fear of death, of grief, of creativity, of what I may find when I delve deeply into myself. And I am glad to have lost the feeling of being late for my own life. I finally feel as if I'm on time, beginning to live an authentic life that comes from soul inspiration, not external aspirations or goals that other people have set for me. Did Stephen have to die for me to arrive at this place? I don't know. I suppose I would eventually have found these blessings as I continued on my journey to self-realization; losing him has certainly accelerated that process.

Even though I had bottomed out in the sadness of giving up Bentley, actually climbing out of grief's dark waters was not a one-time event. During the next few weeks I found myself plunging in again and again like a diver hunting for pearls along the sea's murky bottom. Every so often, I would discover a new insight that would push me up to the surface; but then the light would fade, and I'd find myself back in the watery gloom.

Trying to be grateful for what I was learning, I did a twenty-day journal exercise on the concept of living abundantly in the present moment. A friend and I attended a seminar by Dannion Brinkley, an expert on near-death experience, who was speaking about his new book, *Secrets of the Light: Lessons from Heaven.*[18] So much of what he said confirmed my own feelings about life, death, and what comes after.

"I don't want you to be afraid of death," he said passionately to his audience. "When you're not afraid, you think about how much fun life is." I suppose someone like Dannion, who has actually died three times and come back to tell the tale, can speak with great authority on how exhilarating it is to simply be alive. I was trying very hard to feel the fun through my friendships and personal creativity projects, but doing so remained a daily challenge.

In April I turned sixty and went on a weekend retreat with members of my book group. It was good to be with friends who had stood by me during Stephen's illness and death and who would let me talk about him. Some days it seemed that all I wanted to do was talk about him—to anybody who would listen. Telling his story was another way to keep him close; but as the weeks passed, maintaining that closeness became increasingly difficult.

May 2, 2009

There is always such a void when I finish a round of writing about Stephen, which means putting it away for a while. It is then that his physical absence takes over. My "Stephen tanks" are just about empty. He was never a big hugger and would sometimes tease me by refusing to hug me, even when I asked him. So I don't have a large store of physical comfort memories, which actually makes my body ache. I miss his maleness, the feeling of his incredible strength. I would not wish him back because we both need to move on. Still, I do wish he would visit once in a while—just to hold me, to tell me what he's doing on the Other Side. Just to give me a glimpse, a kiss, and a reassurance that I can do whatever is next for me. And for us.

Around this time I felt myself moving into a new cycle of change that was really uncomfortable because all around me things started breaking. My document shredder jammed and had to be replaced; the vacuum cleaner started pumping out smoke and fumes; the brickwork on my patio crumbled when the satellite-dish installer used it as a stepladder. Light bulbs were burning out in ceiling fixtures that I couldn't reach without teetering on a high ladder.

I was overwhelmed by the natural tendency of physical things to decay, and I was discouraged by the fact that I no longer had a man around the house to fix anything that broke. All of my neighbors were elderly, or single women like me, or simply unavailable. Stephen's brother and father would have helped, but they lived too far away to come over and change light bulbs. I just wanted to go to sleep forever.

May 10, 2009

I feel another layer of Stephen-essence slipping away. I deleted his e-mail account yesterday—just one more item on a checklist that makes his absence more permanent. How could that adorable smile be forever banished from this earth? It's so hard to realize that he won't be dropping in one of these days.

Actually, he did drop by at Christmastime. It was a dream, yet much more than a dream. It really felt like a visitation. I remember saying as he held me in his arms, "Thanks for coming back for me; I couldn't bear your being gone." I can still see him, dressed in a white shirt and jeans, no longer sick, once more strong and smiling. It never happened again.

I wish I could really connect with him; but when I think that, what I hear is "You're not ready." I guess this means I still have a lot of healing to do first. I have to be much stronger before I can move into the next phase of my life.

May 15, 2009

Exactly seven months since Stephen has been gone and tonight all I can think is: Why did you leave me and why can't I go too? I have erected the beginning of a new life and it's totally meaningless without you. It's empty and cold because you're not in it. I'm sad and alone and my heart is absolutely broken.

I would be perfectly content to just end it all now. Get off this crazy planet before the whole civilization crumbles. Half of the money you worked so hard to save has disappeared in the stock market. Now I have to find a way to make it back.

I know I have work to do, but I miss you so much. Every fifteenth of the month you're just that much farther away from me. Will I ever catch up to you? Will I ever find you again? Or is the whole idea of life everlasting just a myth? Were those eighteen years of marriage all we'll ever have?

I did such a bad job during most of them. I was so selfish and crabby. I just need you to hold me and tell me you forgive me for not loving you better. I hope I made it up to you in the end, but I could have been so much kinder before you got sick. I don't know why I fought you—why I couldn't seem to trust you or follow your suggestions before life got so hard.

Several nights later I had another dream of Stephen holding me, wrapping me in his forgiveness. He is tender in these dreams, like he was just before he died. When he was alive, there was a sting about him sometimes if I was out of alignment with him or my authentic self. These dreams were different. I woke up with a feeling of closeness that kept me going for several days—or at least until other obligations captured my attention.

May 24, 2009

Tonight I was writing in my journal after a long conversation with a friend whose cousin had just died. She was very upset, so I tried to comfort her with some of the perspectives that have been coming to me as I write about my life with Stephen. Suddenly, I found myself

writing what seemed to be a strong message from him, not the usual
inner voice that sometimes appears in my journals:

*You must try harder to reach me where I am on the Other Side. I can
come only so far. Still your mind and heart and come to me. I am here.
Where are you?*

This was the kick in the pants I had been waiting for. I had to find
a way to stay connected with Stephen. To do that, I knew I had to
leave the safe cocoon I had built around myself in the last several
months. I needed to get away from the house I still identified only
as the place where Stephen and I used to live together—not as *my*
home. I needed a better way through the labyrinth of feeling that
had become my life. And to find all this, I felt called to venture far
across the sea.

Twenty-eight

THIN AS GOSSAMER

Hence in a season of calm weather,
Though inland far we be,
Our Souls have sight of that immortal sea
Which brought us hither.

—William Wordsworth

STEPHEN'S CHALLENGE FOR ME to find him was not a new inspiration. In fact, it confirmed an earlier call to travel that had come through my friend Mimi. "I think you should go on the Celtic Spirituality pilgrimage this summer," she had said, quite out of the blue. Our mutual friend John—a gifted counselor and spiritual facilitator—was taking a group to Ireland to visit sites considered sacred to the Irish and their progenitors, the Celts.

"I went several years ago," Mimi told me, "and I was deeply moved by the sacred energy I felt in the land as well as the ancient sites. You would absolutely love it, and getting away could be so good for you. John said there is still one place left for July. Why don't you see if you can get it?"

So I did. All the plans fell into place with free airline tickets, upgrades, and hotel rooms from business travel points, plus the promise of generous hospitality from family and friends in both the U.S. and the U.K. I decided to make an adventure of it: after visits in Southampton in the south of England and Leeds further north, I would have several days exploring on my own before joining John's group at the retreat site near Dublin.

"What do you hope to get out of this trip?" a curious friend asked over dinner one evening.

"I have an itinerary, but no real expectations," I replied. Actually, that wasn't quite true. I wanted very much to be transformed and enlightened by the magical quality of Ireland that Mimi said she had experienced. I didn't know what I would feel, but I was confident that *something* would happen in the land of my own Irish ancestors—the Laffertys and the Patricks.

I read up on the Celts, an ancient pagan people who had a surprisingly open relationship with both the beginning and ending of life. When they were not waging fierce and noisy battles against one another, many were keen observers of the heavens and deeply connected to the land. Even after they embraced St. Patrick's Christianity in the fifth century AD, their spirituality remained wild and pungent, retaining the rich flavor of a natural world they passionately inhabited.

To the Celts, God was personal, strongly feminine, and available, even to the simplest of persons. Life was a circle from birth to death and rebirth; and the cycles of the sun, moon, stars, and seasons were cause for celebration with rituals, prayers, and exuberant festivals.

Early in my own path of self-discovery, I had been drawn to the way of the Celts by their belief that death was not an end, simply another state of being that was more like walking into another room than going off to a separate existence (or nonexistence, as the case may be). For the Celts, the veil between this world and the next was "thin as gossamer."[19] They believed it was possible to flow between matter and Spirit, and their daily lives reflected an easy comfort with the Divine.

As my favorite Irish writer, John O'Donohue, put it, "For the Celts, the eternal world was so close to the natural world that death was not seen as a terribly destructive or threatening event."[20] When you pass over to the Other Side, you are going home to a place of eternal light and love.

In my current circumstance, I had to believe the Celts were right. So, with great anticipation, I was off on a three-week trip that would end in Ireland—land of the "thin" places—to discover if the visions of my youth were true. To learn if the glimpse into the afterlife I had shared with Stephen was real. And to find out if I could somehow reach across the barrier separating me from my beloved, into the land where the eternal is now and love never dies.

July 3, 2009

This daytime flight across the Atlantic is a dream! Avoiding the bargain red-eye flight meant using thousands of frequent-flier miles to upgrade to business class; but this is, as they say, the only way to fly! Great food, comfy accommodation in one of those new lie-flat seats, non-intrusive seatmate, on-demand movies, and wonderful service. I could get used to this treatment.

So far the oddest part of the trip has been how often I have found myself wanting to tell Stephen about who and what I've been seeing—family in New York, a revival of *West Side Story* on Broadway, the Guggenheim Museum, Central Park, and friends in Washington, D.C. Of course, every time I think, *I have to call Stephen,* I realize he didn't leave a number where I could reach him. I can't call him, even though it seems like he should still be at home, sitting in his chair in the living room, watching the New York Yankees win another ballgame—right by the phone he always answered when I was traveling for work. But he's not there; and if I call, I'll only hear my own voice on the answering machine at the other end of the line.

If your primary interest when visiting a new place is food, fun, and conversation, you are a tourist, not a pilgrim. Touring was certainly my focus during the July Fourth weekend, which I spent in

Southampton, England, with my dear friend Judi and her adorable
family. It was an absolute whirlwind of sightseeing, excellent meals,
and nonstop conversation.

One thing I remembered from visiting this same part of England
on a theater study tour between my freshman and sophomore years in
college was the generous hospitality of the British. Judi, her husband,
and their two sons did not disappoint. We packed as many adventures
as possible into Saturday and Sunday, visiting Salisbury Cathedral,
Stonehenge, the New Forest, and the seaside at Bournemouth—even
finding some old haunts from my visit there forty years earlier. They
offered to keep me if I wanted to stay permanently, and I was sorely
tempted to accept. However, more adventure beckoned as I made
my way north.

July 6, 2009

I'm on the train from Southampton to Leeds in the center of
England where I will spend two nights with Leslie, the wife of my
colleague Dave who passed away so suddenly two years ago. Leslie
and I have met only once in person, but we've built a solid friendship through the e-mails we have been exchanging since Dave's death.
It's been over two years since he died, so she's ahead of me in some
aspects of the grieving process—although it's not really a race, is it?

We're really looking forward to sharing experiences and insights
about what to do with the next few decades—for ourselves and for
others like us who, at a relatively young age, have already found and
then lost the love of our lives.

The day after I arrived in Leeds, Leslie's friend Sarah joined us for
wine, cheese, and group therapy. Her husband (also named Dave,
but younger, at only forty-five) had died just five months earlier from
colon cancer. The three of us were curious to discover what we might
learn from each other because we are all writers, life coaches, and
professional-development trainers.

Leslie and Sarah had been talking about what sort of counseling
or training is available for "people like us." As Leslie put it: "women

and men who have experienced the dying or death of a beloved partner and who want to be powerful around it, finding a way to be with death that is empowering and also honors the grief and the really crappy parts."

Both of them felt that the support available to them was limited and many of the grief-counseling-type approaches were not getting to the deep places they wanted to explore. They agreed that some self-development programs that focused on taking immediate action in your life were great, but didn't speak directly to the experience of bereavement and were sometimes not appropriate, especially for someone in the early days of grief.

So the question for Sarah, Leslie, and me was: What kind of workshops or training could we develop to help ourselves and others "be" with death and grief and our new lives? How could we move forward with the intention of allowing myriad emotions to wash through us without getting stuck in separation and suffering? Leslie had set up the conversation beautifully in an e-mail she'd sent me in June:

> I was thinking about how for Dave and me our wedding vows created the context of our marriage. We often talked about our commitment to love each other without condition, to stay in integrity with each other, to honor each other as whole and complete, and to choose each other every day. We didn't succeed in doing that every day, and we still drove each other crazy on occasion; but it was all within the context we had created. It was the foundation of our relationship and we kept it in mind (most of the time!) in speaking to each other, especially when were having difficult conversations.
>
> I always felt that Dave was better at that than I was. But the truth is that I created that too, and I can continue to be committed to that for myself—to love myself without condition, to stay in integrity with myself, to honor myself as whole and complete, and to choose to be who I am every day. That's what I got out of being married to Dave.

What Leslie was describing was the essence of a workshop experience we wanted to provide for people who wanted to turn loss into a new approach to personal wholeness, whatever kind of relationship they might have had with the person they were grieving. In a way, our conversation that afternoon was a microcosm of how one of those interactive workshops might look and feel:

We maintained an attitude of inquiry to see what might arise during the conversation. We had no specific agenda for what we should discuss or accomplish. We shared experiences, but we did not spend a lot of time revolving the details of the dying process or its meaning—the why's and why not's of what had happened to us.

We paid attention to how our bodies were reacting and took little breaks for more food and wine and chocolate—which we heartily agreed are an important part of this kind of sharing (in moderation, of course). We allowed ourselves to laugh at how crazy you become in the midst of caregiving or sudden loss, and we cried when something touched us deeply.

We avoided the pitfalls of competitive grieving, which can arise sometimes in groups: "You think you had it bad, just listen to this!" And none of us tried to "fix" or even counsel the others.

We honored both the similarities and the differences in our situations. We agreed that gratitude opens the door for the universe to supply all our needs. We focused on being powerful in our new lives. And we each left the conversation feeling more enthusiastic and more able to do just that.

I came away from our afternoon together with seven pages of notes and a profound appreciation for these two brightly creative women who were so intent on being present with their experience of the "now"—even when it was devastatingly painful. I was especially impressed with their idea that faith and belief are not the same, especially in relation to death and grief.

As Leslie explained it, faith is the perfection of the present moment; belief is whatever story about our experience we accept as true. Faith is liberating because in the "now" we feel the continuity of consciousness—our own and that of our beloved. We may feel pain in the moment, but we do not resist it; and, therefore, we do not suffer.

What gets us into trouble are the stories we believe and repeat to ourselves because they are about the past or the future, not the present. When those stories are about our dead husbands, they too easily focus on separation. We get tangled up in the saga of our aloneness, not in the continuum of life where we are still one. And in that state of separation, we suffer.

Twenty-nine

LOST IN MY STORY

*And my desire to understand became so
intense that even my sleep was disturbed.*

—*The Way of the Pilgrim*

THE NEXT MORNING, Leslie dropped me at the train station, where
I caught the 10:51 to Cumbria and the Lake District in northwest-
ern England. I would have preferred to take the 8:50 a.m. train, but
getting up that early would have been difficult. In addition to our
afternoon with Sarah, Leslie and I had worn ourselves out with a
couple of day trips around Yorkshire, while talking nonstop about
our shared experience of losing brilliantly self-aware husbands.

I was excited to finally reach the rugged land of Wordsworth and
Coleridge that Stephen and I had always wanted to visit. Or at least
I had. He was never crazy about traveling anywhere he couldn't
drive—and there was that uncomfortable business of flying across
the Atlantic Ocean to get there.

July 8, 2009
    I just love England! The scene is picture-perfect as the train
passes soft, green fields demarcated with waist-high hedges or stone

walls made from the ubiquitous gray slate stone that must have totally covered Yorkshire and points north when the country was first inhabited. The English may have used up most of their timber over centuries of building, but they seem to have enough stone to last another millennium.

It took several hours to get from Leeds to Preston, change point for the train to Windermere. I knew I had to take a bus from Windermere to Ambleside, where I had booked two nights at a local bed-and-breakfast; but I had no idea where any of these places were in relation to one another. For some reason, I hadn't bothered to buy a map of England or even pick up a railway schedule—very unlike me. I hadn't needed them until now because in New York and D.C. I was familiar with the local transportation systems; and in England, so far, I had been with friends who knew their way around. This journey to the Lake District was the first time in over ten days that I had been completely on my own in unfamiliar territory.

As the train rambles on toward the homeland of Stephen's favorite poet, the absence of a traveling companion and the realization that he's neither here nor there descend like a dark blanket around me. Are the towns and villages in this part of England actually dingier than what I've seen before, or is it only my perception? Somehow the Lancaster area seems less quaint, harder hit by the economic down-turn. Or am I projecting my feelings onto the landscape?

Outside of Oxenholme, quite near to Windermere, the land opens up. We're in Cumbria now with a lovely lake on the left and some rugged hills off in the distance. Now there are camping parks and, judging by the variety of foreign accents, families on holiday. Many of these people have probably grown up coming to this part of the world every year for retreat from the hubbub of daily life. I'm beginning to see why. Even from the train, the views are spectacular.

Thanks to some kind locals on the bus from Windermere to Ambleside, I managed to find my B&B—one of the more distinctive accommodations in an area overflowing with endlessly quaint places to stay because the owners are beekeepers.

> The Kingswood Bee & Bee is darling. After dragging my suitcase halfway up a steep, curving lane, I found it nestled behind a stone wall, overlooking the narrow, main road that winds through what must be one of the most charming villages on earth. Ambleside is all gray slate, but it's not in the least gloomy. In fact, the stones almost glisten in the dappled sun that slides in and out of damp clouds. And there are flowers everywhere. The gardens here are soft, bright, and luscious. The whole place has been scrubbed and painted. My little ground-floor room used to be a scullery. It includes a tiny bath and a clothes cupboard I have to bend down to access because it's tucked under the stairway to the second floor. Of course, they call it the Harry Potter room.

I had arrived about 2:00 p.m., in plenty of time to hastily unpack and find my way to Grasmere, about three miles away, where Wordsworth's famous home, Dove Cottage, is located. I could have taken a bus, but I wanted to go on foot—to get a feel for where the Wordsworths would have walked and what they might have seen along the way. Both William and his sister, Dorothy, were enthusiastic walkers, and it's still a favored way of getting around here. Ambleside was overflowing with shops that carried hiking boots, backpacks, and walking sticks.

The weather was perfect for my hike—mostly cool but warm enough to work up a serious sweat on the rustic footpath that I managed to lose, then find, then lose again, and find once more as it descended immediately behind the home where Wordsworth wrote his most famous poems.

The view of lakes and hills was glorious along the steep, stone-laden trail called the Coffin Road because they used to carry coffins over these hills from Ambleside for people who were required by local ordinance to be buried in Grasmere—no doubt resulting in a high mortality rate for pallbearers. I had trouble just hauling myself over the path, more like a streambed than a major hiking trail.

I truly felt like a pilgrim now, thrilled at the thought of visiting what was to me a shrine—home of the man whose poems had been a source of inspiration and consolation to Stephen and me. In a way, it was Wordsworth's deep insight "into the life of things" that had drawn me into Stephen's inner world at a time when I was having trouble getting there.

As I walked, absorbing the views the great man himself had once seen and written about, I remembered how Stephen would read Wordsworth's poetry aloud to me. I thought how he would have loved roaming through the rugged Cumbrian hills that had inspired such lines as these from the *Prelude*:

> The rains at length have ceased, the winds are stilled,
> The stars shine brightly between clouds at rest,
> And as a cavern is with darkness filled,
> The vale is by a mighty sound possessed.

Stephen would have relished the hike, although he would have gone more slowly than my hurried pace. Even when you don't get lost, the walk to Grasmere takes more than two hours; so I just barely made it in time for the afternoon's final tour of Dove Cottage.

I paid the entrance fee and entered the simple gate with a sense of reverence and awe. Here was the garden where William had sat lost in thought. Here was where Dorothy had written her *Grasmere Journals* that detailed so much of their daily lives. Here was where William's wife, Mary, and their first couple of children had lived and where a ceaseless stream of visitors had stayed for extended periods of time. The most famous of these overnighters were Samuel Taylor Coleridge and Robert Southey—the other two Lake Poets who were William's friends, collaborators, and sometime competitors.

But everything was so small and dim. The cottage had been a tavern before it was home to a poet laureate, and it was low and dark—not at all as I had expected. I was shocked that I could detect no feeling of the Wordsworth family here. It seemed to have been long ago siphoned off by thousands of tourists clomping through, led by pleasant tour guides who could recite a bit of "Daffodils" but who conveyed none of Wordsworth's passionate Romanticism.

There was nothing here of the spiritual insights he had gleaned while exploring the lakes and crags that were home and inspiration to his soul, as in these lines from one of Stephen's favorite poems, *Lines Written a Few Miles above Tintern Abbey*:

> Five years have passed; five summers, with the length
> Of five long winters! and again I hear
> These waters, rolling from their mountain-springs
> With a soft inland murmur.—Once again
> Do I behold these steep and lofty cliffs,
> Which on a wild secluded scene impress
> Thoughts of more deep seclusion; and connect
> The landscape with the quiet of the sky.

There was no visionary energy here that I could feel. In fact, I found the whole collection of small slate buildings around Dove Cottage to be quite lifeless. Most everything was closed when I came out after the tour—even the shops in Grasmere Village, just a short walk across the stream.

Sadly disappointed, I wandered through Grasmere until I found a restaurant serving dinner. There were only a few tables filled, and the whole place felt deserted. Nevertheless, the setting was pretty; and I noticed the Wordsworth graves in the churchyard across the way. I decided to pay my respects after dinner and then walk home—along the lakeside road this time. There was nothing to rush back for; in this northern latitude it was still hours before sunset.

Not only could I not feel the fire of Wordsworth, I could not feel Stephen. It was if I had been abandoned in a lonely universe with only distant memories to keep me company. Somehow I had expected to be uplifted to an exalted state of awareness just from being in the Lake District—as if merely landing in the place would confer spiritual insight.

Stephen and I had always agreed that Wordsworth's visions

were probably more a result of his own predisposition to such experiences than of some intrinsic character of the landscape itself. While the grandeur of nature can inspire feelings of transcendent oneness, the seed of consciousness must first exist in the individual mind and heart.

And yet, I couldn't help looking for the spirit of Wordsworth in the place that had been his home. I suppose it was nostalgia for the way things used to be that made me want to visit here in the first place. And, of course, they never are the way they used to be; things are only what they are today.

July 9, 2009

Before he died, Stephen told me not to try to find him—that he would not be hanging around—and I believed him. Yet, in the days immediately following his transition and in many moments since (including the Christmas visitation-dream), I have wondered if perhaps he was mistaken. Perhaps he was surprised and then delighted to discover he could actually commune with me occasionally while continuing his studies in the universities of the Spirit—but I could never be absolutely certain. And now that I feel so utterly alone, it seems clear he was right the first time. Any "presence" I may have felt has probably just been wishful thinking on my part.

This trip is convincing me I don't like traveling solo. I feel desperately alone and missing Stephen so acutely I just want to go home. I've been out for two weeks, which is too long. I was fine as long as I was visiting people, but this singular sightseeing is lonely. The fact that my first pilgrimage visit has left me utterly bereft of any deep spiritual encounter just makes the whole experience worse.

Today I felt quite ill, probably because yesterday I walked so vigorously from Ambleside to Grasmere and back. Only the prospect of missing a yummy breakfast this morning got me up and dressed.

Later I took a bus to the village of Keswick—crowded and too commercial—and then an hour's boat ride on the Derwentwater, which is truly as beautiful as the guidebooks had promised. But Stephen wasn't there to put his arm around me as we sped across the lake, gazing at the expansive views, or to suggest that we hop off at one of the many piers where hikers then climb the hills called the Catbells or continue on around the shore on foot. He was always the great initiator of side trips. Left on my own, I just stayed on the boat, made the loop around the lake, wandered through an outdoor street market in Keswick, and took the bus back to Ambleside. I am sad and ready to end the trip now.

Actually, there had been a chance that my trip would be cut short. Michael and Andrea—our hosts at Avelin, the retreat center in Ireland—had been in a terrible car accident over the July Fourth weekend. Andrea was slightly bruised, but Michael was in bed with a serious back injury. There had been a flurry of e-mails back and forth as they tried to locate members of our little group, some of whom were traveling in France, apparently without Internet access. I was actually hoping we could just call it off, but alternate arrangements were made. This meant that the next morning I would continue on to Dublin, where I had booked a free night at the five-star Conrad Hilton, followed by five days at Avelin for our pilgrimage into Celtic spirituality.

July 10, 2009

I'm waiting for my flight to Dublin at the ridiculously small Blackpool International Airport, and I'm not in very good shape. Last night I gave up on sightseeing. I ate some tasty, yet truly greasy, fish-n-chips and then packed my bags while watching a DVD of the movie *Miss Potter*, which showed many of the Lake District sites I've missed by not being here longer. I woke up this morning with a feeling of abject despair after an oddly disturbing dream about Stephen— something about my driving him off. He was really upset with me, and I couldn't seem to reach him. The separation was excruciating.

Last night, the B&B owner volunteered to take me to the train in Windermere after breakfast; however, I was up very early this morning with a strong prompting to leave immediately. I have learned to obey those urgings, so I left a note apologizing for being rude and slipped off to catch an earlier train.

It's a good thing I did. I had in mind that my plane departure time was 1:00 p.m., but that is actually the Dublin *arrival* time. Somebody was looking out for me there. Last night I tried to book my train ticket online, but the reservation wouldn't go through. Again—a good thing because I would have taken the wrong train and ended up miles from the Blackpool Airport. As it is, I'm here in plenty of time—sadly, feeling more like a refugee than a pilgrim.

Thirty

DARK NIGHTS OF EIRE

*There is a land of the living
and a land of the dead,
and the bridge is love.*

—Thornton Wilder

EVERY PILGRIMAGE BEGINS with a call in the heart that says:

Follow me. Leave the comfort of your home and venture with me into Spirit's depths. The destination is vague. There are no maps or obvious markers. Oh, there are signs, if you can see them, but you will not find them if you're looking with material eyes, and they lead only to the next bend in the road. So will you come? If you will, treasure awaits. So come, and be glad in the jouney.

Many are called to pilgrimage; few can hear—and even fewer answer. Yet, when the answer is given—"Yes, I'll come"—it is as if a little bell rings in the farthest reaches of heaven. And when the bell sounds, it starts up a cosmic engine, or perhaps a great clock—with giant wheels, and cogs, and gears, and spinners—all working according to the timeless principles of pilgrimage that govern each phase of the seeker's journey. Like countless travelers over the centuries, we walk our own path according to these principles, though we cannot see the pattern until the journey is done.

Along the way, there are hardships, challenges, and disappointments—all designed to transfigure the hard places of separation within us. We can try to delay the process, as I did by visiting lots of friends and tourist sites before I got to Ireland. Eventually, however, we can no longer hold back the tide of self-transformation that we set in motion the day we said, "Yes, I think I'll go on a pilgrimage."

It is as if, in stepping out into the unknown, we journey to the center of our own being where, even if we are not grieving the actual loss of a loved one, the cleansing fires of grief ignite. Before we can reap the insight that often follows pilgrimage, we must first leave something behind, allowing outworn modes of thought and feeling to be seared in the flames of loss. And in the process, we suffer.

July 10, 2009

I'm here in Dublin, not sure what I feel about the whole "pilgrimage" idea. I couldn't find my hotel because the airport bus driver missed the turn and let me off on a corner instead, saying, "Oh, it's just down the street and over a bit to the left." Of course, I couldn't see it, even when I was practically in front of the building.

Fortunately, the hotel bellman just happened to be chatting with some cabbies whom I asked for directions. He immediately took my bag and led me to the front desk, announcing me to the clerk as if I were a visiting dignitary rather than a weary American here for a free night on hotel award points. I have enjoyed a luxurious hot bath and am now eating a lovely dinner that includes a free glass of wine, which I definitely need. The hotel is across the street from St. Stephen's Green, an inviting patch of color in an otherwise gray city that I may or may not explore tomorrow. I mostly just want to rest.

July 11, 2009

So far it seems as if my journey has been mostly outward—at least proving that I can navigate all manner of transportation modes, extend myself to reconnect with family and friends, and venture somewhat courageously to visit new places.

Now it is time for another try at going within. The Dove Cottage visit was a failure in that regard—perhaps from too many expectations. So what will I find now that I am finally in Ireland? Will I be able to appreciate Dublin without a traveling companion who enjoys the same things I do? I am forcing myself to get out into the city, even though sitting here at breakfast I feel perfectly miserable, desperately alone, and in disbelief that Stephen could be gone.

On one hand, I feel like I am carrying him in my heart, perhaps even at my side, imagining what he would like or dislike along the way. Then I feel how difficult it is for me to function without him. I get so confused. It's a good thing that angels seem to be watching out for me because without them I would not be doing well in the concrete world—successfully completed bus journeys notwithstanding. Stephen's mastery of the physical had been sufficient for both of us, and I'm not there yet.

I spent the morning walking around the streets of Dublin close to my hotel. St. Stephen's Green provided a scenic thoroughfare to Grafton Street and on to Trinity College where I managed a quick entry to see the famous illuminated New Testament text known as the Book of Kells. Miraculously, it has been preserved since the Middle Ages.

Even early in the morning, the scene outside presents a long queue of tourists waiting to squish through the jammed museum shop that leads to the exhibit. But inside, the actual display is beautifully arranged with videos demonstrating how the intricate designs were painstakingly created on calfskin vellum that took weeks to prepare, even before the first inked letters could be applied. I was deeply moved to see pages of the actual volumes that are over one thousand years old and that remain a profound testimony to what people will create out of sheer devotion and determination.

Perhaps even more breathtaking was exiting the museum through the Long Room of Trinity College Library. I was not prepared for the sight of this enormous room with shelves of ancient books rising two stories to the vaulted, barrel-shaped ceiling. The musty smell of old paper and leather bindings was intoxicating, and I envied the students who were actually allowed in the stacks.

St. Patrick's Cathedral was likewise inspiring. I must have had at least one pleasant embodiment as a medieval nun because, whenever I entered one of theses old gothic churches—as I had also recently done at Salisbury Cathedral—I got the feeling of being at home. There was something so familiar about the stonework, the altars, the rows of candles, and the statues of saints. Today I was fortunate to hear a free concert of ancient sacred music presented by a girls' choir from Norwich. The experience was sublime; I was once more a hopeful pilgrim.

So, Saturday was an inspirational day after all. After my Dublin walking tour, I still had time for a late lunch back at the hotel before I had to catch my bus for Michael and Andrea's retreat house, where I finally settled in.

But getting there was a bit of a nightmare. John, my seventy-year-old psychologist friend from Denver who was the sponsor of this pilgrimage, had said the bus from Dublin went right past Avelin. *That should be easy enough to find,* I thought. This is true—*if* your cell phone works so you can call ahead, which mine didn't; *if* the driver knows where or what Avelin is, which this one didn't; and *if* you are sitting on the right side of the bus so you can see the retreat house as the bus streaks by it, which I wasn't. So, I rode all the way to the end of the line, to the little village of Ballymore Eustis, without seeing Avelin or having any idea how to find it.

"I'll be here for twenty minutes, if you want a ride back," said the bus driver as she went off to the market for a snack. Feeling more and more like a displaced person, I set off with my bags to the first business that looked clean and inviting. Turns out it was an off-track betting place where a couple of older men (actually they were probably my age—when did that get to be older?) were watching horse races on television, and a woman behind the counter said she had no idea where I was going.

Fortunately, a lovely Irishman with sparkling blue eyes appeared behind me. He looked like a cousin of the Dublin bellman and was equally helpful. "I know exactly where you're going," he said. "Now let's go find your bus driver so I can give her directions." He helped me back on the bus and confidently explained to the driver, "Avelin's back down the road to Dublin. Go past the football field, down the hill, and just past Angler's Rest where you can pull over."

None of these residences have street numbers and the road is so narrow there really isn't room for the bus to pull over to make unscheduled stops. But sure enough, we followed my blue-eyed savior's directions and there it was—marked with the most discreet and undetectable of signs.

I knocked on the front door and there was my dear friend John. He had cut short his vacation in France to run the Celtic retreat in Michael and Andrea's stead. Michael, a minister/psychologist like John, was usually the pilgrimage guide as well as host, but his accident had rendered him incapable of doing either.

"Come in!" John beamed. Then his face changed from joy to concern at my bedraggled appearance. I must have looked like someone who has given up on life, which was certainly how I felt at that moment. Every logistical or physical challenge seemed to absolutely crush my energy and resolve.

However, the house was lovely, and two ladies who had already arrived for our retreat were sweetly comforting; so I tried to calm down and be grateful. Sipping a welcome cup of tea, John and I talked about the expectations we bring to pilgrimage.

"I didn't know it was going to hurt," I said, trying to explain why I was getting so weepy. "I've been open to everything but the pain of missing Stephen, of him not being with me in all these places he would have loved."

"I think you miss Stephen so bad because he is actually so near, not because he is so far away," said John. "You sense him, but you can't touch him. When you walked into the house, my first impression was that he was right there with you. I think you should go to bed early, write some poetry, do some journaling, and see what comes up for you that way."

Oh, how I wanted to believe John. I excused myself and went to my little room at the end of the hall. I was sobbing again as I closed the door and took up my journal. Almost immediately a poem formed—and then, amazingly, a dialogue.

The Pain of Pilgrimage

> There are things I will never do again
> Songs I will never sing
> Hands I will never touch
> Lips I will never kiss
> Arms that will never hold me
> And a heart that has long since
> > ceased to beat
> > in my ear from the
> > breast that will never
> > again cradle me in its warmth.
> I must forge a new path—
> A path I do not want
> A path I cannot or will not see
> > because it leads away
> > from all I hold most dear—
> > except, of course, from God.

Did I have to come to Ireland to cry all of my tears? To visit the scenes of our partings? Or did I have to come to where the veil is thinnest so you could reach through? Oh, speak to me, my darling—so I may know it's you. Help me on my way. Crack my heart wide open so I may write from that open space where love would flow out.

I expected deep spiritual encounter and a way to frame my writing. I did not know it would hurt to find it. Am I already past the end of our story? No. I'm still in the midst of it because every night I go to bed alone. And every day I wake up slightly more alone than I was the day before because I am that much farther away from the day you died.

But no, he says, as I write. *You only think you are. Be patient, my darling, and walk on. I did not know you would suffer so,* he says. *Who could have known how many tears would fall and yet will come before we're joined once more? Have faith, my love. Can you feel me here?*

No, I say. I want to, but I don't. I can sense you in my aura, around my head, in my mind. No, wait, I do feel something. (Do I really feel myself being embraced—or am I just imagining that I do because I want to so badly?)

All I want to do is weep from the bottom of my soul. Because somehow I thought when I found you again this time it would be forever—but it wasn't. Time and again I've lost you, then found you, thinking, *Surely not again*—and then you die. Sometimes all too soon; sometimes after many years. But it's always the same—you die!

This time was different. This time you were more able to teach me. More able to get me ready—although just barely. This time you held on until you knew I understood what you were trying to teach me. This time I can break the cycle of getting lost without you. This time I can live to tell the tale of how you laid down your life for me so I could also find the Divine. Is this a pact we made in heaven—a drama we would play out? To prove to me that love truly is eternal and to show others that death is just an interval on the soul's great pilgrimage?

So speak to me, my darling. And show me how to love God more than I love you. Help me open my heart. Help me dive into the pain and find there bliss and holiness and your own sweet self—my partner forever. I am crying down the centuries tonight. Oh, may these tears cleanse a thousand years of heartache so that joy may come again.

Pay attention to when you feel the tingle of holiness, he says. *That will be the sign I am near—and at peace. Remember how I calmed you down. That is the peace of my presence and yours. Your job is to learn to do that on demand, to still yourself, and just "be" in the sacredness of silence. You are making it too hard. Be gentle as you reach for the secret places of your soul.*

July 12, 2009

I slept soundly last night but awoke this morning remembering a strange dream: I'm off rushing around, doing "outside" kinds of things—totally separated from Stephen—although this time I am actually able to get him on the phone. We apologize to each other. I tell him he is the love of my life and that I cannot bear to be apart from him. He agrees and we are instantly back together. Waking, I remembered his eyes and feeling him next to me. I always feel him to the right of me in these dreams, holding me, present in my aura.

I feel him there right now. Can I learn to carry his presence? I don't know how I can endure these years of separation unless I can learn to go deeply within and reach across the divide that separates us. It is so hard not to be unspeakably sad. So much of the time I just want to die. Every month seems to get harder. I want Stephen back and that's all I want. I long for him. I am in despair that I can't get to him. I want to go home and I want to be with Stephen. That's it. Everything else is just pretend.

Thirty-one

THE ENCOUNTER

In a dead wall a new window opens,
in dense darkness a path starts to glimmer,
and into a broken heart healing falls like morning dew.

—John O'Donohue

IT IS NO EXAGGERATION TO SAY I was not fit for human consumption as the retreat got underway. I was tired and grumpy, and—although I tried hard not to show it—I found my fellow pilgrims a bit intrusive. I knew I needed people, but I didn't want to be around them.

I began to think that Stephen and I had switched roles—which I suppose happens to people who have been married a long time. He was an introvert, never comfortable around groups of people. With me, he had become more open to relationships; in some ways— especially as he got sicker—I had become less so. He had learned to flow and I had learned boundaries. Unfortunately, when he died, he took the relationship with him, leaving me stuck with too many psychological fences.

I was increasingly protective of my space, lest I be overwhelmed by other people's energy—something that had always been a problem for me when fatigued. Now, here in Ireland, on pilgrimage—which is best done with an intention of serene attention and openness to whatever may arise along the way—I felt broken and brittle, sadly unwilling or unable to create new relationships.

I felt compelled to keep moving. I rushed about from place to place, unable to be still long enough for the gentle energy of Ireland to reach me. I was like a wounded animal that runs from the very people who want to heal it, afraid their touch will only cause more pain.

July 12, 2009—evening

Today was a weird day. The problem is that, except for John, I do not know the other people on the retreat and I feel that the six of us are not all on the same wavelength. I guess I had expected everybody in the group to be interested in the same kind of philosophical conversations John and I have during the lunches we share every few months, but their interests seem to be more social. I know this is my problem, not theirs; I just don't know how to fix it. I am trying to be responsive, but so far, this is not the transformative experience I was expecting.

I have read that the early Celts looked upon wells and natural springs as openings into the body of the goddess Brigid, who is the personification of the land of Ireland. I have always interpreted this belief symbolically—as a way of getting in touch with the sensuality and intuition that are aspects of the Divine Feminine. But now I find myself with people who seem to interpret the belief literally, walking in reverent silence through an overgrown field as if going to see a holy relic rather than a spring that flows quietly out of the ground.

These are good people, but I feel out of step with them and very uncomfortable with the prospect of spending five days riding around in the tiny six-seater sedan we've crammed into, waiting for water to speak. At the well, I did my best to enter into the experience that was clearly moving to them; but after standing stock-still for over twenty minutes, trying to calm my agitated mind and just "feel something!" from the land, to me, it was still just rocks and water.

I do admit that a cup of water from the little grassy spring felt alive when it was poured into my hands before we left the site. Yet the question remains: Was the water itself holy, had it absorbed the vibration of the collective prayers of the pilgrims who viewed it as sacred, or was my mind simply primed to receive a blessing? I still don't know for sure.

Now that we have returned to Avelin this evening, one of the men suggested something we could think about for our next excursion: "Where does the stream of the sacred flow out of you into the world?" Now, this was more like what I had expected from the group; and yet, my rather abrupt response was, "Words—and I need silence to contact my own stream."

For right now, achieving silence means I should remain at the retreat house tomorrow morning rather than going out on another day trip, especially one that promises to be very long. I'm a bit torn about missing some of the archeological sites because everyone says these ruins really "speak" to them. But, frankly, I doubt I will hear a thing except my own critical thoughts.

Giving myself permission to stay home on Monday was a relief, but, as it turned out, not a workable solution, because Michael and Andrea needed the house to themselves. So I pulled myself together and put on a happy attitude, trying to act as if I was having a good time. As we drove along, I did actually begin to relax and bond with my fellow pilgrims (who were trying so hard to be kind to me), and the six of us thoroughly enjoyed the ancient sites of New Grange, Slane, and Tara—even though we saw the last two in a blowing rain. I now fully understood how people used to catch a sudden chill and die in this climate. We were damp to the bone when we got back to Avelin.

The next day, our little group drove to Kildare as part of our pilgrimage to the sites of Ireland's three great saints: Patrick, Kevin, and Brigid, who embodied both the pre-Christian and the Christian Celtic traditions. Our first stop was a neat modern condo that serves as the home and welcome center for the Brigidine Sisters, who are an official restoration of the fifth-century Catholic Order of St. Brigid of

Kildare. They also hold great reverence for Brigid the goddess, who is often shown bringing a rainbow light to ancient Ireland, in this case beautifully rendered in a large fabric hanging on a prominent wall of their center. They receive pilgrims from all over the world, so Sister Mary Minehan received us warmly.

Gathered with my fellow travelers around a large candle in the center of her reception room, I instantly felt my spine tingle with energy as she lit the flame and began her invocation to St. Brigid. *Oh, my God,* I declared to myself, *this woman is the real spiritual deal I've been looking for ever since I left home.*

For over two hours we experienced what I would call "darshan," a Hindu term for receiving a blessing from being in the presence of a deity, revered person, or sacred object. Spiritual teachers may consciously convey such a blessing to their followers during a formal audience or informal presentation. My sense of Sister Mary was that she did so unconsciously.

This unassuming Catholic nun, who prayed with the voice of divine realization, was absolutely grounded in practicality; and when she fixed her gaze upon us, she looked straight into our hearts, filling them with pure loving-kindness. She knew we were there as pilgrims and so she spoke to us of that ancient practice.

"As a pilgrim, you must know your roots—where you have come from," Sister Mary began. "You must be aware of where you are now—in this moment, in this place. And then you must be able to say where you are going. You cannot change what's over; you must become who you are to build a new life of beauty and holiness within you." She was very firm on this point.

"A powerful way to do so is to walk in the footsteps of the formidable presence of the Divine Feminine in the person of St. Brigid of Kildare," she went on. "Her mission was and is to help people 'bridge it'"—Sister Mary laughed at her own joke—"to literally bridge the gap between the mundane and the Divine.

"Billions of years ago we were all dreamed into existence as part of the whole of creation. We are all of the same sap, and it is the earth that will bring us together in this new millennium. I believe the resurgence of interest in Celtic spirituality is because it awakens the soul from the ground of being where it slumbers."

Sister Mary had been a great soul friend to John O'Donohue, the former Catholic priest and popular author, poet, and Celtic wise man who had died suddenly on January 3, 2008, two days after his fifty-second birthday. The next thing she said flew like an arrow into my heart.

"When our loved ones die, they do not go away; we just can't see them any more," she said. "I feel John with me always." Then she spoke of his humility and brilliant use of simple language. "He was a genius and a great healer," she said with obvious tenderness. "He would ask my opinion, even though I felt like a worm next to a giant. He had a way of hearing the heartbeat of the Divine in every person who crossed his path and he was always in tune with what he called 'the music of what's happening' in the present moment."

As our visit wound to a close, my companions thanked Sister Mary and went back to the car with mementos of jewelry and candles the Brigidine Sisters sell to raise money for the pilgrimage center they are planning to build on the outskirts of Kildare. I hung back for a final word with this incredible woman.

"I just want to tell you how much it meant for me to meet you today," I said, with tears brimming in my eyes. "I lost my husband last October and he was my *anam ċara*."

"Then, of course, your heart is fractured, isn't it?" Sister Mary said, looking at me with immeasurable tenderness.

"Yes. And it's almost more than I can bear."

"But he's not gone, you know," she smiled. "He's right here." Pulling a copy of *Benedictus* from her shelf, she said, "Let me read you the blessing John O'Donohue wrote 'On the Death of the Beloved.'" She read several passages, ending with an invitation to the departed to be with us until we meet again in a place where we will never be separated or alone.[21]

It was all I could do not to dissolve on the spot. Sister Mary steadied her gaze into mine. "You're strong," she said, taking both my hands in hers. "I feel your strength. You can do this. But you know you cannot walk around your grief; you must walk through it."

"I know," I said through my tears, accepting in my heart that the pain of being separated from Stephen might never really go away. "And I will do it. Thank you for everything."

We smiled deeply at each other. Sister Mary enfolded me in her arms; and, with the simplicity of a hug, she took away my pain.

"I thought you were going to stay!" exclaimed one of my fellow pilgrims when I finally returned to the car. She said that while sitting next to me during our conference with Sister Mary, she had actually felt my heart leap in response to Mary's request for younger sisters to join them in carrying the light of Brigid to the world.[22] Of course, I wasn't going to suddenly become a Catholic nun; but I had felt the flame of the Divine Feminine surge within me at that moment.

"I think I just had a healing," I said rather weakly to the group. I was dazed, stunned, even a little wobbly in the knees at the sudden absence of the pain that had so nearly crippled me for days.

"Do you want to say anything about it?" asked John.

"Not right now," I said. "I have to think about this a while." Throughout the rest of the day, as we explored Kildare and other sites having to do with Brigid the goddess and the saint, inspirations came to me—impressing themselves into my consciousness, resting with a gentle peace until I could write them down in my journal.

July 14, 2009, evening

So what is the lesson of today? On my own, I would have fully embraced the idea that Stephen is just on the other side of the veil between life and the afterlife; but he believed he would be going on, not hanging around. So I have been conflicted about entertaining the possibility that he could be right here with me.

Nobody knows until they get to the Other Side exactly what they will find or what they will be able to do. So he must have been surprised at his ability to reach me—and my pushing him away must have caused him pain. We don't often think of the departed as suffering, but I think they do. This trip has been agonizing (probably for both of us) because I have been concentrating on Stephen's absence, not his presence.

Has he been with me all the time but I haven't been letting him through? My heart burns at that notion—and I suddenly get an image of Stephen reaching across the veil of time and space, which had thinned during my conversation with Sister Mary and may not even exist in her awareness. It is as if my willingness to bear the pain of separation, together with Sister Mary's recognition of Stephen's presence, somehow allowed us to reconnect through her. However it happened, I am definitely not the same person as the gloomy one who walked into an unassuming condo in the village of Kildare this morning.

So where shall we go tomorrow, my dear, on our last day in Ireland? It's time to move from pain to joy—to be in that space that will encourage me to love others as the Divine loves them. To be committed to the path as you were and as Sister Mary so clearly demonstrates by simply being her authentic self. The past few days have been the final dark night of grief—the valley of the shadow of loss I had to cross before I could start "Brigiding" the gap between the visible and the invisible. Now my heart soars in delight—which, according to my friend John, is the Aramaic meaning of the word *will*.

July 15, 2009

Today is exactly nine months since Stephen died—and the entire day has felt like a rebirth celebration. This was the first brilliantly sunny weather we have had on our tour, and it was perfect for our excursion to Glendalough, the site of St. Kevin's seventh-century dual monastery and community. The group marveled at how happy I seem. Indeed I am because I feel Stephen with me, almost as if I have become a combined being: Cheryl-plus-Stephen—with one whole person living in the material world and another whole person living in the ethereal. Separate no more.

The countryside seemed especially vibrant as we zipped down the narrow, grass-lined roads, over the heather-strewn mountains of the

Wicklow Gap where the movie *Braveheart* was filmed, past the ever-present fields of sheep, and along the lakes and streams that feed into the lush valley that has been a holy place for over fourteen hundred years. I can't say the graveyards and ruined chapel buildings particularly spoke to me, but on this day I didn't mind. The archeologist in me found them intriguing, and the setting was beautiful.

After shopping for sweaters and enjoying an especially well-prepared lunch at a local hotel, we headed back to Avelin with a drive over the Sally Gap in the Wicklow Mountains. Here the landscape looked like Colorado, with high tundra, pine forests, and wide-open valleys. It was raining, but brilliant sun intermittently broke through the clouds.

"I'll bet we see a rainbow," I predicted confidently; although my hope began to fade as we drove on. Then, suddenly, just over a rise that offered an expansive view of mountains and valleys in the distance, there was a rainbow. Not a vibrant spectrum such as we see in the Rocky Mountains, but a softer, wider arc that was actually three rainbows side by side, filling the entire valley with color and light.

> There are so many meanings attached to rainbows: My friend Cindy says a rainbow is God's promise of his threefold presence with us. Tibetan Bardo tradition encourages departing souls to aim for the rainbow light on their way to higher spheres. My spiritual teacher used the symbol of a circular rainbow to represent our treasures of past loving words and deeds that are stored in heaven. And St. Brigid is pictured as bringing a rainbow light to Ireland.
>
> Today the rainbow felt to me like a sign from Stephen that we have both been healed of the pain of separation. That we are growing into our new relationship—on opposite sides of the veil, but very present, one with the other. And that we will never, ever lose each other again.

Thirty-two

THE RETURN

The heart that has truly loved never forgets.

—Thomas Moore

August 20, 2009

Today I had lunch at an outdoor café with my friend Pat, who is a talented painter of portraits and southwestern landscapes as well as a gifted psychologist. Several years ago, she lost her husband and soul mate, Ted. They had worked together for over twenty years as group facilitators and trainers. Her experience and counsel have been invaluable to me in my own journey with loss.

As we enjoyed the warm summer breeze that already carries a slight tinge of autumn crispness in the air, I told her about my trip to Ireland and my sudden decision to go back to school for a master's degree in psychology—something I have wanted to do ever since Stephen and I left Montana almost twelve years ago. Pat is glad to hear that I'm moving on, but she is concerned with my pace.

"I'm glad to hear you really grieved," she said. "I was afraid you were too 'okay' too soon. It's been six years since Ted's been gone, but last spring I found another new layer of grief and understanding. It's really a process that never quite finishes."

I can understand her concern. As a psychologist, she is very familiar with Elisabeth Kübler-Ross's five steps of facing death: denial, anger, bargaining, depression, and acceptance. She knows that Stephen and I went through our own experience with these stages as he was dying, but she wants to be sure I understand that they do come up again for the survivor who is dealing with the loss.

Pat is okay with my not getting angry and she understands that sometimes it's still hard for me to believe that Stephen is really gone. Still, she doesn't think it's possible or healthy to get to the acceptance stage as quickly as I appear to have done.

Of course, she wasn't with me for the meltdown in February over re-homing Bentley or the nights I've cried myself to sleep after soaking boxes of tissues with tsunamis of tears. I'm not big on public blubbering, but I've definitely had my days. Grief has its own timetable and its own way of unfolding, and that process is different for each of us.

In some ways, I think my career as a professional-development trainer may have been a detriment to really "working my grief," as Leslie's friend Sarah put it, because, when I talk with others about losing Stephen, it has been too easy for me to slip into trainer mode—telling them stories with the idea of helping *them* process *their* feelings about my situation. This type of interaction puts me at a bit of a distance from my most painful feelings and more in touch with those of the person I'm talking to. Plus, I'm always concerned about not burdening others with too much sadness. I haven't wanted my friends to pull away because I'm such a drag to be around.

So I can see Pat's point. I know I am nowhere near to being finished with grief; but after going through the abject despair I experienced in Ireland, I also know I'm in a much healthier place today than I was before I embarked on a pilgrimage.

My experience tells me that certain levels of grief simply must be experienced in all their awfulness if we are to move on to whatever life holds for us in the future. What I did not realize when setting out on my three-week adventure in late June is that, when you identify any portion of your journey as a spiritual pilgrimage (which was the point of the Ireland visit), the entire journey becomes a pilgrimage— even if you think you're only playing tourist along the way.

In a way, life itself is a pilgrimage of self-discovery that begins as soon as we leave the womb's cozy comfort. Celtic spirituality expert Edward Sellner has developed a one-day pilgrimage model that lets us experience some of the practice's transformative power without going far away.[23] However, true pilgrimage conveys the sense of mystery—even danger—that only happens when we find ourselves alone in the numinous world of the Unknown.

In that unfamiliar setting, we enter into a relationship of co-creation with the Divine. Our willingness to be transformed allows Spirit to dissolve old patterns of thought and feeling we have brought along as so much excess baggage. And in releasing those patterns, we discover new levels of insight and finer communion with higher realms of awareness that elude us in the concrete environment of our daily lives.

I think this is another reason why travel is so much a part of pilgrimage. New patterns are hard to accept when we're surrounded with the old ones. Creativity is influenced by environment. And, even though it's spiritual inspiration we are seeking, finding and deeply connecting with it often happens through a sensual interaction with elemental forces of earth, air, water, and fire.

In my case, pilgrimage was literally burning me up. Almost as soon as I arrived in the Lake District, I started waking up in a pool of sweat with my face burning. This heat was not the same as menopausal night sweats (with which I am well acquainted). It felt like sunburn, but it was coming from the inside. It got so bad in Ireland that I gave up wearing makeup because I had to keep slathering on moisturizing cream, which dried up as soon as I put it on. I might have expected such facial desiccation in the high-desert climate of Colorado, but not in the pervasive dampness of England and Ireland.

"This feels karmic," I wrote in my journal—as if ancient memories were being torched while I slept and useless ideas consumed in a spiritual fire that was also mental, emotional, and physical. Despite the healing I had received at Sister Mary's and the incredible closeness I now felt with Stephen, it was not until days after my return home that the interior fire completely subsided.

Dream expert Robert Moss says he interprets dreams literally and daily life metaphorically.[24] I'm not sure I entirely agree with him; but while on pilgrimage, many of the daily steps you take do feel metaphorical—especially the final step that returns you to the "real world," as I found on my last day in Ireland.

Before our little band of seekers left Glendalough on that gloriously sunny day in July, I found a labyrinth carved into the lawn at the visitors' center. As others in my group gathered one by one from their rambles around St. Kevin's valley, I slowly entered the path designed to resemble a huge tree, thinking about the amazing journey I had been on, feeling that walking this labyrinth was indeed a metaphor for my pilgrimage. Reflecting on the experience that day, I wrote a final journal entry in Ireland:

> You walk a circuitous route that doubles back on itself—that may even become tedious, as the goal often appears to recede from sight. Then, almost by surprise, you are in the calm center and from that vantage point the pilgrim's path looks easy, making you wonder why it took you so long to find your way to the middle point of insight and inspiration.
>
> You rest a while in peace. You may want to stay there forever; but then you must return, winding your way out by the same way you came in, because all pilgrimages must end. You must return to the life you left behind, now in a different guise. When you reach the outside, you breathe a silent prayer of gratitude and then rejoice—for you are no longer who or what you were. Your transformed life begins anew. It is a blessed feeling.

Thirty-three

A GIFT OF PEACE

The deeper that sorrow carves into your being,
the more joy you can contain.

—Kahlil Gibran

ABOUT A YEAR BEFORE STEPHEN DIED, a longtime friend who was teaching a computer course in Denver came over to our house for dinner. "Your home feels so peaceful," he remarked, perceiving at once our strongest intention: to be at peace with our lives and our love, and to let nothing—not even cancer—intrude upon that state of being.

Stephen's meditation practice had made him a master of equanimity and I did my best to follow his lead. Since his death, I have discovered that entering fully into the grieving process has brought me a profound sense of peace about my life and how I can "be" with that life until the end of my days. We each have our own way to peace; the point is to find it.

I think one reason we may fall apart in the face of great loss—getting angry, taking up alcohol or drugs, or immediately looking for another partner—is that, in this modern world, we have never been taught how to experience authentic grief. We (and others) want our mourning to be tidy, polite, and over in a day or two so we can get on with our busy, outwardly focused lives. We are afraid of grief's primitive rawness that can completely overwhelm us with its own agenda.

One day soon, I hope our society will return to an acceptance of death as a natural part of life. Then perhaps grief counseling will focus not only on alleviating our pain but also on teaching us how to dive into the absolute depths of it—even making friends with our sorrow as the Celts did—sitting with it, asking what it wants to teach us.

Even more than their irrepressible joy in life, a rich legacy the Celts have bequeathed us is their passionate embrace of loss as a bridge to the invisible world. They made a great ritual of grief. In some villages, local women still keen the dead with a haunting, mournful sound that is perhaps meant to plunge all those present into the rich melody of loss. And then the wake calls friends and family to a circle of love and remembrance that weaves together laughter and tears—another opening to the holy sorrow of the soul.

This is a poetry we've lost in our modern lives and a comfort that escapes us when facing death. This is what I went to Ireland to find—a return to the deep rhythm of my soul, a love for the wild, free shelters of my heart. And the experience of living in the thin places of my spirit where the brush of an angel's wing is not uncommon.

Death carries the poetry of the unseen—the darkness, not only of grief and loss, but also of life's most profound mystery. Grief unlocks the song of the soul in great waves of longing. We cry for the lost touch, the warmth of a body lying next to us, the comfort of the smile or soft word. But if we follow grief down the gaping hole it has bored through the heart, winding down and down as it spirals into unknown caverns of being, we may find there, not pain, but a love of unspeakable tenderness and a peace that affirms we are not alone.

This is the profound longing of the soul for its Creator. And here is a mystery safeguarded by the great mystics: There is a price for such intimacy, for we must spend all of our tears. To become one with the peace-commanding presence of Spirit we must be willing to plumb the depths of our aloneness. Something of our brittle former self must die in the funeral pyre of our grief if we are to guide our lives forward in the way our loved ones would have us go. For only in profound loss is the heart free to experience the agony of physical separation that leads to the ultimate bliss of spiritual union.

If death is the doorway to heaven for the departed, then perhaps grief is the portal for those who remain. We tend to think that the ones who die first take the better part because they go home to a world of light and love, while we who cherished them must abide to suffer their absence. But I am beginning to see it is also a blessing to grieve, because the soul-wrenching pain, which accompanies the loss of innocence that deep grieving causes, leaves in its wake a sublime awareness that comes only from the total surrender such suffering demands.

It is the utter vulnerability of grief that propels the soul up and in to its Creator, who is its only true solace. In that moment of abject emptiness, the Divine Presence rushes in to make it whole, to cradle the heart and comfort the soul in the sweet insight that only in becoming truly helpless do we find the enduring help of the Other Side.

We can keep God at a distance for eternity if we choose. But the Divine within is meant to bridge us from one world to the next. "Don't shut yourself off from an entire universe of friendship and comfort," it declares. "The invisible world is surely teeming with angels, masters, and loved ones who are eager to partner you through life."

For me, this is what walking up to the door of death with Stephen has actually come to mean. And here, I believe, is the real secret of communion between the unseen and the seen: Until we achieve the ultimate union with Spirit, we are neither all living nor all dead. We are always a bit of both. The ongoing death and rebirth of some part of us is always being played out—certainly at the body's cellular level, and likely in our minds and hearts too. Our job in this life is to champion that which endures, and we do so by entering into life's many challenges as well as by welcoming its blessings.

If we embrace whatever life brings us, I believe death can be beautiful because we will have prepared for it by dealing with many lesser transitions. Long before we find ourselves visited with great loss, we will have learned that the authentic self goes on, the soul does not

die, and love lives forever. That is the life raft we build through all of
our striving—constructed of a million right decisions and countless
acts of love that are the very warp and weft of our being.

So in a way, I think we make our own grace for the end of our
days. Our choices in this life determine much about how we will die
into the next—not so much the outer circumstances, but the inner
conditions of heart, mind, and soul.

Even if we should die suddenly, like my dear friend Dave, we
can be prepared. His wife, Leslie, told me there was nothing unsaid
between them. Of course, there were regrets for projects left undone,
for experiences they would never have together. But there were no
lingering angers or misunderstandings. Despite their normal human
foibles, they were able to fully express their love, mutual appreciation,
and forgiveness for being less than perfect. And together they shared
a remarkable joy in being alive to whatever each day presented. This
was how Dave lived his life and how he was able to enter death—even
without knowing that he would not live to see another day.

Stephen was likewise prepared—and so he was at peace. He was
not worried about meeting God face to face because he had practiced
meeting him every day. He could just as easily have gone in a flash,
like Dave; so I cannot help feeling that his much slower death from
cancer was in part a service to our families, to help them adjust to
saying good-bye. And a generous opportunity for me to "get it"—to
finally understand who was this man I married on faith as well as
love because God spoke into my heart and said, "He's the one."

As a result of Stephen's determination, endurance, and great love, I
was given the gift of a lifetime: to go through the dying process with
my beloved. To catch a glimpse of eternity as it impinged upon his
consciousness. And to feel the ecstasy of his release from embodiment
as he made his way to higher spheres, into the arms of angels that
awaited him, just as I am convinced they wait for each of us.

I must admit, having gone through what I did with Stephen, I
would be quite happy to make a fast exit from this world when my
time comes. Yet, in the end, I believe that what matters most is not so
much the method that takes us as who we are being when we go.

In our lifetime, we are offered countless paths to the Divine. The grace is this: We can embody that sweet presence now by embracing life in all its complexity—every day—before our time here on earth expires. Surely such opportunity is a grace, a gift of profound inner peace. Because in the simplicity of right now, this moment is perfect, everything is good, and that is truly beautiful.

QUESTIONS FOR
REFLECTION

We all have reservoirs of life to draw upon,
of which we do not dream.

—William James

RESERVOIRS OF LIFE

Today I see that even death can be a form of healing.

—Bernie Siegel

WHEN I WROTE *A Beautiful Death*, I hoped it would be read in three ways: first, as an inspirational story that would comfort and inspire the reader; second, as a book that would encourage open discussion of the very difficult subjects of death, loss, and grief. And third, as reassurance that you have what it takes to face the end of life with grace and confidence.

Confronting the inescapable fact of death and its many implications can be frightening and confusing. It can revive distressing or even traumatic memories of loss, regret, disappointment, anger—the entire range of human emotions. But if psychological health and emotional well-being are important to us, then discussing this most difficult of subjects is vital.

Stephen and I believed that talking about death and the dying process with open minds and hearts allowed us to set the tone for his transition. We could continue to reinforce our faith in the continuity of life from this world to the next. We could share our beliefs with friends and family in hope that the power of our convictions would comfort them and perhaps offer them a different perspective. And we could, by the example of our service to one another, demonstrate a way through life to death that would inspire others to accept this final act on the stage of life as not just a terrible end, but as a glorious new beginning.

We found that our discussions about dying usually began with reflection upon life—its content, its meaning, and the unfolding processes that allowed us to experience it most profoundly. Throughout his illness, we returned again and again to five basic concepts we had actually been working with long before he got sick. After his diagnosis, they became even more important in our striving for peace of mind and heart.

Eventually I distilled these issues into the questions that follow—questions for the one who is dying as well as for those who love and care for that person. Even if you are not facing death now, contemplating these questions—on your own, with a study group, or in professional therapy—can also serve as deep meditation on life and may well help prepare you for its end.

Because this work is ongoing and very personal, I suggest you use a journal or notebook to record the reactions and inspirations that arise as you make your way through this material. Although I have arranged the questions in an order that I feel reflects the five parts of the book, this is not a linear activity. So you needn't move sequentially through the questions. Just answer them if and when they move you.

I believe there is a compassionate inner wisdom that permeates life, death, and grief—and that unfolds in loops and circles, often returning to the same lesson multiple times. In living with Stephen's illness, his death, and my loss, I found that I learned more, suffered less, and grew immeasurably as a person when I simply allowed that wisdom to carry me through the process. I pray that, in reading our story and contemplating these questions, you will find the same comfort and support.

You probably already have your own library of inspirational material. However, when life gets rough, you may actually forget to return to the texts that have brought you solace before. Please consider this a gentle reminder. To help you on your journey, I am including just a few of the books and audio recordings Stephen and I found most inspiring. Many additional resources are also available on my website at www.abeautifuldeath.net.

HOW HAVE I BEEN PREPARED?

Yet Hope again elastic springs,
Unconquered, though she fell;
Still buoyant are her golden wings,
Still strong to bear us well.

—Charlotte Brontë

I HAVE HEARD IT SAID we are never given more in this life than we can handle. This can be difficult to accept if we are facing death. But I have seen that we can grow profoundly in the midst of our greatest trials if we recognize the unique personal qualities we bring to the situation.

So the questions we must ask early in our journey are about gaining an appreciation of exactly what we are dealing with and how our individual gifts of faith, knowledge, talent, and experience may actually have prepared us for this moment—even if we feel completely unprepared. When we know that we do have the personal resources to carry on, it is much easier to be courageous—for ourselves and for those who depend on us.

The Preparation Questions

1. What is my current difficulty?

Write out just the facts of the situation without using emotional language to describe what is happening. Articulating your problems factually can sometimes make them seem less overwhelming and easier to deal with one at a time. Try just making a list of details, listing each one separately.

2. **What life experience has prepared me for the challenge I am now facing?**

Here you are looking for similarities between what you are facing now and other life events that may not seem obvious at first, but are actually similar in some way. If it seems you have never dealt with anything remotely similar, perhaps you have learned applicable lessons from the experiences of other people you know.

3. **What specific knowledge do I possess that has prepared me for the challenge I am facing?**

Has a piece of information recently come to your awareness that gives you exactly the perspective you need right now? Perhaps your education or professional training—even a book you've read or a conversation you've had—has prepared you.

4. **What qualities of personality, soul, character, physical strength, intelligence, sensitivity, or faith do I possess that make me especially able to face this situation?**

These are the personal physical, mental, and spiritual resources at your disposal for meeting the difficulty in which you now find yourself. If it's hard to think of these qualities, ask yourself what blessing or help to others would be missing if you were not here.

5. **How do I feel now that I have answered these questions?**

Reflect on what you've experienced while answering the first four questions. Did articulating your personal experience and naming your personal resources change your perception of your ability to meet your current challenges? If so, how? If not, don't be concerned. This work often bears fruit later with an insight that comes just when you need it most.

Suggested Reading

Excuse Me, Your Life Is Waiting: The Astonishing Power of Feelings, by Lynn Grabhorn (Charlottesville, VA: Hampton Roads, 2000).

This is one of my favorite approaches to reframing persistent problems into solvable situations. Grabhorn's style is humorous, slightly irreverent, and highly practical. She doesn't take herself too seriously and her easy practices can help you do the same— even while dealing with extremely serious challenges.

Now, Discover Your Strengths, by Marcus Buckingham and Donald O. Clifton, Ph.D. (New York: The Free Press, 2001).

This is primarily a professional development book written for a business audience. I recommend it here because purchasing the book gives you one-time access to the Gallup Organization's online "Strengths Finder" tool, a quick and very accurate way to identify your top five strengths. Another way to discover your strengths is to ask several trusted friends or family members what qualities they most admire about you. You may be surprised at how they agree on qualities that are obvious and deeply important to them but hidden from or inconsequential to you because you take these qualities for granted.

The Artist's Way: A Spiritual Path to Higher Creativity, by Julia Cameron with Mark Bryan (New York: Jeremy P. Tarcher/Putnam, 2002).

Although expanding your creativity may not be high on your priority list right now, Cameron's seminal work is a powerful introduction to the practice of journaling as a way to process your thoughts and feelings. Following her recommendation of "morning pages" (or "evening pages," as I found more useful) can help unlock your inner resources of intuition, creative problem-solving, and self-confidence. Allowing yourself even half an hour of this daily "me" time can reap amazing benefits in the midst of great personal difficulty.

HOW AM I STAYING AFLOAT?

If a man wishes to be sure of the road he treads on,
he must close his eyes and walk in the dark.

—St. John of the Cross

IF THEY ARE NOT ACTUALLY FRIGHTENED of death, most people are at least apprehensive because there are so many unknowns: Where do we go when we die? Is there an afterlife or do we just disappear into oblivion? Do we face an eternity of love or damnation? These questions are disturbing enough on their own, but even more unsettling is the prospect of facing the Great Void without knowing who or what it is we take with us after death. Who is the "I" that actually makes the transition from this world to the next? What part of me (if any) goes on to another kind of existence in the invisible realm? How do I reach the Promised Land?

Stephen deeply pondered these matters. He felt that beliefs are like a boat that carries us over life's rough waters—so that, when we get from one harbor to the next, we are not only safe and secure, we are also blessed with greater understanding of our own path through life. We may employ many "boats" before our final crossing, but the key is for each new boat to take us closer to our inner reality than its predecessor.

Stephen believed we are supposed to eventually become the boat ourselves. At some point in our lives we are meant to have internalized life's lessons so completely that we sail into our final hours on the life raft of a profoundly genuine self. Here's how he explained it to me: It is as if we can become our own Noah's Ark, which we build with our own two hands—board by board, plank by plank—gathering in, two-by-two, the spiritual resources our soul will need to survive after the physical body passes away.

If we are fortunate to live to an advanced age (not quite like Noah's six hundred years, of course), we will have constructed a mighty ship before the rains come. Of course, most of us are not going to live that long, and sometimes the thunder booms and the lightning strikes before we barely have the hull in place. So what do we do?

Being with Stephen throughout his dying process taught me that every day we must ask ourselves: If the rains come today, will my boat float? How many positive qualities of self will it be carrying if this is all the time I have left? Perhaps I don't consider myself particularly enlightened, but what "soul stuff" have I gathered into my ark that will go with me to the far-distant shore? This was Stephen's greatest concern as he approached the end of his life, and it is certainly a motivation for me now.

So the purpose of the following reflection questions is self-discovery—finding our authentic self in the midst of great difficulty. It is in these moments that we often discover the very best of who we are—and that we have actually been building a strong inner life raft for quite some time.

The Life Raft Questions

1. **What is my present belief system and how is it helping me navigate the rough waters of adversity?**

   The beliefs you identify can be formal or informal, and they need not be spiritual. In answer to this question, you can also describe your personal code of ethics, morality, or sense of right and wrong.

2. What is my state of being right now?

A good way to determine the nature of your inner life raft is to consider various aspects of your "self." For example, what physical sensations do you notice in your body—is there tension, pain, relaxation? What emotions are you experiencing—worry, joy, anger, frustration, peace? How would you describe your frame of mind—balanced, scattered, confused, centered? You don't have to use words; sometimes doing some kind of free-form artwork can be very revealing as well as therapeutic. Many counselors use art therapy as a way of helping their clients access this deeply personal information.

3. How can I stay balanced amid what is happening right now?

This could include exercising or centering practices such as meditation. If you don't have such a practice, simply going for a walk can clear your head. If that is not possible, take five minutes and just focus on breathing slowly and deeply. Doing something creative such as painting, drawing, singing, or dancing can help. Drinking more water during a time of crisis is very important, as is eating foods you find nourishing and balancing.

4. How can I be present with what is arising in my thoughts, feelings, and outer experience?

It is so difficult to stay in the "here and now" when it is filled with pain. But, instead of panicking or going numb, can you pay attention to what is going on right now in the present moment, rather than imagining a better or worse future? Living each day as it comes and dealing with just what happens in that day can help you feel less overwhelmed.

5. What am I learning about myself and/or my loved one(s) through this experience?

Facing death teaches many lessons, some comforting and some

not particularly pleasant. Creating a beautiful death has a lot to do with allowing yourself to be taught—and being gentle with yourself when the lessons are difficult or painful. You will undoubtedly add to this list of lessons as your journey unfolds. I do suggest making note of your insights as they occur. I was amazed at what I learned during Stephen's illness and how those lessons continued to help me long after he was gone. For the person who is dying, these lessons are absolutely invaluable as their final hours approach.

SUGGESTED READING

Anam Čara: A Book of Celtic Wisdom, by John O'Donohue (New York: Harper Perennial, 2004).

The world lost a great man when John O'Donohue passed away in 2007. A former Catholic priest from the west coast of Ireland, he was a brilliant poet, philosopher, and scholar. His wisdom and deeply compassionate insight never fail to inspire me. To my mind, *Anam Čara* is the definitive illumination of the Irish imagination and a profound exploration of the human heart and soul. This is a perfect bedside book to savor a few pages at a time.

Talking About Death, by Virginia Morris (Chapel Hill, NC: Algonquin Books, 2001).

If you find exploring these issues alone or with your loved one(s) difficult (most people do), I suggest this book as a practical resource for beginning the conversation. Stephen and I found that the more we talked, the more we learned and the less we were afraid.

The Miracle of Mindfulness, by Thich Nhat Hanh (Boston: Beacon Press, 1976).

If you want to delve further into the idea of living in the present moment, the work of Vietnamese monk Thich Nhat Hanh is ideal. His gentle presence simply radiates from the page, offering comfort, hope, and peace.

The Power of Now: A Guide to Spiritual Enlightenment, by Eckhart Tolle (Novato, CA: New World Library, 2004).

This could be one of the most important books you will ever read. Tolle's clear style perfectly explains what "living in the now" means. You may quickly find yourself considering your current circumstances from a different, more useful perspective.

SUGGESTED AUDIO RECORDINGS

Christian Meditation: Entering the Mind of Christ, by James Finley (Boulder, CO: Sounds True, 2003).

Author, retreat leader, and psychotherapist James Finley left home at the age of eighteen for the Abbey of Gethsemani in Trappist, Kentucky, where he lived and studied with Thomas Merton for five and a half years. Informed by Merton's respect for all faiths, Finley's approach to meditation is both practical and easy to follow. If you have trouble stilling your mind to meditate on your own, letting him guide you is a comforting experience.

I Want Burning: The Ecstatic World of Rumi, Hafiz, and Lalla, by Coleman Barks (Boulder, CO: Sounds True, 2001).

I am particularly fond of the poetry of Rumi, the Sufi mystic who— like the Christian mystic St. John of the Cross—wrote about his very personal spiritual experiences while in an ecstatic state. The sensual nature of Rumi's work may surprise a first-time listener, but I encourage you to let the words carry you into the deeply spiritual world that Rumi conveys—and that is so beautifully read by Coleman Barks.

WHAT DO I NEED RIGHT NOW?

Needs do not cease to be because they have been ignored.

—Thomas J. Leonard

BEING A CAREGIVER CAN BE BRUTAL, even if the role comes naturally and you are surrounded by a good support system. You are, of necessity, intensely focused on the other person's needs—and those needs can be all-consuming. Sometimes, there is not much to be done externally, but you must be ready to act instantly. Things are changing, but often only inside the person who is ill. There is little you can fix, but you must attend just the same.

It is unfortunate that the caregiver role often falls to the elderly or others who lack the physical stamina necessary to endure the relentless stress and hyperattentiveness involved in caring for someone who is dying. It is also not surprising that many people who are highly attuned to the needs of others are often woefully unaware of their own. Or if they do know what they need, they allow their personal interests to be subsumed by those who are more vocal or whose needs they perceive as being more important.

Even the best caregivers need loving support, and something else that may seem radical to those who are giving their all for another: self-care. We are better able to help our loved ones make their final journey when we are strong in body as well as determined in mind and spirit. People who are dying are often highly sensitive and easily disturbed. If we allow our own fatigue or negativity to creep into the way we approach the dying person, we may inadvertently inflict harm upon those we love the most.

When we feel overwhelmed, asking ourselves some simple questions can provide clarity and suggest an action plan. These questions are equally applicable to the one who is dying.

The Needs Questions

1. Who or what makes up my support system and what do the various individuals or groups do for me?

Identifying who you can turn to and for what purpose is really important, especially when you get frazzled or start feeling overwhelmed.

2. What do I want or need in this moment?

If you are cranky or out of sorts, your own well-being may need some help. Paying attention to the present moment is your best resource here. Get someone to cover for you for a while so you can sit quietly and sense how and what you are feeling. What thoughts, emotions, and physical sensations are you experiencing? The body lives in the "now" and tells the truth, so practice noticing what it may be telling you to do for your own health and stability. Learning to do this for yourself will also help you become more skilled at identifying the patient's needs.

3. What will my fulfilling that desire actually accomplish?

Sometimes what we think we want may not satisfy the underlying need. For example, a patient may complain of discomfort in order to get attention; but if the pain has been managed and the patient continues to call for assistance, the real issue may be loneliness. So when you express a desire, you may have to ask, "What is it for?" in order to get what you actually need.

4. What will it take to fulfill that want or need?

This could mean money, time, help from others, or a change in environment. You have to know what constitutes successful fulfillment of your need so you can ask for the right remedy.

5. How or from whom do I get it?

Try to set up your network of support before you actually need it—see question #1.

6. Who will really listen to me so I can express my deepest feelings and craziest thoughts?

It is important for caregivers and patients alike to have a sounding board. We can't always talk to our loved ones about our desires, fears, or regrets; but we do need to discuss these things. Support groups specifically designed for caregivers provide a safe environment in which to discuss difficult issues. Expressing yourself openly and honestly will make all the difference in your ability to stay afloat. If you find it just too hard to broach certain subjects on your own, do not hesitate to ask a counselor or clergyperson to assist you in conducting the conversation. Hospice chaplains and counselors are also very adept at encouraging discussion of uncomfortable subjects.

SUGGESTED READING

Energy Medicine, by Donna Eden with David Feinstein (New York: Jeremy P. Tarcher/Putnam, 1998).

Eden's work may be too radical for some, but the principle of tapping various parts of the body to energize or calm is strongly supported by many alternative-healing modalities. Many of Eden's exercises are simple and quick, which is useful when your time is not your own.

Honor Yourself: The Inner Art of Giving and Receiving, by Patricia Spadaro (Bozeman, MT: Three Wings Press, 2009).

This lovely book, written by a dear friend, is one of the best compilations of self-care wisdom I have ever read. The author's insights into living with paradox are well considered, and the exercises she includes are very practical.

The Way of Qigong: The Art and Science of Chinese Energy Healing, by Kenneth S. Cohen (New York: Ballantine, 1997).

The practice of Qigong (pronounced chee-gung) is the foundation of many martial arts. The exercises are gentle but extremely powerful—calming if you feel frantic and energizing if you feel tired. Stephen was able to continue doing Qigong exercises after he could no longer work out. We both found them very helpful.

WHAT MUST I LET GO OF?

The result of letting go is that you discover
a bank of self-existing energy
that is always available to you—
beyond any circumstance.

—Chögyam Trungpa

LETTING GO OF our loved ones is excruciating. The attachments are not just emotional or spiritual, they are physical. It is as if our very cells have been knit together and when our loved one leaves, the parting feels surgical. The only thing that makes the separation bearable is knowing that the person is in a better place.

I suppose this is one of the few blessings of a lingering illness: the realization that the body has worn out and the soul longs to be liberated from the physical shell that has become a virtual prison. So the pain of staying outpaces the sorrow of going—which is when we find ourselves whispering, "I'll be okay. You can go on if you need to."

This is what love does: It lets go of love for love's sake. But more subtle, and frequently more difficult to surrender, than love are the lingering feelings of hurt or injustice for past wrongs (real or imagined) committed against us. These are the "unforgiveables" we hang on to—sometimes for years. And it is these feelings that need to be surrendered if we are to be freed in mind and spirit as the dying are more dramatically freed of their bodies.

About twenty-four hours before my father slipped into a coma, he and my mother were talking about their fifty-seven years of marriage. "We'll just remember the good things," my mother said to him, gently patting his hand, "not the things that went wrong." "Did anything go wrong?" my father responded with genuine surprise. He was already tipping over to the Other Side, where only love and forgiveness prevail.

Apparently, this is not uncommon. Medium Concetta Bertoldi[25] reports that countless spirits who communicate with her speak in terms of universal love, not recrimination. The atmosphere on the Other Side seems to be one of pervasive forgiveness that prompts the departed to urge their embodied friends and families to bury the hatchet, to treat one another with kindness, and—most importantly—to forgive themselves with the unconditional mercy of the Divine Presence. Only then can all parties be truly free.

It is easy to see how this could be true. Observe the workings of your own psyche. You may have noticed how, when you learn the lesson of a difficult situation or resolve your differences with a certain person, it is as if the problem never existed. It is dissolved, even transformed, possibly resulting in friendship where once there was only enmity. That is the alchemy of forgiveness—to heal that which was broken, to beautify that which was ugly, to elevate that which was debased. Forgiveness releases the pent-up energy of negativity and transmutes it into the power of good. When we truly forgive another person, we let go of the negative image in which we have imprisoned him or her, and in the process we ourselves are released—because it takes a lot of energy to hold on to hatred or anger. Humans are essentially loving beings. All forgiveness does is return us to our natural state.

Of course, the most difficult person to forgive is often oneself. We may forgive others for great abuses but we cannot seem to forgive ourselves for our humanity. Nobody is perfect, but somehow we expect that we should be. Depending on our life experience and upbringing, we may kick ourselves around the block for things we should or should not have done, thought, or said. Where others may see our special gifts, we acknowledge only imperfections. We create an icon of our failings that is impervious to the ministrations of all but the most determined of angels.

But if we are to move on—especially after great loss—we must surrender our most passionately held erroneous beliefs and learn to forgive ourselves as the Divine has already done. We must free ourselves before we can truly liberate others. In the conversations Stephen and I had before he died, we were able to confront our fears and regrets and let them go. By the time he passed away, we were not hanging on to past hurts or grasping at future miracles. We were simply present for each other.

The questions in this section are some of the most difficult any of us ever attempt to answer. For that reason, if you are not accustomed to doing deeply introspective personal-growth work, I highly recommend that you work through this material in the company of a counselor or clergyperson. This is especially true when dealing with strong emotions such as anger or fear.

The Letting Go Questions

1. What expectations do I hold for myself and/or others in dealing with this death? Are these expectations reasonable?

It is all too easy to burden ourselves with expectations of how death *should* take place, what we *should* be doing, how we *should* be reacting. The final hours of life are a time to practice great gentleness with self and others. Emotions are likely running high and no one can predict exactly how the end will come. So identifying our expectations and giving ourselves permission to simply do the best we can is very important.

2. What am I most afraid of?

Sometimes merely identifying our greatest fears can help alleviate them. If we don't talk about fear, it can grow to overwhelming proportions. I continue to ask myself this question, especially if I notice that I'm anxious or worried or cranky. Fear lies at the bottom of most—if not all—of our worries and concerns. This question is akin to asking, "What is it for?" Until you become adept at this work, identifying underlying fears is often best done with a counselor.

3. Do I have any regrets or unresolved feelings about this death?

Even when we have done everything "right," we may feel that we could have or should have done more to help our loved ones. I found it hard not to criticize myself for not holding Stephen's hand at the end or for dozing off just as he was about to die. These expectations are unreasonable and can be the cause of painful regret. You can help reduce this regret if you are able to talk about troubling thoughts, express deep emotions, and discuss how the dying person wishes to experience his or her final hours. Please do so before the end of life is upon you.

4. What does this death mean to me?

Almost immediately upon my father's passing, my mother exclaimed, "Now I'm a widow!" For her, his death meant the sudden realization of her aloneness. But death has many deep meanings—not all of which are negative. Exploring those meanings can lead to wonderful insight and encouragement for the future. You may not find them right away. Answering the loss questions in the next section may provide additional insight.

5. How can I be at peace that everything is being done that the dying person wants to be done?

Sometimes, everything that *can* be done as a medical intervention is more than the patient *wants* to have done. Be sure to ask for complete explanations of treatment options and consequences and keep asking until you are satisfied. Pain is often what frightens people the most. Hospice workers are especially knowledgeable about palliative-care options.

6. How can I let go and allow this death to unfold naturally?

I believe we do eventually reach a point when we can let our loved one go on—and the person who is dying also comes to the place where letting go is the most natural response. This is one question that hospice counselors and chaplains are particularly well trained to help you answer. You can begin to answer this question yourself by noticing what it is that you are most afraid of losing.

7. What else must I let go of?

The answer to this question may feel like an unending list, but you can do it. Just take one step at a time. Long before Stephen passed away, we had let go of expectations for a miracle cure. Stephen let go of any remaining fear of death. I had to let go of my desire to know what was going to happen and when it would happen. I think the short answer to what to let go of is this: Let go of anything that pulls you out of the present moment. Letting go really means being able to live right now with whatever is arising in this moment.

SUGGESTED READING

Broken Open: How Difficult Times Can Help Us Grow, by Elizabeth Lesser (New York: Villard, 2005).

This is a powerful work that is especially helpful in letting go of a sense of injustice or resentment that life and death are not fair.

Dying Well: Peace and Possibilities at the End of Life, by Ira Byock, M.D. (New York: Riverhead, 1997).

A deeply compassionate book written by one of the primary

proponents of the hospice movement. Dr. Byock has dedicated his life to the premise that nobody should have to die in pain and nobody should have to die alone. The stories he tells of families he has worked with will inspire and encourage you in your own walk with death. It includes guidelines for talking with medical personnel, friends, family, and all concerned with making the end of life meaningful.

Final Gifts: Understanding the Special Awareness, Needs, and Communications of the Dying, by Maggie Callanan and Patricia Kelley (New York: Bantam, 2008).

This was the most important book I read before Stephen's passing. The authors—who are hospice nurses—create a vivid picture of what happens as death approaches. This single volume made all the difference in my being able to enter into Stephen's final hours and walk with him to the open door he had to pass through alone.

Grace and Grit: Spirituality and Healing in the Life and Death of Treya Killam Wilber, 2nd ed., by Ken Wilber (Boston: Shambhala, 2000).

Stephen and I read this book together when we learned his cancer was terminal. I read it again in his final year of life. More than any other, Ken and Treya's story gave us the inspiration, courage, and conviction that we could make of Stephen's passing a beautiful and deeply spiritual experience. *Grace and Grit* is also an excellent introduction to Wilber's philosophy.

Necessary Losses: The Loves, Illusions, Dependencies, and Impossible Expectations That All of Us Have to Give Up in Order to Grow, by Judith Viorst (New York: The Free Press, 2002).

A brilliant book that articulates why loss and letting go of who and what we love most dearly may be one of life's most important lessons. Part IV is especially apropos.

WHERE DO I GO FROM HERE?

Your inner purpose is to awaken.
It is as simple as that.

—Eckhart Tolle

REGARDLESS OF THE PATH YOU FOLLOW, there are no short cuts through grief or any other process of personal transformation. You have to walk through it. Skipping steps actually slows down the process. As Judith Viorst says in her book *Necessary Losses,* "Losing is the price we pay for living."[26]

The questions that follow can be asked both before and after a death has occurred. As I worked through them, I gained insight and clarity, which I consider two of the most valuable elements of personal growth and psychological health. I rediscovered the incredible legacy of practicality Stephen left me. And I began to construct a new life built on healthy expectations, a deep sense of positive self-regard, and personal responsibility for the feelings that can still swamp me with grief—but that, more often now, simply remind me of how tenderly and completely I was loved.

These are perennial questions we may ask at many times in our lives—when circumstances change, when we change, or when desired change seems to elude us. What is important is that we give ourselves time to let the answers bubble up from deep places of heart and soul where the desire for truth abides. In the silence of contemplation, creative solutions will arise. It is from this foundation that we raise our eyes up to what is next, not only back to what was.

Because these questions penetrate so deeply into awareness, you may want to engage a trained therapist to accompany you in this exploration. And be gentle with yourself here. You may not be able to answer some of these questions right away. Let the answers unfold in their own time.

These questions can also be answered by the person who is dying—before death begins its final approach. Exploring them can lead to a beautifully peaceful crossing over.

The Loss Questions

1. What am I losing or what have I lost?

Make a list of everything that death has taken or will take from your life—physical, mental, emotional, and spiritual. You will no doubt discover there are wonderful things you miss but also some not-so-wonderful ones you don't. This is no disrespect to the departed. Nobody is perfect—which means you may have been carrying some burdens while your loved one was alive that you are glad to no longer be bearing.

2. What am I gaining or what did I gain?

Again, it is no disrespect to the living or the dead to realize that death has pushed you forward in personal growth, perhaps even opening opportunities that were not present before. This is a good place to articulate the blessings or healings you may have received while walking this path with your beloved. For the dying person, acknowledging what you have learned through your journey can be a profound declaration of life that will carry over from this world to the next.

3. What is calling to me?

Answering this question means being willing to hear the call to do something new—perhaps embarking on an adventure or a challenge, or merely taking the next step in regaining your emotional footing. If you are the person who is dying, are you feeling called to the Other Side?

4. What nurtures me at the deepest levels of my being?

Knowing what feeds the soul is so important during the sensitive time before death or as we begin to rebuild our lives—and what feeds us will change over time. This is one of the key elements of following your own path to wholeness. If you are the person who is dying, it's important to know what will help you attain the kind of death you want. Stephen and I both knew he needed a peaceful environment and we did our best to achieve it so his dying process was not disrupted.

5. Who or what is toxic to me and how can I remove myself from that situation?

This question is meant to identify situations, activities, or interactions that are potentially tiring or even dangerous to you—especially when you are in the vulnerable state of dying or grieving. Hospice workers are very sensitive to things that agitate the person who is dying. They emphasize that the first responsibility is to the dying person, second to the caregiver, and third to family and friends.

6. What is my sense of personal identity at this point in my life?

Stephen identified himself as rich in spirit—a devoted son of God who was going home to his Heavenly Father. Before his death, I identified myself as the champion of his dying process. After his death, it was difficult not to identify myself as the gaping hole that death left in my heart. Gradually, I came back to a sense of myself as a person with a mission and a deep connection to Spirit. Answering this question with the help of a counselor is a gentle way to allow your answer to change over time.

Suggested Reading

Healing After Loss: Daily Meditations for Working Through Grief, by Martha Whitmore Hickman (New York: Avon, 1994).

> A dear friend recommended this book before Stephen passed away, and it has been a comforting bedside companion ever since. Sometimes we just need a simple reminder to put one foot ahead of the other as we find our way through the wilderness of grief. Hickman's meditations are gently powerful.

The Seeker's Guide: Making Your Life a Spiritual Adventure, by Elizabeth Lesser (New York: Villard, 1999).

> One of the best and most comprehensive books ever written about the spiritual path. Lesser has seen it all and still managed to emerge as a balanced voice for practical spirituality. Regardless of your belief system, you will find great wisdom in these pages.

The Three "Only" Things: Tapping the Power of Dreams, Coincidence & Imagination, by Robert Moss (Novato, CA: New World Library, 2007).

> I have included Moss's book here because he is such a master of synchronicity, creating a fascinating dialogue between the waking and dreaming states. Dreams can provide profound insight and comfort to the person who is dying. For the survivor, as you build a new life, paying attention to your dreams and life's many coincidences can help strengthen the bridge between this world and the next—a constant reminder that the Other Side is just a dream away.

Transitions: Making Sense of Life's Changes, 2nd ed., by William Bridges, Ph.D. (Cambridge, MA: Da Capo, 2004).

Bridges's book was the first place I ever read about the "neutral zone"—that odd, in-between place of not being your old self and having no idea what your new self will be. A valuable resource for navigating the first stages of loss.

ACKNOWLEDGEMENTS

AT SOME POINT IN THE LIFE OF A BOOK, it ceases to belong solely to the author. At that point a gifted team is necessary to cut and polish this rough stone of a story into a gem that will stand out in a dizzying array of books in stores and online catalogs. For assembling such a group of talented professionals, my deepest thanks go to long-time friends and colleagues Nigel J. Yorwerth and Patricia Spadaro of www.publishingcoaches.com. I will be forever in your debt for believing in this book and for lending the full weight of your experience and expertise to every step of its publication and success.

To cover designer Nita Ybarra and interior designer Alan Barnett, my sincere gratitude to you both for so beautifully capturing the essence of the story and for creating designs that perfectly reflect the sense of peace and support I wanted to convey from first impression to final word.

To my brilliant editor, Anne Barthel, a million thanks for your time and talent, for long, productive lunches in New York City, and for becoming a cherished friend during our many months of collaboration. You have been nothing less than a godsend for this project, proving once more that an author is nothing without a patient, perceptive, and skillful editor.

Throughout my life, and especially during Stephen's illness and death, I have been blessed with friends and family who have loved and supported me in my darkest hours and who have cheered me on during the process of completing this book. First of all, to my dear mother, life is too short to express the fullness of my gratitude for your unconditional love and belief in me. To Stephen's family, may I simply say that it remains a gift and an honor to be one of you.

To my book group friends, Evelyn Bowman and Mimi Michel, I hope you know how fondly I cherish your love, your insights, and the wonderful retreats that keep us all growing in wisdom and grace. To my soul sister and partner in grief, Kathleen Brand, I am profoundly grateful for the opportunity we have had to support each other during some of the most difficult years of our lives. To Pat Pendleton, deepest thanks for your wisdom and insight that helped me through some very rough times. To Leslie Holmes and Sarah French, I truly appreciate your willingness to share so openly your feelings and reflections on losing your own husbands. And to John Lee, thanks for getting me to Ireland and for putting up with my woeful condition when I got there.

To Theresa McNicholas, Susan Harrow, and numerous others who read a very rough early manuscript, I am grateful for your patience, for helpful insights and suggestions, and for challenging me to think more deeply about the path and purpose of the story. To Ann Klaiman, thank you for a lifetime of friendship and lately your literary eagle eye. And deepest gratitude to Henry Klaiman for helping Stephen finish his final woodworking project when he no longer had the strength to do so.

I remain deeply grateful to our team from The Denver Hospice for your care, understanding, and ever-available support. Because of you, Stephen was able to die at home as he wanted, and I was able to be with him every step of the way. I honor you for your service and thank you for your presence in our lives.

To my dear friends from our teacher's community—now scattered around the world—my heartfelt thanks for love and prayers, for generous hospitality when I needed a bed during my travels, and for being an important part of the ongoing path I am privileged to walk with you.

Finally, and most humbly, I wish to thank my darling Stephen for finding me again, for all that you taught me in our eighteen years together, and for never really leaving me. I am grateful beyond words to the universe of angels, masters, and beings of Spirit who have guided and guarded my path through life. And to beloved Morya El, as my teacher once said, "I loved you before I knew you." Whatever blessing may come from this book is because of you. The faults are mine alone.

NOTES

Chapter 10. Surfing the Waves

1. Ken Wilber, *Grace and Grit: Spirituality and Healing in the Life and Death of Treya Killam Wilber.* 2nd. ed. (Boston: Shambhala, 2000).
2. Ibid, 372.

Chapter 11. Putting Cancer Behind Us

3. See www.integralinstitute.org and Ken Wilber, et al, *Integral Life Practice Starter Kit:* Version 1.0 (Boulder, CO: Integral Institute, 2005).

Chapter 16. A Promise to Keep

4. Wilber, *Grace and Grit,* 244–45. I highly recommend that you read the entire chapter titled "What Kind of Help Really Helps." For additional information on *tonglen* practice and its foundation in Tibetan Buddhism, see Pema Chödrön's audio program *Good Medicine: How to Turn Pain into Compassion with Tonglen Meditation.* (Boulder, CO: Sounds True, 2001).

Chapter 17. Accepting What Is

5. See Ira Byock, M.D., *Dying Well: Peace and Possibilities at the End of Life* (New York: Riverhead, 1997) and Maggie Callanan and Patricia Kelley, *Final Gifts: Understanding the Special Awareness, Needs, and Communications of the Dying* (New York: Bantam, 2008).
6. *The Urantia Book* (New York: Uversa Press, 2005), 48:7.16.

Chapter 18. Running the Race

7. El Morya Khan, from the Agni Yoga books written by Russian mystics Nicholas and Helena Roerich. El Morya is identified as an ascended master and a founding sponsor of Theosophy and other occult or spiritual organizations, including that of my teacher.
8. Antoine de Saint-Exupéry, *The Little Prince,* trans. Richard Howard (New York: Harcourt, 2000).

Chapter 19. Approaching Death

9. John 14:2.
10. *The Psalms* read by Alex Jennings (Franklin, TN: Naxos AudioBooks, 2005).

Chapter 21. What Do the Signs Say?

11. Callanan and Kelley, *Final Gifts,* 96.

Chapter 22. Through the Doorway

12. Sogyal Rinpoche, *The Tibetan Book of Living and Dying* (New York: HarperCollins, 1993), 102.

Chapter 23. The Genuine Heart of Joy

13. Chögyam Trungpa, *Shambhala: The Sacred Path of the Warrior* (Boston: Shambhala, 1984), 27–32.

Chapter 24. With Sheer Determination

14. Pablo Neruda, "XCIV" in *100 Love Sonnets: Cien sonestos de amor,* trans. Stephen Tapscott (Austin: University of Texas Press, 1992), 199.

Chapter 25. The Postcard from Heaven

15. See Marie Antoinette Kelley's website, www.portraitsofthesoul.com, for more examples of her beautiful custom portraits. The "Postcard from Heaven" can be seen in the Celestial Signatures gallery.

Chapter 26. Touching Bottom

16. Matthew Fox, *Radical Prayer: Love in Action* (Boulder, CO: Sounds True, 2003).

Chapter 27. The Middle Place

17. William Bridges, Ph.D., *Transitions: Making Sense of Life's Changes.* 2nd ed. (Cambridge, MA: Da Capo, 2004), 133–155.
18. Dannion Brinkley and Kathryn Brinkley, *Secrets of the Light: Lessons from Heaven* (New York: HarperOne, 2008).

Chapter 28. Thin as Gossamer

19. George MacLeod quoted by J. Philip Newell, *Listening for the Heartbeat of God: A Celtic Spirituality* (New York: Paulist Press, 1997), 93.
20. John O'Donohue, *Anam Ċara: A Book of Celtic Wisdom* (New York: Harper Perennial, 2004), 206.

Chapter 31. The Encounter

21. John O'Donohue, *Benedictus*, published in the United States as *To Bless the Space Between Us* (New York: Doubleday, 2008), 171.
22. The Sisters of St. Brigid are in the midst of a massive fund-raising campaign to build a proper welcome center in which to receive the thousands of pilgrims who come to Kildare each year. They also want to expand the services they can provide for education, especially about care of the earth, which they consider of vital importance for the future of mankind. For more information see www.solasbhride.ie.

Chapter 32. The Return

23. Edward C. Sellner, *Pilgrimage: Exploring a Great Spiritual Practice* (Notre Dame, IN: Sorin Books, 2004), 206–207.
24. Heard at a seminar on dreams conducted by Moss. For more information about consciously working with dreams and the imagination, see Robert Moss, *The Three "Only" Things: Tapping the Power of Dreams, Coincidence & Imagination* (Novato, CA: New World Library, 2007).

Questions for Reflection

25. Concetta Bertoldi, *Do Dead People Watch You Shower? And Other Questions You've Been All but Dying to Ask a Medium* (New York: HarperCollins, 2008).
26. Judith Viorst, *Necessary Losses: The Loves, Illusions, Dependencies, and Impossible Expectations That All of Us Have to Give Up in Order to Grow* (New York: The Free Press, 1986), 325.

DEATH CAN BE
BEAUTIFUL WHEN . . .

- We are not afraid of life or death
- We can discuss and prepare for death as an inevitable part of life
- We have reconciled with our loved ones
- Our loved ones have assured us they will be okay without us
- We are open to the experiences that approaching death can bring
- We have an advocate who can help us articulate our wishes to others and run interference for us when problems arise
- Our caregivers understand the dying process and support us, even when we don't make sense
- Our caregivers don't take it personally when we struggle to get comfortable—when nothing seems to work
- We can talk with loved ones or counselors about our fears, hopes, dreams—even our disappointments
- We are in the care of hospice or other patient-centered professionals who keep us comfortable and treat us with dignity and respect
- Our pain is compassionately managed and we are included in decisions being made about our care
- Caregivers and medical professionals allow the body to dictate our passing rather than prolonging life when we are ready to go on
- We can die in the presence of many others, just a few, only one, or none—according to our own desires
- We have faith that we live in a merciful universe
- We are at peace with the future in whatever form we envision it
- We die in love.

Photo by Larry Stanley

CHERYL ECKL is a writer, speaker, professional-development facilitator, and personal life coach. Since the death of her husband in 2008, she has focused on developing resources and workshops to help others who are facing death—either their own or that of someone they love. A former singer and actress, Cheryl is a world-class communicator who delivers her practical wisdom with intelligence, humor, and real-life stories. She lives in Colorado and is currently completing a master's degree in Transpersonal Psychology.

For additional information and resources on end-of-life issues, visit her website at www.abeautifuldeath.net. There you will find essays, stories, interactive links, suggestions for caregivers, answers to frequently asked questions, and links to organizations that offer services and support for all phases of illness, caregiving, the dying process, loss, and grief. Also available online is a free study guide for reading groups.

If you would like to share your own story of witnessing a beautiful death, please send an e-mail to: stories@abeautifuldeath.net.